PIAGET *and His School*

A Reader in Developmental Psychology

with contributions by members of the faculty of the
Faculté de Psychologie et des Sciences de l'Éducation,
University of Geneva:

JEAN PIAGET
Honorary Professor of Psychology
Director of the International Center
for Genetic Epistemology

BÄRBEL INHELDER
Professor of Genetic and Experimental Psychology

GUY CELLÉRIER
Professor of Cybernetics and Epistemology

ELSA SCHMID-KITSIKIS
Assistant Professor in Clinical Psychology

HERMINE SINCLAIR
Professor of Psycholinguistics

MAGALI BOVET
Research Associate

PIERRE MOUNOUD
Professor of Early Childhood Development
Professor of Psychology at the University of Lausanne

HAROLD H. CHIPMAN
Research Associate
Lecturer in Psycholinguistics at the University of Fribourg

CHARLES ZWINGMANN
Professor of Psychology
Psychotherapist
Medico-psychological Consultant

PIAGET
and His School

A Reader in
Developmental Psychology

editors
BÄRBEL INHELDER *and*
HAROLD H. CHIPMAN

CHARLES ZWINGMANN
coordinating editor

SPRINGER-VERLAG
New York   Heidelberg   Berlin
1976

editors:

BÄRBEL INHELDER, Faculté de Psychologie et des Sciences de l'Éducation,
Université II, 24 rue du Général Dufour, 1211-Genève 4

HAROLD H. CHIPMAN, Faculté de Psychologie et des Sciences de l'Éducation,
Université II, 24 rue du Général Dufour, 1211-Genève 4

coordinating editor:

CHARLES ZWINGMANN, 5, avenue J. Trembley, CH-1211 Geneva, Switzerland

LIBRARY OF CONGRESS CATALOGING IN PUBLICATION DATA

Main entry under title:
Piaget and His School: A Reader in Developmental Psychology
   Bibliography: p. 281
   Includes indexes.
    1. Cognition (Child psychology) 2. Piaget, Jean, 1896-
3. Geneva. Université. Institut des sciences de l'éducation
(Institut J. J. Rousseau) I. Inhelder, Bärbel. II. Chipman, Harold,
1947-   III. Zwingmann, Charles.
BP723.C5P54   155.4′13′0924   75-8903

ISBN 0-387-07248-9 Springer-Verlag New York Heidelberg Berlin

ISBN 3-540-07248-9 Springer-Verlag Berlin Heidelberg New York

Foreword

In introducing this volume I have great pleasure in thanking the editors for the idea of bringing together a number of recent studies (1960–70) of the Geneva School of Psychology and the Center for Genetic Epistemology, and above all in thanking my closest collaborator, Professor Bärbel Inhelder, for the care and perspicacity with which she chose these texts, without forgetting the valuable help provided by her assistant Harold Chipman.

Two aspects of this volume impress me particularly. The first is that, though I have retired—from teaching, not from research—the Geneva School is not only very much alive, but is seen to be continually pursuing new paths if we consider the variety of the problems investigated and the increasing diversification of disciplines: research on learning and the functional processes of development, developmental psycholinguistics, cross-cultural investigations, research into clinical and educational applications, as well as innovative work on a number of epistemological questions taken up more recently. Nothing can be more surprising or satisfactory for an author at the end of his career than to see some of his subject matter which seemed exhausted (e.g., conservation research) giving rise to a whole new series of studies.

My second impression is that of the unity of our various investigations, despite the diversity of perspective so clearly brought out by B.

v

Inhelder in her introduction. The reason for this unity is that explanatory adequacy can be attained only by exploring the formative and constructive aspects of development. To explain a psychologic reaction or a cognitive mechanism (at all levels, including that of scientific thought) is not simply to describe them, but to comprehend the processes by which they were formed; failing that, one can but note results without grasping their meaning.

JEAN PIAGET

Preface

Man distinguishes himself from other creatures primarily by his abstract reasoning capacity and his ability to communicate his knowledge by highly complex symbolic processes. What is called "humanity" and progress is to a large degree a measure of his consciousness and the deployment of his creative potentials.

There are few scientists who have explored the universe of cognition, and contributed to the understanding of the realm of knowledge, with greater genius, care, and scientific intuition than Jean Piaget and his longtime collaborator Bärbel Inhelder.

Professor Inhelder and her assistant Dr. Harold Chipman realized this book in spite of the heavy load of research, teaching, and administrative duties in a rapidly expanding Institute. It is therefore a particular pleasure for me to present this book.

Bärbel Inhelder has succeeded Jean Piaget as professor of genetic psychology at the University of Geneva. It is difficult to decide which of her attributes should be mentioned first—her brilliance, her modesty, or her kindness. The latter can be confirmed by all those who have direct contact with her—we have become friends in the course of this project. The former is evidenced by her contributions to this book. As S. Farnham mentions in an editorial which refers to her outstanding work on information processing in cognitive learning," she has evolved a unique research style combining the sensitivity of the Piagetian méthode clinique with an objectivity and precision favored by American experimentalists. The result is a type of analysis that draws the Piagetian program firmly into an information processing framework." Under her guidance, the Piagetian conception of the child which has become famous, among other things, as a result of direct observation and dialogue with children, clear theoretical formulations with high inferential and application value (for the normal as well as the deviant child), will be continued and extended.

May this book convey the great significance of this approach to the child and stimulate further research in the area of human development.

CHARLES ZWINGMANN

Acknowledgments

1. "Piaget's theory," by J. Piaget, appeared originally in *Carmichael's Manual of Child Psychology* (P. H. Mussen, editor), 3rd Edition, Vol. 1. New York: John Wiley and Sons, Inc., pp. 703–710. © 1970 by John Wiley and Sons, Inc. Reprinted by permission.

2. "The gaps in empiricism," by J. Piaget and B. Inhelder, appeared originally in *Beyond Reductionism* (A. Koestler and J. R. Smythies, editors). London: Hutchinson, pp. 118–148. © 1969 by Hutchinson Publishing Group, Ltd. Reprinted by permission of A. D. Peters and Co.

3. "Information processing tendencies in recent experiments in cognitive learning—Theoretical implications," by G. Cellerier, appeared originally in *Information Processing in Children* (S. Farnham-Diggory, editor). New York: Academic Press, pp. 115–123. © 1972 by Academic Press, Inc. Reprinted by permission.

4. "Biology and cognition," by J. Piaget, appeared originally in *Diogenes*, (54): 1–22 (1966). Reprinted with the permission of *Diogenes*, an International Review of Human Sciences published parallelly in English, French, and Spanish, 1 rue Miollis, Paris-15.

5. "The affective unconscious and the cognitive unconscious" is an original translation of "Inconscient affectif et inconscient cognitif," by J. Piaget, which appeared originally in *Raison Présente*. Paris, 19: 11–20 (1970)

6. "The development of concepts of chance and probability in children," by B. Inhelder, was written especially for this volume. It will also appear in *Knowledge and Development: Advances in Research and Theory*, Vol. 1. New York: Plenum Press (in press).

7. "Identity and Conservation," by J. Piaget, appeared originally in *On the Develop-*

ment of Memory and Identity. Barre, Mass.: Clark University Press. Reprinted by permission.

8. "Memory and intelligence in the child," by B. Inhelder, appeared originally in *Studies in Cognitive Development* (D. Elkind and J. H. Flavell, editors). New York: Oxford University Press, pp. 337–364. © 1969 by Oxford University Press, Inc. Reprinted by permission.

9. "Information processing tendencies in recent experiments in cognitive learning— Empirical studies," by B. Inhelder, appeared originally in *Information Processing in Children* (S. Farnham-Diggory, editor). New York: Academic Press. © 1972 by Academic Press, Inc. Reprinted by permission.

10. "Operational thought and symbolic imagery," by B. Inhelder, appeared originally in *European Research in Cognitive Development* (P.H. Mussen, editor). Monograph of the Society for Research in Cognitive Development, pp. 4–18. © 1965 by the Society for Research in Cognitive Development. Reprinted by permission.

11. "The sensorimotor origins of knowledge," by B. Inhelder, appeared originally in *Early Childhood: The Development of Self-regulatory Mechanisms.* New York: Academic Press, pp. 141–155. © 1971 by Academic Press, Inc. Reprinted by permission.

12. "The development of systems of representation and treatment in the child," is an original translation of "Le dévelopement des systèmes de représentation et de traitement chez l'enfant," by P. Mounoud, which appeared originally in *Bull. Psychologie Paris,* 296 XXV: 261–272 (1971–1972). Reprinted by permission.

13. "Developmental psycholinguistics," by H. Sinclair, appeared originally in *Studies in Cognitive Development* (D. Elkind and J. H. Flavell, editors). New York: Oxford University Press, pp. 315–336. © 1969 by Oxford University Press. Reprinted by permission

14. "Epistemology and the study of language," by H. Sinclair, appeared originally in *Epistemology and the Study of Language.* Paris: CNRS (1971). Reprinted by permission.

15. "Some pathologic phenomena analyzed in the perspective of developmental psychology," by B. Inhelder, appeared originally under a different title in *Merril-Palmer Quart. Behav. Develop.,* 12 (4): 311–319 (1966).

16. "Operatory thought processes in psychotic children," by B. Inhelder, appeared originally under a different title in *Measurement and Piaget* (D. R. Green, M. P. Ford, and G. B. Flamer, editors). New York: McGraw-Hill, pp. 163–167. © 1971 by McGraw-Hill Book Company. Used with permission of McGraw-Hill Book Company.

17. "Need and significance of cross-cultural studies in genetic psychology," by J. Piaget, appeared originally [in French] in *Int. J. Psych.,* 1: 3–13 (1966) and [in English] in *Culture and Cognition* (J. W. Berry and P. R. Dasen, editors). London: Methuen (1974). Reprinted by permission of the International Union of Psychological Science and Dunod Editeur, Paris.

18. "Piaget's theory of cognitive development and individual differences," by M. Bovet, appeared originally under a different title in the *Procedings of the Peabody–NIHM Conference, Part 1.* New York: Appleton-Century-Crofts, pp. 59–70. © 1970 by Appleton-Century-Crofts. Reprinted by permission.

Contents

Introduction

BÄRBEL INHELDER

Throughout his career, Piaget has always concerned himself with problems of genetic epistemology, for to him the question of what is contributed to human knowledge by the knowing subject and what by the object to be known can be answered scientifically only if the question is asked in terms of growth—and hence of transformations—of knowledge. In other words, for Piaget knowledge does not exist in static form but is a constructive process characterized by its origin and development. As his field of study he consequently chose children's ideas at various stages of cognitive development. The method of investigation that has now been used by Piaget and his co-workers for some 50 years is psychogenetic experimentation, which seeks to determine the stages or levels in the construction of knowledge, their developmental links, as well as the mechanisms through which a consistent system of logical reasoning and of explaining the physical world is built up.

One example among many to show the interaction between epistemological and psychologic preoccupations is the development of the concept of chance in the mind of the child, a study suggested by a mathematician and pursued by psychogenetic methods; its results attracted the attention of a number of physicists on the occasion of the

Translated by Morris Sinclair.

fiftieth anniversary of the Niels Bohr Institute. The concept of chance turns out to be a late ontogenetic conquest, just as it is a latecomer in the history of scientific thought. Not until the child has attained a certain level of reversibility in operations and of reasoning by combinatory systems is he capable of gradually understanding, by contrast, the irreversible sequences that characterize chance events.

The pursuit of such interests, which go beyond the bounds of psychology properly speaking, have provided us over decades of research with insight into the often surprising but coherent universe of the child.

Piaget's discoveries relating to the development of concepts of quantity conservation (number, spatial categories, time, causality, and logic) commanded the sometimes critical attention of psychologists all over the world and gave rise to innumerable replication studies which vouch-safed world renown for Piaget as the greatest of child psychologists. His discoveries furthermore threw a new light on certain fields that had been investigated by experimental psychology since its very beginnings, e.g., mental images and memory.

The extreme positions adopted by the associationists and the *Denkpsychologie* of the Würzburg school may be recalled: the former treated the image as a perceptual residue that played an essential part in the building up of associations of ideas; the latter, by contrast, reduced it almost to nothing in a system of thought that proceeded without images. Developmental psychology now seems to have shown that the image as the figurative aspect of cognitive functions takes on the status of a symbol by which it is possible to represent, to evoke, or to anticipate changes in reality (i.e., translations, rotations, and transformations of figures in space). Through our approach, it has been shown that these figurative symbolizations develop along with, and closely depend on, the corresponding cognitive operations.

An interesting complementary finding was provided by the study of certain aspects of memory in its relationship to the genesis of the operations and fundamental concepts of knowledge. The memory code, far from being immutable or only subject to deterioration in the course of time, is transformed and elaborated through the influence of the general forms of action and thought that constitute it and on which the memory-images are in turn dependent.

To put it another way, Piaget in his theoretical approach is constantly drawing on the resources of several disciplines so as to achieve their effective interaction: his epistemology informs his psychology and vice versa, just as both are fertilized by his biologic perspective, which in turn is enriched by both the other disciplines.

Piaget considers himself a naturalist though not a positivist. He is a naturalist by inclination and education. From research on molluscs in Switzerland, to which in his early days he devoted his doctoral thesis in zoology, through his fine study on *Limnaea stagnalis* to his detailed and delightful observations of various phenotypes of the species *Sedum*, which inspired his most recent publication, Piaget has always been concerned with problems of the functional adaptation of the organism to its environment. On the biologic level, this adaptation is considered in terms that are as far removed from Lamarckian empiricism as they are from classic Darwinism. Between the theory of mutations with *post hoc* selection and that of hereditary variations as an exclusive function of the environment, Piaget sees a third possibility: regulatory mechanisms of endogenous origin, modifiable through interaction with the environment.

Piaget's point of view converges with that of certain modern schools of biology, especially Waddington's with regard to his work on embryogenesis in which he brought to light the powerful regulatory mechanism (homeorhesis) that gives direction to the functional interactions between the hereditary program commanding the ontogenesis of the nervous system and the stimulations provided by the environment. This temporal regulatory process is what allows structural equilibrium (homeorhesis) to be installed.

On the psychologic level, similar regulatory systems would account for the installation of cognitive behaviors and would ensure a continuity between biologic and psychologic adaptation. Such continuity becomes apparent in the sensorimotor beginnings of knowledge. The first forms of cognitive adaptive behavior arise from functional assimilatory processes based on preestablished biologic structures. The earliest manifestations of mental activity consist in incorporating, or indeed assimilating, new elements to the hereditarily programmed structures. Through repetition and generalization, this assimilatory activity leads, by differentiation and accommodation, to the construction and subsequent coordination of action forms or patterns ("schèmes"). This activity is thus the basis for the subject's first cognitive systems. The action patterns with which the child explores the world become coordinated and their integration by reciprocal assimilation creates new forms of behavior that are not part of the hereditary organic structures.

Such a biologically oriented conception differs considerably from classic learning theories which refer to connections and conditionings imposed from without, whereas the assimilatory concept always implies the integration of new elements into earlier structures and the elaboration of new structures by the subject in interaction with the environment.

Such a conception is equally far removed from preformism, which is again being cultivated to some extent, in particular under the influence of rationalistic psycholinguistics, which presupposes linguistic structures and thence rational structures written into the hereditary program.

All of Piaget's work stems from a constructivist approach which tends to show a continuity between lower and higher functions without, however, reducing the latter to the former. To account for this continuity as well as for the novelty of cognitive structures, Piaget invokes regulatory mechanisms that operate according to the different levels of achievement and their modes of formation.

Piaget has been called "a cybernetician before cybernetics" because in his early work he presented biologic equilibrium not as a balance of opposing forces but as the result of a kind of mutual support of the parts in relation to the organisms as a whole. Since then, he has consistently taken up the same problem; for, if the origins of knowledge are biologic but not innate, and if the sensorimotor forms of intelligence and logicomathematical thought constitute a continuum, then an explanatory theory has to be based on regulatory systems. Piaget has often stressed the very general character of such systems, whereas heredity can take very different forms in the various biologic groups. The regulatory mechanisms, which are operative at all levels, naturally start by being unconscious and only much later give rise to deliberate and systematic efforts of consistency. The unconscious is not the exclusive preserve of the emotions, as Piaget explained in a paper given to the American Psychoanalytic Society. He has constantly stressed that equilibrating mechanisms govern emotional as well as cognitive processes. This continuous autoregulatory process tends toward ever greater equilibration of which the logical and mathematical operations constitute a perfect form of equilibrium. The second issue of *Etudes d'Epistémologie Génétique* was already devoted to logic and equilibrium, but Piaget now finds it inadequate and has taken up the problem again in a new work published under the title *L'Equilibration des Structures Cognitives* (1975).

The equilibration theory is not a completed system; on the contrary, with its strong heuristic component it opened up unsuspected possibilities of research into a variety of fields including learning theory, developmental psycholinguistics, cross-cultural comparisons of cognitive development as well as psychopathology.

It may come as a surprise that Genevan psychologists have taken an interest in the processes of learning which—by classic standards—presuppose a subject subordinated to the demands of reality. In our interactionist and constructivist view, however, the advance of knowledge results from encounters between the subject's budding patterns of action and thought on the one hand, and reality on the other. It follows that our learning situations are constructed to maximize the possibilities of such encounters occurring. The results of a whole series of research projects first of all have shown that the scope and the quality of the progress achieved during and after learning sessions varied significantly with the subject's level of cognitive functioning which, interpreted in ontogenetic biologic terms, would mean "with his level of competence." The research brought out especially the dynamic aspects of new cognitive discoveries, such as the growing awareness of contradictions between different conceptual subsystems as well as between these systems and the interpretation of reality. The attempts made by children to reconcile, often by way of compromise, their various approaches and interpretations of experimental situations allows us to follow, as through a magnifying glass, the gradual development of knowledge. The fundamental concepts essential to knowledge are not in fact developed in isolation but are continually in interaction; this interaction and its regulatory dynamics seem to play a fundamental part in the development of knowledge by ensuring a kind of equilibration which Piaget calls "majorizing" in order to emphasize that equilibration means a continual search for a better equilibrium rather than only a return to a previous equilibrium following some imbalance. Our learning experiments do not only show behavior that is due to corrective, *post facto*, regulations but also behavior that implies self-regulatory and therefore self-organizatory mechanisms.

A theory of development should also account for the role played by the cultural environment. In our research we concentrated on the construction of the most general forms of knowledge and not on the content of collective beliefs nor on particular performances acquired through social transmission. As regards the construction of the general forms of knowledge there are two extreme theses: on the one hand, universality of human reason and, on the other, its infinite variability and its plasticity in the face of social impact. From the developmental and constructivist point of view, it seems possible to suggest a third interpretation according to which the solicitations and inhibitions of cultural origin would not directly be reflected in the construction of knowledge but would also be subordinate to regulatory mechanisms inherent in the adaptive activity of the subject.

Several of our co-workers have for years been pursuing research in nonEuropean cultures. Such work calls for theoretical rigor as well as great adaptability to the variable conditions and often surprising situations arising in the field. Close collaboration with the local people is of course essential in this type of work. The results obtained so far show considerable convergence. Children growing up in very different cultural settings all show, at one period or another of their development, the same patterns of cognitive assimilation and the same structural coordinations. Divergences appear to be mainly of a temporal nature: already at the sensorimotor level, advances and delays can be observed, and certain acquisitions that seem to be closely linked in one culture may be clearly separated in time in another. More importantly, M. Bovet was able to show that, though certain concepts might, at certain times and because of cultural influences, arise along different pathways than those observed in Switzerland, there was again convergence once the concept was fully acquired. All this tends toward the general conclusion that, though there

5

may be secondary, particularly temporal variations in the acquisition of concepts, the order of acquisition is broadly the same wherever it has been studied.

Research on the psychopathology of thought, originally started in response to a practical need for diagnosing and assessing certain forms of intellectual deficiencies and maladaptations gave rise to several research projects whose results, in turn, gave unexpected support to the psychogenetic theory.

Dissatisfied with the customary approach to testing used in the diagnosis of mental handicap—an approach that relies on performance rather than on the subject's potentialities and that usually lacks a theoretical basis—we sought many years ago (and work in this direction has continued) to find a way of adapting our experimental situations and methods of questioning of developmental psychology to this purpose.

Though pathologic forms of thought show characteristic functional divergences from normal thought patterns, certain basic resemblances again bear witness to the universality of the laws of cognitive development. In mental retardation the hierarchical and integrative order is the same as in normal development, but the constructions remain incomplete; they result from a lower rhythm of development with certain stoppages of development leading to closures or ceilings which, unlike the normal equilibration levels, do not provide the possibility of further elaboration.

An interesting aspect of the breakdown of reasoning in senile dements is that by and large it seems to follow development in reverse order. The breakdown also occurs in the senile dements' production of certain syntactic forms that are closely linked to logical operations. Concepts belonging to the different fields of knowledge (logicomathematical, physical, spatiotemporal) do not seem to disintegrate homogeneously. Moreover, figurative aspects of thought seem to be more subject to deterioration than operative aspects, and the latter can help to compensate for any shortcomings of the former.

In certain forms of child psychoses it is interesting to see to what extent disturbances in the regulatory mechanisms that normally govern the interactions between the subject and the physical and human objects of his environment may hinder the construction of the fundamental framework of knowledge. Psychotic children capable of elementary logical reasoning have particular, insurmountable difficulties with the idea of "chance" as an indeterminate, irreversible type of event.

Another area where new directions of study have opened up under the impact of Piaget's epistemological and psychologic theories is that of psycholinguistics. H. Sinclair and her collaborators are investigating the acquisition of language within a Piagetian developmental framework and a number of experimental studies on the comprehension and production of certain sentence patterns are beginning to yield some insight into the different strategies young children use in the conquest of the creative, but rule-bound, system of their mother tongue.

Epistemological preoccupations thus led to psychologic and even psychopathologic studies, and this extension of the field of investigations allows us gradually to define more clearly the possibilities and limitations of certain modes of adaptation, a direction in which E. Schmid is pursuing her research. Certain hypotheses suggested by cognitivist theory receive support from such more psychologically oriented studies. The fact that deterioration may follow development in reverse is in some respects a stronger confirmation of the concept of developmental stages than that provided by cross-cultural studies since it converges with Jackson's idea of hierarchical dissolution. By accentuating the discordances among aspects of thought which in development are formed simultaneously—such as the operative and figurative aspects of the various types of scientific knowledge—psychopathology enables us to understand better their various roles. The distortions in the representation of reality engendered by disturbances in the regulatory mechanisms convince us—if that were still necessary—of the primordial importance of the equilibration processes for the development of creative thinking.

ONE

Theoretical Aspects

1

Piaget's Theory

JEAN PIAGET

The following theory of development, which is particularly concerned with the development of cognitive functions, is impossible to understand if one does not begin by analyzing in detail the biologic presuppositions from which it stems and the espistemological consequences in which it ends. Indeed, the fundamental postulate that is the basis of the ideas summarized here is that the same problems and the same types of explanations can be found in the three following processes:

a. The adaptation of an organism to its environment during its growth, together with the interactions and autoregulations which characterize the development of the "epigenetic system." (Epigenesis in its embryologic sense is always determined both internally and externally.)

b. The adaptation of intelligence in the course of the construction of its own structures, which depends as much on progressive internal coordinations as on information acquired through experience.

The present chapter is, in part, the expansion of an article on my conceptions of development published in *Journal International de Psychologie*, a summary of previous publications, but it also takes into account recent or still unpublished work by the author or his collaborators and colleagues. As a matter of fact, "Piaget's theory" is not completed at this date and the author of these pages has always considered himself one of the chief "revisionists of Piaget." (Author's note)

11

c. The establishment of cognitive or, more generally, epistemological relations, which consist neither of a simple copy of external objects nor of a mere unfolding of structures preformed inside the subject, but rather involve a set of structures progressively constructed by continuous interaction between the subject and the external world.

We begin with the last point, on which our theory is furthest removed both from the ideas of the majority of psychologists and from "common sense."

THE RELATION BETWEEN SUBJECT AND OBJECT

1. In the common view, the external world is entirely separate from the subject, although it encloses the subject's own body. Any objective knowledge, then, appears to be simply the result of a set of perceptive recordings, motor associations, verbal descriptions, and the like, which all participate in producing a sort of figurative copy or "functional copy" (in Hull's terminology) of objects and the connections between them. The only function of intelligence is systematically to file, correct, etc., these various sets of information; in this process, the more faithful the critical copies, the more consistent the final system will be. In such an empiricist prospect, the content of intelligence comes from outside, and the coordinations that organize it are only the consequences of language and symbolic instruments.

But this passive interpretation of the act of knowledge is in fact contradicted at all levels of development and, particularly, at the sensorimotor and prelinguistic levels of cognitive adaptation and intelligence. Actually, in order to know objects, the subject must act upon them, and therefore transform them: he must displace, connect, combine, take apart, and reassemble them.

From the most elementary sensorimotor actions (such as pushing and pulling) to the most sophisticated intellectual operations, which are interiorized actions carried out mentally (e.g., joining together, putting in order, putting into one-to-one correspondence), knowledge is constantly linked with actions or operations, that is, with *transformations*.

Hence the limit between subject and objects is in no way determined beforehand, and, what is more important, it is not stable. Indeed, in every action the subject and the objects are fused. The subject needs objective information to become aware of his own actions, of course, but he also needs many subjective components. Without long practice or the construction of refined instruments of analysis and coordination, it will be impossible for him to know what belongs to the object, what belongs to himself as an active subject, and what belongs to the action itself taken as the transformation of an initial state into a final one. Knowledge, then, at its origin, neither arises from objects nor from the subject, but from interactions—at first inextricable—between the subject and those objects.

Even these primitive interactions are so close-knit and inextricable that, as J. M. Baldwin noted, the mental attitudes of the infant are probably "adualistical." This means they lack any differentiation between an external world, which would be composed of objects independent of the subject, and an internal or subjective world.

Therefore the problem of knowledge, the so-called epistemological problem, cannot be considered separately from the problem of the development of intelligence. It reduces to analyzing how the subject becomes progressively able to know objects adequately, that is, how he becomes capable of objectivity. Indeed, objectivity is in no way an initial property, as the empiricists would have it, and its conquest involves a series of successive constructs which approximates it more and more closely.

2. This leads us to a second idea central to the theory, that of *construction*, which is the natural consequence of the interactions we have just mentioned. Since objective knowledge is not acquired by a mere recording of external information but has its origin in interactions between the subject and objects, it necessarily implies two types of activity—on the one hand, the coordination of actions themselves, and on the other, the introduction of interrelations between the objects. These two activities are interdependent because it is only through action that these relations originate. It follows that objective knowledge is always subordinate to certain structures of action. But those structures are the result of a *construction* and are not given in the objects, since they are dependent on action, nor in the subject, since the subject must learn how to coordinate his actions (which are not generally hereditarily programmed except in the case of reflexes or instincts).

An early example of these constructions (which begin as early as the first year) is the one that enables the 9- to 12-month-old child to discover the permanence of objects, initially relying on their position in his perceptual field, and later independent of any actual perception. During the first months of existence, there are no permanent objects, but only perceptual pictures which appear, dissolve, and sometimes reappear. The "permanence" of an object begins with the action of looking for it when it has disappeared at a certain point A of the visual field (for instance, if a part of the object remains visible, or if it makes a bump under a cloth). But, when the object later disappears at B, it often happens that the child will look for it again at A. This very instructive behavior supplies evidence for the existence of the primitive interactions between the subject and the object which we mentioned (¶ 1). At this stage, the child still believes that objects depend on this action and that, where an action has succeeded a first time, it must succeed again. One real example is an 11-month-old child who was playing with a ball. He had previously retrieved it from under an armchair when it had rolled there before. A moment later, the ball went under a low sofa. He could not find it under this sofa, so he came back to the other part of the room and looked for it under the armchair, where this course of action had already been successful.

For the scheme* of a permanent object that does not depend on the subject's own actions to become established, a new structure has to be constructed. This is the structure of the "group of translations" in the geometric sense: (a) the translation $AB + BC = AC$; (b) the translations $AB + BA = O$; (c) $AB + O = AB$; (d) $AC + CD = AB + BD$. The psychologic equivalent of this group is the possibility of behaviors that involve returning to an initial position, or detouring around an obstacle $(a$ and $d)$. As soon as this organization is achieved—and it is not at all given at the beginning of development, but must be constructed by a succession of new coordinations—an objective structuration of the movements of the object and of those of the subject's own body becomes possible. The object becomes an independent entity, whose position can be traced as a function of its translations and successive positions. At this juncture the subject's body, instead of being considered the center of the world, becomes an object like any other, the translations and positions of which are correlative to those of the objects themselves.

The group of translations is an instance of the construction of a structure, attributable simultaneously to progressive coordination of the subject's actions and to information provided by physical experience, which finally constitutes a fundamental instrument for the organization of the external world. It is also a cognitive instrument so important that it contributes to the veritable "Copernican revolution" babies accomplish in 12 to 18 months. Whereas before he had evolved this new structure the child would consider himself (unconsciously) the motionless center of the universe, he becomes, because of this organization of permanent objects and space (which entails moreover a parallel organization of temporal sequences and causality), only one particular member of the set of the other mobile objects which compose his universe.

3. We can now see that even in the study of the infant at sensorimotor levels it is not possible to follow a psychogenetic line of research without evolving an implicit epistemology, which is also genetic, but which raises all the main issues in the theory of knowledge. Thus the con-

---

* Throughout this chapter the term *scheme* (plural, *schemes*) is used to refer to *operational* activities, whereas *schema* (plural, *schemata*) refers to the figurative aspects of thought—attempts to represent reality without attempting to transform it (imagery, perception and memory). Later in this chapter the author says, ". . . images . . . , however schematic, are not schemes. We shall therefore use the term schemata to designate them. A schema is a simplified image (e.g., the map of a town), whereas a scheme represents what can be repeated and generalized in an action (for example, the scheme is what is common in the actions of 'pushing' an object with a stick or any other instrument)."

struction of the group of translations obviously involves physical experience and empirical information. But it also involves more, since it also depends on the coordinations of the subject's action. These coordinations are not a product of experience only, but are also controlled by factors such as maturation and voluntary exercise, and, what is more important, by continuous and active autoregulation. The main point in a theory of development is not to neglect the activities of the subject, in the epistemological sense of the term. This is even more essential in this latter sense because the epistemological sense has a deep biologic significance. The living organism itself is not a mere mirror image of the properties of its environment. It evolves a *structure* which is constructed step by step in the course of epigenesis, and which is not entirely preformed.

What is already true for the sensorimotor stage appears again in all stages of development and in scientific thought itself but at levels in which the primitive actions have been transformed into *operations*. These operations are interiorized actions (e.g., addition, which can be performed either physically or mentally) that are reversible (addition acquires an inverse in subtraction) and constitute set-theoretical structures (such as the logical additive "grouping" or algebraic groups).

A striking instance of these operational structurations dependent on the subject's activity, which often occurs even before an experimental method has been evolved, is *atomism* invented by the Greeks long before it could be justified experimentally. The same process can be observed in the child between 4 to 5 and 11 to 12 years of age in a situation where it is obvious that experience is not sufficient to explain the emergence of the structure and that its construction implies an additive composition dependent on the activities of the subject. The experiment involves the dissolution of lumps of sugar in a glass of water. The child can be questioned about the conservation of the matter dissolved and about the conservation of its weight and volume. Before age 7 to 8 the dissolved sugar is presumed destroyed and its taste vanished. Around this age sugar is considered as preserving its substance in the form of very small and invisible grains, but it has neither weight nor volume. At age 9 to 10 each grain keeps its weight and the sum of all these elementary weights is equivalent to the weight of the sugar itself before dissolution. At age 11 to 12 this applies to volume (the child predicts that after the sugar has melted, the level of the water in the container will remain at its same initial height).

We can now see that this spontaneous atomism, although it is suggested by the visible grains becoming gradually smaller during their dissolution, goes far beyond what can be seen by the subject and involves a step-by-step construction correlative to that of additive operations. We thus have a new instance of the origin of knowledge lying neither in the object alone nor in the subject, but rather in an inextricable interaction between both of them, such that what is given physically is integrated in a logicomathematical structure involving the coordination of the subject's actions. The decomposition of a whole into its parts (invisible here) and the recomposition of these parts into a whole are in fact the result of logical or logicomathematical constructions and not only of physical experiments. The whole considered here is not a perceptual "Gestalt" (whose character is precisely that of *non*additive composition, as Kohler rightly insisted) but a sum (additive), and as such it is produced by operations and not by observations.

4. There can be no theoretical discontinuity between thought as it appears in children and adult scientific thinking; this is the reason for our extension of developmental psychology to genetic epistemology. This is particularly clear in the field of logicomathematical structures considered in themselves and not (as in ¶ 2 and ¶ 3) as instruments for the structuration of physical data. These structures essentially involve relations of inclusion, order, and correspondence. Such relations are certainly of biologic origin, for they already exist in the genetic (DNA) programming of embryologic development as well as in the physiologic organization of the mature organism before they appear and are reconstructed at the different levels of behavior itself. They then become fundamental structures of behavior and of intelligence in its very early development before they appear in the field of spontaneous thought and later of reflection. They provide the foundations of these progressively more abstract axiomatizations we call logic and mathematics. Indeed, if logic and mathematics are so-called "abstract" sciences, the psychologist must ask: Abstracted from what? We have seen their origin is not in objects alone. It lies, in small part only, in language, but language itself is a construct of intelligence. Chomsky even ascribes it to innate intellectual structures. Therefore the origin of these logicomathematical structures should be sought in the activities of the subject, that is, in the most general forms of coordinations of his actions, and, finally, in his organic structures themselves. This is the reason why there are fundamental relations among the biologic theory of adaptation by self-regulation, developmental psychology, and genetic epistemology. This relation is so fundamental that if it is overlooked, no general theory of the development of intelligence can be established.

ASSIMILATION AND ACCOMMODATION

5. The psychologic meaning of our previous points (¶ 1 to 4) is that the fundamental psychogenetic connections generated in the course of development cannot be considered as reducible to empirical "associations"; rather, they consist of *assimilations*, both in the biologic and intellectual sense.

From a biologic point of view, assimilation is the integration of external elements into evolving or completed structures of an organism. In its usual connotation, the assimilation of food consists of a chemical transformation that incorporates it into the substance of the organism. Chlorophyllian assimilation consists of the integration of radiation energy in the metabolic cycle of a plant. Waddington's "genetic assimilation" consists of a hereditary fixation by selection on phenotypes (phenotypic variations being regarded, in this case, as the genetic system's "answer" to stresses produced by the environment). Thus all the organism's reactions involve an assimilation process which can be represented in symbolic form as follows:

$$(T + I) \rightarrow AT + E \tag{1}$$

where T is a structure, I the integrated substances or energies, E the eliminated substances or energies, and A a coefficient > 1 expressing the strengthening of this structure in the form of an increase of material or of efficiency in operation.* Put in this form it becomes obvious that the general concept of assimilation also applies to behavior and not only to organic life. Indeed, no behavior, even if it is new to the individual, constitutes an absolute beginning. It is always grafted onto previous schemes and therefore amounts to assimilating new elements to already constructed structures (innate, as reflexes are, or previously acquired). Even Harlow's "stimulus hunger" cannot be reduced simply to subordination to the environment but must rather be interpreted as a search for "functional input" ("éléments fonctionnels") that can be assimilated to the schemes or structures actually providing the responses.

At this point it is appropriate to note how inadequate the well known "stimulus-response" theory appears in this context, as a general formulation of behavior. It is obvious that a stimulus can elicit a response only if the organism is first sensitized to this stimulus (or possesses the necessary reactive "competence" as Waddington characterizes genetic sensitization to specific inducers).

When we say an organism or a subject is sensitized to a stimulus and able to make a response to it, we imply it already possesses a scheme or a structure to which this stimulus is assimilated (in the sense of incorporated or integrated, as defined previously). This scheme consists

---

* For example, take T to be an already established classification on a set of objects, O, which divides it into two distant subclasses. I is a set of new objects that are added to the original ones and to which the classification T must be extended. When this is done (I has been assimilated to T), it turns out that there are say two new subclasses (the whole structure is now AT) and some properties of the new objects I (e.g., the number of elements in I, or their shape, size or color) have been neglected in the process. We now have $T + I \rightarrow AT + E$, where $T =$ the two original subclasses, $I =$ the new elements. $AT =$ the four subclasses, and $E =$ the irrelevant properties of the new elements, that is, the properties which are not used as criteria for classifying in this specific instance.

precisely of a capacity to respond. Hence the original stimulus-response scheme should not have been written in the unilateral $S \to R$ form, but in the form:

$$S \rightleftharpoons R \qquad \text{or} \qquad S \to (AT) \to R \qquad (2)$$

where AT is the assimilation of the stimulus S to the structure T.

We thus return to the equation $T + I \to AT + E$ where, in this case, T is the structure, I the stimulus, AT the result of the assimilation of I to T, that is, the response to the stimulus, and E is whatever in the stimulus situation is excluded in the structure.

6. If assimilation alone were involved in development, there would be no variations in the child's structures. Therefore he would not acquire new content and would not develop further. Assimilation is necessary in that it assures the continuity of structures and the integration of new elements to these structures. Without it an organism would be in a similar situation to that of chemical compounds, A, B, which, in interaction, give rise to new compounds C and D. (The equation would then be $A + B \to C + D$ and not $T \to AT$).

Biologic assimilation itself, however, is never present without its counterpart, accommodation. During its embryologic development, for instance, a phenotype assimilates the substances necessary to the conservation of its structures as specified by its genotype. But, depending on whether these substances are plentiful or rare or whether the usual substances are replaced by other slightly different ones, nonhereditary variations (often called "accommodates") such as changes in shape or height may occur. These variations are specific to some external conditions. Similarly, in the field of behavior we shall call accommodation any modification of an assimilatory scheme or structure by the elements it assimilates. For example, the infant who assimilates his thumb to the sucking schema will, when sucking his thumb make different movements from those he uses in suckling his mother's breast. Similarly, an 8-year-old who is assimilating the dissolution of sugar in water to the notion that substance is conserved must make accommodations to invisible particles different from those he would make if they were still visible.

Hence cognitive adaptation, like its biologic counterpart, consists of an equilibrium between assimilation and accommodation. As has just been shown, there is no assimilation without accommodation. But we must strongly emphasize the fact that accommodation does not exist without simultaneous assimilation either. From a biologic point of view, this fact is verified by the existence of what modern geneticists call "reaction norms" —a genotype may offer a more or less broad range of possible accommodations, but all of them are within a certain statistically defined "norm." In the same way, cognitively speaking, the subject is capable of various accommodations, but only within certain limits imposed by the necessity of preserving the corresponding assimilatory structure. In Eq. 1 the term A in AT specifies precisely this limitation on accommodations.

The concept of "association," which the various forms of associationism from Hume to Pavlov and Hull have used and abused, has thus only been obtained by artificially isolating one part of the general process defined by the equilibrium between assimilation and accommodation. Pavlov's dog is said to associate a sound to food, which elicits its salivation reflex. If, however, the sound is never again followed by food, the conditioned response, or temporary link, will disappear; it has no intrinsic stability. The conditioning persists as a function of the need for food, that is, it persists only if it is part of an assimilatory scheme and its satisfaction, hence of a certain accommodation to the situation. In fact, an "association" is always accompanied by an assimilation to previous structures, and this is a first factor that must not be overlooked. On the other hand, insofar as the "association" incorporates some new information, this represents an active accommodation and not a mere passive recording. This accommodatory activity, which is dependent on the assimilation scheme is a second necessary factor that must not be neglected.

7. If accommodation and assimilation are present in all activity, their ratio may vary, and only the more or less stable equilibrium which may exist between them (though it is always mobile) characterizes a complete act of intelligence.

When assimilation *outweighs* accommodation (i.e., when the characteristics of the object are not taken into account except insofar as they are consistent with the subject's momentary interests) thought evolves in an egocentric or even autistic direction. The most common form of this situation in the play of the child is the "symbolic games" or fiction games, in which objects at his command are used only to represent what is imagined.* This form of game which is most frequent at the beginning of

---

* The categories of play defined by Piaget (in *Play, Dreams and Imitation*, 1961b, for example) are the following:

a. Exercise Games. These consist of any behavior without new structuration but with a new functional finality. For example, the repetition of an action such as swinging an object, if its aim is to understand or to practice the movement, is *not* a game. But the same behavior, if its aim is functional pleasure, pleasure in the activity in itself, or the pleasure of "causing" some phenomenon, becomes a game. Examples of this are the vocalizations of infants and the games of adults with a new car, radio, etc.

b. Symbolic Games. These consist of behaviors with a new structuration, that of representing realities that are out of the present perceptual field. Examples are the fiction games where the child enacts a meal with pebbles standing for bread, grass for vegetables, etc. The symbols used here are individual and specific to each child.

c. Rule Games. These are behaviors with a new structuration involving the intervention of more than one person. The rules of this new structure are defined by social interaction. This type of game ranges over the whole scale of activities, starting with simple sensorimotor games with set rules (the many varieties of marble games, for instance) and ending with abstract games like chess. The symbols here are stabilized by convention and can become purely arbitrary in the more abstract games. That is, they bear no more relation (analogy) with what they represent. (Translator's note) representation (between 1½ and 3 years of age), then evolves toward constructive games in which accommodation to objects becomes more and more precise until there is no longer any difference between play and spontaneous cognitive or instrumental activities.

Conversely, when accommodation prevails over assimilation to the point where it faithfully reproduces the forms and movements of the objects or persons which are its models at that time, representation (and the sensorimotor behaviors which are its precursors and which also give rise to exercise games that develop much earlier than symbolic games) evolves in the direction of imitation. Imitation through action, an accommodation to models that are present, gradually extends to deferred imitation and finally to interiorized imitation. In this last form it constitutes the origin of mental imagery and of the figurative as opposed to the operative aspects of thought.

But as long as assimilation and accommodation are in equilibrium (i.e., insofar as assimilation is still subordinate to the properties of the objects, or, in other words, subordinate to the situation with the accommodations it entails; and accommodation itself is subordinate to the already existing structures to which the situation must be assimilated) we can speak of cognitive behavior as opposed to play, imitation, or mental imagery, and we are back in the proper domain of intelligence. But this fundamental equilibrium between assimilation and accommodation is more or less difficult to attain and to maintain depending on the level of intellectual development and the new problems encountered. However, such an equilibrium exists at all levels, in the early development of intelligence in the child as well as in scientific thought.

It is obvious that any physical or biologic theory assimilates objective phenomena to a restricted number of models which are not drawn exclusively from these phenomena. These models involve in addition a certain number of logicomathematical coordinations that are the operational activities of the subject himself. It would be very superficial to reduce these coordinations to a mere "language" (though this is the position of logical positivism) because, properly speaking, they are an instrument for structuration. For example, Poincaré narrowly missed discovering relativity because he thought there was no difference between expressing (or translating) phenomena in the "language" of Euclidian or of Riemanian geometry. Einstein was able to construct his theory by using Riemanian space as an instrument of *structuration*, to "understand" the relations between space, speed, and time. If physics proceeds by assimilating reality to logicomathematical models, then it must unceasingly accommodate them to new experimental results. It cannot dispense with accommodation because its models would then remain subjective and arbitrary. However, every new accommodation is conditioned by existing assimilations. The significance of an experiment does not derive from a mere perceptive recording (the "*Protokollsätze*" of the first "logical empiricists"); it cannot be dissociated from an *interpretation*.

8. In the development of intelligence in the child, there are many types of equilibrium between assimilation and accommodation that vary with the levels of development and the problems to be solved. At sensorimotor levels (before 1½ to 2 years of age) these are only practical problems involving immediate space, and as early as the second year, sensorimotor intelligence reaches a remarkable state of equilibrium (e.g., instrumental behaviors, group of displacements; see ¶ 2). But this equilibrium is difficult to attain, because during the first months, the infant's universe is centered on his own body and actions, and because of distortions due to assimilation not yet balanced by adequate accommodations.

The beginning of thought creates multiple problems of representation (which must extend to distant space and can no longer be restricted to near space) as well as the problem of adaptation no longer measured by practical success alone; thus intelligence goes through a new phase of assimilatory distortion. This is because objects and events are assimilated to the subject's own action and viewpoint and possible accommodations still consist only of fixations on figural aspects of reality (hence on states as opposed to transformations). For these two reasons—egocentric assimilation and incomplete accommodation—equilibrium is not reached. On the other hand, from the age of 7 to 8 the emergence of reversible operations ensures a stable harmony between assimilation and accommodation since both can now act on transformations as well as on states.

Generally speaking, this progressive equilibrium between assimilation and accommodation is an instance of a fundamental process in cognitive development which can be expressed in terms of centration and decentration. The systematically distorting assimilations of sensorimotor or initial representative stages, which distort because they are not accompanied by adequate accommodations, mean that the subject remains centered on his own actions and his own viewpoint. On the other hand, the gradually emerging equilibrium between assimilation and accommodation is the result of successive decentrations, which make it possible for the subject to take the points of view of other subjects or objects themselves. We formerly described this process merely in terms of egocentrism and socialization. But it is far more general and more fundamental to knowledge in all its forms. For cognitive progress is not only assimilation of information; it entails a systematic decentration process which is a necessary condition of objectivity itself.

THE THEORY OF STAGES

9. We have seen that there exist structures which belong only to the subject (¶ 1), that they are built (¶ 2), and that this is a step-by-step process (¶ 7). We must therefore conclude there exist stages of development. Even authors who agree with this idea may use different criteria and interpretations of stage development. It therefore becomes a problem that requires discussion in its own right. The Freudian stages, for instance, are only distinct from each other in that they differ in one dominant character (oral, anal, etc.) but this character is also present in the previous—or following—stages, so that its "dominance" may well remain arbitrary. Gesell's stages are based on the hypothesis of the quasi-exclusive role of maturation, so that they guarantee a constant order of succession but may neglect the factor of progressive construction. To characterize the stages of cognitive development we therefore need to integrate two necessary conditions without introducing any contradictions. These conditions for stages are (a) that they must be defined to guarantee a constant order of succession, and (b) that the definition allow for progressive construction without entailing total preformation. These two conditions are necessary because knowledge obviously involves learning by experience, which means an external contribution in addition to that involving internal structures, and the strucures seem to evolve in a way that is not entirely predetermined.

The problem of stages in developmental psychology is analogous to that of stages in embryogenesis. The question that arises in this field is also that of making allowance for both genetic preformation and an eventual "epigenesis" in the sense of construction by interactions between the genome and the environment. It is for this reason that Waddington introduces the concept of "epigenetic system" and also a distinction between the genotype and the "epigenotype." The main characteristics of such an epigenetic development are not only the well-known and obvious ones of succession in sequential order and of progressive integration (segmentation followed by determination controlled by specific "competence" and finally "reintegration") but also some less obvious ones pointed out by Waddington. These are the existence of "creodes," or necessary developmental sequences, each with its own "time tally," or schedule, and the intervention of a sort of evolutionary regulation, or "homeorhesis." Homeorhesis acts in such a way that if an external influence causes the devloping organism to deviate from one of its creodes, there ensues a homeorhetical reaction, which tends to channel it back to the normal sequence or, if this fails, switches it to a new creode as similar as possible to the original one.

Each of the preceding characteristics can be observed in cognitive development if we carefully differentiate the construction of the structures themselves and the acquisition of specific procedures through learning (e.g., learning to read at one age rather than another). The question will naturally be whether development can be reduced to an addition of procedures learned one by one or whether learning itself depends on developmental laws which are autonomous.

2

The Gaps in Empiricism

JEAN PIAGET AND BÄRBEL INHELDER

Empiricism has engendered many different ideas, from the naive concepts of knowledge as a copy of reality, to the more refined forms of "functional copy" (Hull's behaviorism) to logical positivism, which aims at reducing scientific knowledge exclusively to physical experience and to language. If we look for common factors in these diverse approaches we find a central idea: the function of cognitive mechanisms is to submit to reality, copying its features as closely as possible, so that they may produce a reproduction which differs as little as possible from external reality. This idea of empiricism implies that reality can be reduced to its observable features and that knowledge must limit itself to transcribing these features.

What we should like to show briefly here is that such a conception of knowledge meets with three fundamental difficulties. Biologists have shown that the relationship between an organism and its environment (at a certain level of scientific study this dichotomy is in itself an abstraction) is one of constant interaction. The view that the organism submits passively to the influence of its environment has become untenable. How then can man, as a "knower," be simply a faithful recorder of outside events? In the second place, among fields of human knowledge and

---

Translated by Mrs. S. Wedgewood (aided by a Ford Foundation grant) with the collaboration of Mrs. H. Sinclair de Zwart.

endeavor, mathematics, for one, clearly escapes from the constraints of outer reality. This discipline deals essentially with unobservable features, and with cognitive constructions in the literal sense of the word. Thirdly, as man acts upon and modifies reality, he obtains, by transforming his world, a deeper understanding than reproductions or copies of reality could ever provide. Furthermore, cognitive activity can be shown to have structural properties: certain broad cognitive structures underlie the thought processes at different levels of development.

BEHAVIORIST EMPIRICISM AND BIOLOGY

The exact counterpart of behaviorist empiricism in biologic theory is a doctrine long since abandoned by biology itself, not because it was wrong in what it maintained, but because it ignored all that has since proved essential to an understanding of the relations between the organism and its environment; we are referring to the Lamarckian theory of variation and evolution. Soon after Hume had sought the explanation of the phenomena of the mind in the mechanisms of habit and association. Lamarck, too, saw the key to the morphogenetic variations of the organism and of organ-formation in the habits adopted under the influence of the environment. Admittedly, he was also speaking of a factor of organization, but he thought of it as a capability of association and not of composition, and the essential aspect of the acquisitions was for him the way in which living beings received, in modifying their habits, the imprint of the external milieu.

These ideas were certainly not entirely wrong, and, so far as environmental influences were concerned, modern "population genetics" has in fact only replaced direct causal action of external factors on the genetic unit (heredity of the acquired characteristics in the Lamarckian sense) by the concept of probabilistic action (selection) of a complex of external factors on multi-unit systems (coefficients of survival and reproduction, etc., of the genetic pool or of differentiated genotypes). But Lamarck's theory lacks the basic principles of an endogenous possibility of mutation and recombination and above all those of an active capacity for self-regulation. When Waddington or Dobzhansky today put forward the phenotype as a "response" of the genetic pool to environmental incitements, this response does not mean that the organism has simply been marked by an external action, but that there has been interaction in the full sense of the term, i.e., that as a result of a tension or imbalance provoked by environmental changes the organism has invented an original solution by means of recombinations, resulting in a new equilibrium.

Thus, when we compare this concept of "response" to that used so long by behaviorism in its famous stimulus-response schema (S–R), we are amazed to find that the behaviorist psychologists have retained a strictly Lamarckian outlook, as if they had ignored the contemporary biologic revolution. Of course, it may well be argued that psychologic and biologic phenomena belong to two different levels since the modifications of behavior studied by behaviorism are exclusively phenotypical, whilst the variations which interest the biologist are hereditary. But we know today that such a distinction cannot be clear-cut and this for numerous reasons, of which the following are the two most important. The first is that the phenotype is the result of continuous interaction between the genes' synthesizing activity during growth and the external influences. The second is that for each environmental influence which can be sufficiently circumscribed and measured, we can determine for a given genotype its "reaction-norms," which give us the range and distribution of the possible individual variations; to ascertain similar reaction norms for behavior we have to make an analysis at all levels of phenotypical reactions.

Consequently, the concepts of stimulus and response must undergo very wide-reaching reorganizations which completely modify their meaning. In fact, in order for the stimulus to set off a certain response, the organism must be capable of providing it. The nature of this capability must therefore first be ascertained. It corresponds to what Waddington called "competence" in the field of embryology (where "competence" is defined as sensitivity to "inductors"). At the outset, it is therefore not the stimulus itself, but the sensitivity to the stimulus which is vital and, of course, the latter depends on the capability of giving a response. The schema must therefore not be written $S = R$ but $S \rightleftharpoons R$, or, more accurately, S (A) R where A is the assimilation of the stimulus to a specific reaction-pattern which is the source of the response.

This modification of the S–R schema is in no way due to a simple desire for theoretical accuracy: it immediately raises what appears to us to be the central problem of mental and, particularly, cognitive development. In the exclusively Lamarckian context of behaviorist theory, the response is simply a sort of "functional copy" (Hull) of the stimuli in their particular succession. Consequently, the fundamental process of acquisition of knowledge is considered a learning process in the empiricist sense of obtaining information through observation of the environment. If this were true, mental development as a whole would then be thought of as the result of an uninterrupted series of "bits" of learning in the above-mentioned sense. If, on the contrary, the basic point of departure is the capability of giving certain responses, i.e., the "competence," learning would not be the same at different developmental levels, and would depend essentially on the evolution of "competences." The true problem would then be to explain their development, and for this the concept of "learning," in the classic sense of the term, would be inadequate.

In our opinion, we cannot but follow the principles discovered by contemporary biology. This means a fundamental change in the psychologic interpretation of mental development. In fact, these new directions in embryology have brought the modern view of biologic development much nearer to our view of psychologic development. As we have long argued, a parallel between biology and psychology does not imply that all is innate in individual development. As we have said, today the phenotype is considered to be the product of an indissociable interaction between hereditary or endogenous factors and environmental influences, so that it is virtually impossible to draw a clear line of demarcation, within behavior patterns, between the innate and the acquired. This is made even more difficult by the presence between the two of the all-important zone of self-regulations.

The linguist N. Chomsky rendered a great service to psychology by providing us with a decisive criticism of Skinner's interpretation of verbal behavior, and by showing the impossibility of representing the process of language acquisition by classic behaviorist and empiricist models. Chomsky has finally chosen the opposite approach insofar as he assumes the existence of an innate kernel* within his transformational grammar. But it is not necessary to take this extreme approach; what Chomsky supposes innate in the capacity for learning language can no doubt be explained by the earlier "structuralizations" due to the development of sensorimotor intelligence (or intelligence preceding language). Generally, even if it is necessary to invoke the endogenous factors disregarded by behaviorism,† it does not mean that everything which is endogenous is hereditary. We still have to consider the factors of self-regulation which are also endogenous but whose content is not innate. As we have just said, between the hierarchical level of hereditary characteristics and that of the acquisitions due to environmental factors, there is a level of self-regulation or equilibration, which plays a vital role in development. This does not oblige or even authorize us to think of everything which is not due to exogenous learning as innate.

Many other lessons of contemporary biology have been ignored by behaviorism, when in fact they are of great psychologic importance. For instance, in addition to homeostasis (often invoked by certain schools of

---

* Mehler and Bever (who consider themselves Chomskyans) regard even the operatory conservations as innate, basing their argument on experiments which have nothing to do with quantitive conservation and which bear witness to the existence at around 2½ and 3 years of a method of numerical evaluation which may be understood as deriving from the quasitopologic criterion of "crowding" and which precedes ordinal evaluation, i.e., evaluation by length.

† It is true that the neobehaviorists are more and more aware of unobservable processes and endogenous factors. However, since they do not use developmental methods of studying these factors and thus do not take into account the different role these factors play at different levels of development, they encounter new difficulties. The theory has been expanded, new hypotheses have been added, but the main theoretical basis has not been changed.

psychology) Waddington has distinguished and labelled "homeorhesis," the sort of kinetic equilibration through which embryonic development, when it has been disturbed, is led back to its necessary paths (which he calls "creodes").

EMPIRICISM AND MATHEMATICS

Insofar as empiricism seeks to limit knowledge to that of observable features, the problem it has failed to solve is the existence of mathematics, and this problem becomes particularly acute when it comes to explaining psychologically how the subject discovers or constructs logicomathematical structures.

Classic empiricism, as argued by Herbert Spencer for example, considered that we derive mathematical concepts by means of abstraction from physical objects: certain Soviet schools of thought share this view, though it is in fact not consistent with the theory of dialectics. In contrast to this attitude, contemporary logical empiricism has well understood the difference between physics, on the one hand, and logic and mathematics, on the other, but instead of seeking a possible common source of knowledge in these respective fields it has maintained that there are two entirely different sources. It has thus aimed at reducing physical knowledge to experience alone (the root of synthetic judgments) and logicomathematical knowledge to language alone (whose general syntactic and semantic features pertain to analytical judgments).

This view poses several problems. Firstly, from the linguistic point of view, while Bloomfield's positivism (and even earlier Watson's behaviorism) aimed at reducing all thought and, in particular, logic to a mere product of language, Chomsky's transformational structuralism reverts to the rationalist tradition of grammar and logic (in doing this, as we have just seen, he exaggerates to the point where he regards basic structures as innate). In the second place, the great logician Quine was able to show the impossibility of defending a radical dualism of analytic and synthetic judgments (this "dogma" of logical empiricism, as Quine amusingly termed it). Moreover, a collective study by our Centre for Genetic Epistemology has been able to verify Quine's objections experimentally by finding numerous intermediaries between the analytic and synthetic poles. Finally, psychogenetically, it is obvious that the roots of the logicomathematical structures must go far deeper than language and must extend to the general coordination of actions found at the elementary behavior levels, and even to sensorimotor intelligence; sensorimotor schemes already include order of movements, embedding of a subscheme into a total scheme and establishing correspondences. The basic arguments of logical empiricism are thus shown today to be refuted in all the linguistic, logical, and psychologic areas where one might have hoped to prove them.

As far as the connections between logicomathematical structures and physical reality are concerned, the situation seems just as clear. It became clarified through experimental analyses of the nature of experience itself. While empiricists aimed at reducing everything to experience, and were thus obliged to explain what they meant by "experience," they have simply forgotten to prove their interpretation experimentally. In other words, we have been given no systematic experimental study on what experience actually *is*.

From our prolonged and careful studies of the development of experience and of the roles which it plays in both physical and logicomathematical knowledge, the following facts emerge.

It is perfectly true that logicomathematical knowledge begins with a phase in which the child needs experience because it cannot reason along deductive lines. There is an epistemological parallel: Egyptian geometry was based on land-measuring, which paved the way for the empirical discovery of the relationship between the sides of a right-angled triangle with sides of 3, 4, and 5 units, which constitutes a special case of Pythagoras' theorem. Similarly, the child at the preoperatory level (before 7–8 years) needs to make sure by actually handling objects that $3+2=2+3$ or that $A=C$ if $A=B$ and $B=C$ (when he cannot see A and C together).

But logicomathematical experience which precedes deductive elaboration is not of the same type as physical experience. The latter bears directly on, and obtains its information from, objects as such by means of abstraction—"direct" abstraction which consists of retaining the interesting properties of the object in question by separating them from others which are ignored. For example, if one side of a rubber ball is coated with flour, the child discovers fairly early on that the further the ball drops in height the more it flattens out when it hits the ground (as indicated by the mark on the floor). He also discovers at a later age (10–11) that the more this ball flattens out the higher it bounces up; a younger child thinks it is the other way round. This is therefore a physical experience because it leads to knowledge which is derived from the objects themselves.

By contrast, in the case of logicomathematical experience, the child also acts on the objects, but the knowledge which he gains from the experience is not derived from these objects: it is derived from the action bearing on the objects, which is not the same thing at all. In order to find out that $3+2=2+3$, he needs to introduce a certain order into the objects he is handling (pebbles, marbles, etc.), putting down first three and then two or first two and then three. He needs to put these objects together in different ways—2, 3, or 5. What he discovers is that the total remains the same whatever the order; in other words, that the product of the action of bringing together is independent of the action of ordering. If there is in fact (at this level) an experimental discovery, it is not relevant to the properties of the objects. Here the discovery stems from the subject's actions and manipulations and this is why later, when these actions are interiorized into operations (interiorized reversible actions belonging to a structure), handling becomes superfluous and the subject can combine these operations by means of a purely deductive procedure and he knows that there is no risk of them being proved wrong by contradictory physical experiences. Thus the actual properties of the objects are not relevant to such logical mathematical discoveries. By contrast, it is just these properties which are relevant when—as in one of our recent experiments—the child is asked questions about how the behavior of pebbles (which stay where you put them) differs from that of drops of water.

The method of abstraction peculiar to logicomathematical structures is therefore different from that in elementary physical experiences. The former can be called a "reflective abstraction," because, when the child slowly progresses from material actions to interiorized operations (by "superior" we mean both "more complex" and "chronologically later") the results of the abstractions carried out on an inferior level are reflected on a superior one. This term is also appropriate because the structures of the inferior level will be reorganized on the next one since the child can now reflect on his own thought processes. At the same time this reflection enriches the structures that are already present. For example, primitive societies and children are already aware of the one-to-one correspondence, but it needed Cantor to discover the general operations of establishing relationships by means of "reflective abstraction" and he needed a second reflective abstraction in order to establish a relationship between the series 1, 2, 3 . . . and 2, 4, 6 . . . and thus to discover transfinite numbers.

In this light we understand why mathematics, which at its outset has been shown to stem from the general coordination of actions of handling (and thus from neurologic coordinations and, if we go even further back, from organic self-regulations), succeeds in constantly engendering new constructions. These constructions must of necessity have a certain form. In other words, mathematical thought builds structures which are quite different from the simple verbal tautologies in which logical empiricism would have us believe.

There is a second difference between physical experience and logicomathematical experience or deduction. Whilst the latter, proceeding by means of reflective abstractions, leads to progressive purification (whose final stages are today those of the formalization peculiar to "pure" mathematics), physical experience is always a sort of "mixture." There is in fact no "pure" experience in the sense of a simple recording of external factors, without endogenous activity on the part of the subject. All physical experience results from actions on objects, for without actions modifying objects the latter would remain inaccessible even to our perception (since perception itself supposes a series of activities such as establishing relationships, etc.). If this is so, the actions which enable us to experiment on objects will always be dependent on the general coordinations, outside of which they would lose all coherence. This means that physical experience is always indissociable from the logicomathematical "framework"* which is necessary for its "structuralization." This logico-mathematical device is in no way restricted to translating the experience into formal language—as if it were possible to have, on the one side, the experience itself and, on the other, its verbal translation.

This brings us back to the central argument of empiricism: that all knowledge should be related as closely as possible to observable facts.

In reality, in every field—from physics to psychology, sociology or linguistics—the essence of scientific knowledge consists in going beyond what is observable in order to relate it to subjacent structures. Firstly, logicomathematical structures must go outside the scope of what is observable, i.e., what is furnished by physical experience in the broad sense (including biologic, psychologic experience, etc.). Infinity, continuity, logical necessity, the hierarchy of constructions and of reflective abstractions are all unobservable realities according to the empiricist, and if they had to be attributed to the simple powers of a "language," this language would have the surprising property of being infinitely richer than that which it describes. Secondly, in physics we might just be justified in regarding as observable features the repeatable relations which functional analysis strives to translate into "laws," but on examination of the actual work of scientists—and not the philosophical statements to which they so often limit themselves—we have to recognize that their systematic and unceasing need to discover why things happen forces them to break through the barriers of the observable. In these last decades, measurement has become a problem and researchers have often sought to identify the structures before attempting measurement. To take just one classic example, no one would dispute that the very widespread success of the application of the group structures in physics means that physicists also subordinate what is observable to systems or models which are not. Present-day achievements of structuralism in biology also provide an example of this and almost all the social sciences are proceeding along the same lines.

* Establishing relationships or logical classes, functions, counting and measuring, etc.

To sum up, the innumerable problems continually being raised by the nature of mathematics and its application to experimental science have moved us further away from, rather than toward, the empiricist ideal of scientific knowledge.

THE NATURE OF INTELLIGENCE

Having thus briefly recalled the difficulties inherent in the empiricist theory of scientific knowledge, we shall now examine the cognitive mechanisms of the human subject in general. First of all, does empiricism in the form of behaviorism give us an adequate interpretation of the nature of intelligence? Behaviorists started off well by studying the subject's actions before his mental mechanisms; these could be studied afterwards by means of the same methods as those used for the actions but extended in scope in order to suffice for their new purpose; G. Miller wittily called this study "subjective behaviorism."

Let us therefore, like the behaviorists, start with the action, but without prejudging the nature of either the external reality or the subject. There is only one profitable method of avoiding such prejudices which result from the fact that we are adults, and as such have certain set forms of thought and behavior. This is the method of developmental psychology in which we follow step-by-step the formation and then the progressive interiorization of actions in our child subjects. This enables us to think of our adult attitudes as the result of a long development, rather than let these attitudes condition our interpretation of the facts. When we proceed in this way we make three fundamental observations. The first is that during the first year of life all actions show an interdependence between the subjects and the objects, which are bound together with no preestablished frontier separating them. There are as yet no objects independent of the subject (object permanency only starts around 9–10 months*) and reciprocally, the subject does not know himself as such, but only in reference to his successive actions. This initial level of complete interaction or radical inability to differentiate between the subject and the objects is important. It is not a question of trying to establish how the subject is going to adapt himself to a reality looked at from outside, but on the contrary, to understand how the succession of action patterns is going to lead to an objectivization of reality (therefore to a construction of objective relations) and to an internal organization of actions.

* Bower showed that if an infant is shown an object which is then hidden behind a screen, from the age of one week he can recognize it when it is shown to him again. This, however, only serves to prove that recognition is a very early phenomenon and in no way does it confirm the permanency or totalization of the object while it is hidden.

The second observation is that an action consists in transforming reality rather than simply discovering its existence: for each new action the acts of discovering and transforming are in fact inseparable. This is not only true of the infant whose every new action enriches his universe (from the first feed to instrumental behavior patterns, like the use of a stick as a means of pulling an object towards one), but it remains true at all levels. The construction of an electronic machine or a sputnik not only enriches our knowledge of reality, it also enriches reality itself, which until then did not include such objects. This creative nature of action is essential. Behaviorists study behavior, therefore actions, but too often forget the "active" and transforming characteristic of an action.

Thirdly, this active nature is inherent in all and not solely the motor aspects of an action. It would thus be very misleading to contrast perception and action as if perception informed us about the world such as it "is in reality" whilst action alone succeeded in transforming it. It can be seen, for example, that if an infant is given his bottle the wrong way up, he tries to suck the wrong end (until about 7–8 months), whilst later he first of all turns the bottle round, so that he can suck from the right end. It is only then that he seems to perceive the bottle as a reversible solid, whose visible sides hide another side which he must find. As, in this particular case, the change in perception is correlative to the discovery of object permanency (whence the "constancy" of its form), it is clear that perception is a basic part of the entire action schematism and cannot be considered a realm apart.

We must therefore conclude from these three observations that an organization of actions, much deeper and richer than a simple set of "associations" between perceptions and movements, is constituted very early on in life. An action which is repeated engenders a *"scheme"* characterized by what is repeatable and generalizable in the original action. The basic property of a scheme (which must not be confused with a figurative *"schema"*—we shall return to this point) is to ensure *"assimilations,"* which, like the judgments of which they are the precursors, may be correct or wrong—which is not the case with associations. For example, when the behavior pattern of the stick becomes established, that is, when the child becomes capable of pulling towards him a desired object with the help of a stick, he may assimilate a metal rod to the stick, which is correct, or a pliable straw to the stick, which is wrong. This system of assimilation schemes presents certain general forms of coordination (order of movements, embedding of a subscheme in a total scheme, establishing correspondences, intersections, etc.), and we must go right back to these forms to find the roots of what will become logicomathematical structures.

Intelligence is thus, in the initial sensorimotor period, the progressive coordination of action schemes. By contrast, with the advent of the semiotic function* (deferred imitation, mental imagery, language, etc.) these actions become "interiorizable" (i.e., they develop independently of externally observable behavior). Thus an uninterrupted series of "reflective abstractions" lead to new constructions. Between 2 and 7–8 years there are no reversible operations, i.e., coordinations which can be effected simultaneously and mentally both ways (unite–dissociate, add–substract, etc.). As a result, when there are transforming actions (transferring a liquid into a bottle of different dimensions, changing the shape of a clay ball, etc.) there are no quantitative conservations. We are, however, already witnessing the formation of a "half logic"—if we may use this term—made up of one-way schemes. For example, the functional dependences $(y=b^{(x)})$, characterized by directed one-way mappings, can be called qualitative but do not yet include reversibility or conservations, whence the noticeable dominance at this level of the notion of order and the widespread use of the ordinal evaluations: "longer" signifies "going further"; "quicker" for a moving object means that it overtakes another, etc.

From 7–8 years, on the other hand, this first half of logic is completed by its second half, in the sense that the child realizes that the most general transformations of action (ordering, uniting, embedding, establishing correspondences, etc.) are reversible (by inversion or reciprocity). The transforming actions are then interiorized as real operations, which combine with each other into a coherent structure and which are stable precisely because they are reversible. These are the operations which enable the construction of seriations $(A>B>C\ldots)$ with transitivity, of classification with understanding of inclusion, of multiplicative matrices (two-way classifications or seriations) and above all of number and measurement (by synthesis of order and inclusion, etc.).

These are the basic operatory mechanisms which, in our opinion, characterize the "concrete" intelligence of the 7 to 10–12-year olds. This intelligence, still linked to the handling of objects, serves as a basis for the

---

* We follow the tradition of the great Swiss linguist de Saussure as regards the different categories of signifiers.

Signifiers that are part of, or caused by, objects or events (for example, the nipple of a baby's bottle, or the traces an animal leaves in the snow, or the smoke of the fire) are called *signals* (in French "indices").

Signifiers that have some resemblance to objects or events (for example, a stick used in play as an umbrella) are called *symbols* (in French "symboles"). Images belong to this same category as do the symbolic gestures which evoke an object, a event, a person, an event.

Signifiers that are conventional and without any direct relation to the significate (for example, words, algebraic signs, numbers, etc.) are called *signs* (in French "signes").

There are many intermediaries between symbols and signs. Symbols become collective symbols which are symbols as well as signs, depending on how much the conventional aspect of the relationship between "signifier" and "significate" is stressed. (For example, the Lorraine Cross was a symbol but has now become a conventional sign designating Gaullism and the original symbolic connection has been almost forgotten.)

later more "formal" structures, which are formed from 11–12 years by the addition of combinatory systems (such as the logic of propositions) and a more general "group" structure coordinating inversions and reciprocities.

But we shall not elaborate on subjects which we have described too often elsewhere (Piaget and Inhelder, 1966b). We have to ask ourselves why the empiricist view in psychology, represented mainly by behaviorism in its many variations, has so frequently neglected the activity of the subject, and why certain authors still refuse to believe in cognitive structures, and consider them to be mere theoretical and logical models made up by psychologists, instead of underlying structures inherent in the cognitive development of the human subject. We see two basic reasons for this.

The first is that psychology is thought of as a science divorced from all others—as if there could be a discipline which is sufficient in itself, when in fact the boundaries between the different sciences are always artificial. We maintain, on the contrary, that it is one of the duties of psychology to try and find the links between behavior and organic life in general and those between man's cognitive development and his important scientific creations. It may well be argued that these are problems of the future, but we think that it is never too early to prepare for the future. The sensorimotor action schemes of the first year of life plunge deep into organic life, and, in a sense, they constitute an intermediate zone between the organic self-regulatory mechanisms and the later logical mathematical operations and their underlying structures. To seek out the possible ways of linking biology to logic and mathematics, is thus no theorist's luxury but the developmental psychologist's duty.

The second reason why so many authors do not understand the significance of such a concept of operations and underlying structures stems, we think, from the superstition of the "observable." If every action is a transformation of reality, it thus constitutes by its very nature a constant sampling of what is observable, and a constant conquest of what is possible—which is still unobservable. Why be afraid of crediting the subject with operatory structures of which he remains unconscious and which are in this sense unobservable, when at the higher developmental levels, these structures will lead logicians and mathematicians to build increasingly rich constructions, culminating in the most far-reaching achievements of the human mind?

Information Processing Tendencies in Recent Experiments in Cognitive Learning— Theoretical Implications

GUY CELLÉRIER

Professor Frijda is reported (by Gascon, 1969) to have said, in an unpublished conference that "Piaget's theory is easier to program than any other existing theory of intelligence." However, my impression is that Piaget's central concepts are not sufficiently specified in their present form to be programmable. His experiments are programmable, but their simulation should only be considered as a means to elucidating the nature of these constructive processes. This is what I wish to submit to a discussion here.

Frijda goes on to say that "programming Piaget does not give rise to problems of principle, but only to practical ones." His examples of practical problems are: how to simulate the processes of abstraction and equilibration; how to make the proper operation and concepts available to the program at the right time; how to formalize the child's environment. If these represent practical problems for the programmer, they also happen to be fundamental problems in Piaget's theory as it stands today. Furthermore, these types of problems would seem to arise whenever we try to convert a structural theory into an information processing one. I would like to add straightaway that I strongly agree with Frijda that all the problems he mentions are fundamental to this conversion. I would only add simulation of *reciprocal assimilation* (the process that coordinates schemes) to his list, and reorganize the list somewhat so as to make it reflect the interdependencies that exist between the problems it mentions.

Piaget himself has never explicitly formulated his views on simulation, so as a first approximation to coordinating his structural approach with simulation problems, I will try to relate this question to Piaget's general position on the nature of explanation.

In Piaget's view, to explain a physical phenomenon (say the expansion of a gas when it is heated) we first discover regular relations between selected properties (pressure, temperature, volume in this case). This is a problem in pattern *recognition*. Then we express these regularities in terms of our own operations (Boyle's equation). This is not an explanation, it simply recodes under the guise of a physical law, a great number of possible experimental situations. This description, however is stronger than the first because the rule allows us to compute what the object will do. We have reconstructed the extension of our experiments and extended it hopefully to all possible experiments. Our new description now allows us to do pattern *generation*. It has, in some sense, captured the *structure* of the task environment—the structural constraints that force it, when it moves, to do so in certain regular paths.

If we now go on to inquire how the object manages to do this computation, we start to move in the direction of explanation. We generally try to discover elementary behaviors of the object (or of its parts) that can be said under some interpretation—again in terms of our operations—to do analog computation of our digital ones, or of their decomposition. Then we show that specific interactions or composition of these elementary behaviors—which may or not be verified experimentally—*necessarily* result in the observed laws and explain them deductively. We now have a process that implements and animates the structure defined by the laws, and we can attribute these lower level operations to the interaction of objects.

The first part of this process—the establishment of structural laws —would describe Piaget's central preoccupation in psychology. He has often compared his representation of the child's stabilized use of rules and concepts to the mathematician's axiomatic representation of an underlying intuitive theory. His succession of *logicomathematical structures* reflects the succession of implicit intuitive theories the child evolves about such concepts as space, time, number, and perhaps truth and its conservation in deduction. This sequence is open at both ends. At the lower end elementary logical operations have their root in psychologic actions on objects or concepts, these actions having their own roots in biologic adaptation. At the upper end the last of the child's structures merge with the first of the adult mathematician's. The child's largely implicit reflective abstraction evolves into the adult's explicit formalization procedures. Moreover, the sequence of mathematical abstractions does not seem to have an upper bound.

This structural approach was dictated, it seems to me, by two main factors in Piaget's thought—one essential, the other somewhat accidental. The first is his fundamental preoccupation with epistemology. He often uses psychology to provide counterexamples to philosophical views on the nature of knowledge. More importantly, however, Piaget's grand design may be characterized as the reconstruction of the Kantian *a priori* categories of knowledge—as developmental necessities. To do this, structures were excellent building blocks. Structures are, in a sense, microcategories. They acquire their normative properties (the quality of deductive necessity) only *a posteriori* through development. Although this developmental aspect refutes the Kantian hypothesis, the Kantian criteria are nevertheless satisfied. Compositions of the structural microcategories generate the Kantian categories. For example, the coordination of class inclusion and seriation generates the concept of number—with all of its Kantian attributes.

The second factor is related to the state of the art in mathematical formalization as it was accessible to the layman (as opposed to the professional mathematician) when Piaget was doing his main work on *groupments* (the INRC group, etc.). The prevalent formalization procedure at the time was what Hilbert called *the postulational method*: we postulate a set of entities, define the operations—i.e., rules for combining them—by their effects on these objects and hopefully proceed to discover and prove interesting properties of these objects and operations. The interesting properties should at least include the intuitive properties attached to the concepts of the underlying (intuitive) theory we are formalizing. This is achieved through an interpretation of the abstract symbols in terms of these underlying, concepts and actions.

This type of representation is at least twice removed, in its degree of abstraction, from the actual actions and situations with which the child or the adult deals. The situations or their internal psychologic representations (concepts, equivalence classes of situations, etc.) are first coded into abstract symbols, elements of a set, and thus divested of their content. The actions (external or internalized) that transform one situation into another are coded into operators that do the same on the symbols. More often than not in Piaget's formalizations, the resulting structure is then defined on the *compositions* of these operators—these compositions reflecting the general coordinations of actions. By way of consequence, the relation of action to situation is also divested of its psychologic means–end dimension. The main point here is that action itself also loses its content in some sense. As it is only defined by its effects or a given extension, the definition of an operator need not incorporate a description of how this result is produced. The operator becomes a black box. The symbol "$+$" represents addition, but does not specify its algorithm.

In brief, I believe these two factors—Piaget's interest in the structure and evolution of concepts, and his use of a postulational method—suffice to account for what has sometimes been called his "sublime disregard of process" in his epistemological analyses. However, it would be grossly misrepresenting his theory to say that process has no place in it. Piaget's insistent characterization of intelligence as an extension of biologic adaptation, and of schemes as the organs of this adaptation are obvious counterexamples.

Definitions of the scheme as goal-oriented sequences of conditional actions and perceptions sound very TOTE-like (Miller *et al.*, 1960) nowadays. I am tempted to speculate that if the genetic or constructive approach to formalization (in Hilbert's terminology), with its representation of processes and its accent on explicit rewriting rules, had been as developed and accessible as it is now, Piaget would have expressed the regularities he observed in behavior in terms of systems of formalized schemes and not of structures. These systems would certainly be easier to simulate, because they would embody the rulelike components of cognition. However, we would still be left with the problem of relating their output to the situation or state-description aspect of knowledge, that is, of interpreting this output in terms of the observed intuitive concepts and representations, as well as of their relations. This would mean constructing a structural theory.

Structure- and scheme-based representations are therefore just two different ways to describe the same observable regularities. Actually, they are not trivially equivalent. Their relations are very similar to the ones we find in many mathematical systems. The same set of strings of symbols can be described as a Boolean algebra in the classic postulational approach, or as "cranked out" by a formal system. Automata have associated semigroups, recurrence relations sometimes have equivalent algebraic forms, and there seems to be no simple way to convert one type of representation into the other. Such a conversion always entails some amount of invention and discovery. Furthermore, the relation is not necessarily one-to-one. We can find an instance of two automata with the same semigroup that cannot be called identical under any reasonable definition of machine homomorphism.

It is quite clear that programming Piaget in the sense of simulating all Piaget-type situations would not be programming the essential Piaget, i.e., the *development* of intelligence. These experimental situations do not cover the whole scope of intelligent behavior in children. Even if they did, we would be left with a juxtaposition of independently evolving programs with no central unity. We would be left also with the job of writing the central coordinator program. However, Piaget's recent experiments on conceptualization of schemes, and on conflicts between schemes, show a significant trend towards a more detailed observation and representation of processes. I think a formulation of these observations in a completely specified algorithmic form is a necessary condition for the realization of this goal.

Nevertheless, these complementary approaches are only descriptive. It we now turn to the second component of explanation—namely, to showing how the observed regularities are produced and implemented by the child—we find the same problem.

In Piaget's language, the succession of stabilized behaviors in seriation gives rise to a sequence of structural representations of concepts, these concepts and their structure evolve. In Gascon's (1969) simulation, the formulation would be: the child uses different rules or algorithms for seriation, that also evolve with age. Furthermore, to each structure in the sequence corresponds a related algorithm—i.e., the sequence of stages is identical in both cases. The remaining problem is also identical: It is to specify what *produces* these successions of rules and concepts. Gascon achieves the simulation of evolution simply by modifying parameters of the program. The main one is the number of relations that must be known about one element of the series before it is put in final position. If this number is one, the program generates a juxtaposition of ordered couples. At the other extreme, if it is six (there are seven blocks to be ordered) it generates a seriation. The formative mechanism that produces the transitions from one extreme to the other is clearly not simulated in any way attributable to some existing mental process in children.

The process of generating uncoordinated couples can be conceptualized in terms of rules: Piaget's *rule of couples*. In terms of structure it is a *classification* into heavy and light blocks. The corresponding conceptualization is that of weight as an absolute, nonrelational property of objects. During the intermediate stage (not simulated by Gascon) the rule of couples may enter into conflict with itself: if $A < B$ is established and by some combination of design and bad luck B is again evaluated to establish $B < C$, A and C can still be classified, but now B cannot be, so the classification is refined and B becomes a medium element. However, now the rule must be changed to accommodate the insertion of any new element into one of *three* classes. This may be done in many ways, but it seems the new stabilized concept emerging from these empirical explorations is that of weight as a relation.* This is linked to the emergence of the rule of *local maxima* as an extension of the rule of couples: [max $(a,b) = a] \Longleftrightarrow (a > b)$ to triples. However, on triples, this entails the em-

---

* In other words, the two nonrelational properties "a is heavy," "b is light" are integrated into the single relation "a heavier than b"—Original editor's note by S. Farnham-Diggory.

pirical discovery of the rule: max [max(ab), c] = max [a, max(bc)] = max (abc).* The extension of this rule to the whole sequence, followed by its systematic repetition, then generates a decreasing series of local maxima (this is the operatory algorithm "determine the heaviest of all, then the heaviest of the rest, etc." . . .).

If we now ask: "How do the new rules and concepts appear," this experiment and many others seem to show the results of a common process. Piaget (1970b) defines it again in a postulational manner, by its effects on the elements—schemes and concepts—it acts upon: "*Reflective abstraction* extracts from the lower structures what is needed for the construction of higher structures. The ordering process in seriation is abstracted from elementary forms that appear in the local orderings of couples, triples or empirical series." To complete the picture, one must add, that the origins of these local orderings can themselves be traced in the general coordinations of sensorimotor actions—i.e., in their sequential character. The second stage of the abstraction process consists in recombining the elementary processes and coordinating them into a new synthesis. The final stage consists in systematizing the coordination process itself, and in extending it to all possible cases. "The self-regulation of the coordination process results in the equilibration of the connections following the two directions (direct and inverse) of possible constructions." The example in seriation would be descending and ascending methods producing decreasing and increasing series, respectively. The achievement of equilibrium produces the *novel* properties of the system compared to the preceding one, their operatory reversibility, for instance. It also preserves some of the essential properties of the lower system as particular cases of the novel one. Piaget's classic example is that of the successive extensions of the concept of number from integers to complex numbers.

What would be the elements of a constructive formulation of the abstraction process? The main idea seems to be that the new rules and concepts arise from recombination of the ones that are present. This recombination relies heavily on the existence of a general purpose representation system that can code both actions and situations, and of a pattern recognition device that acts on these representations to produce rules and concepts—that is, higher order entities such as prescriptions and descriptions. This means the representation system must have some capacity to accommodate new types of input: it must itself be adaptive. Finally, there must exist a decomposition and recombination device that acts on these descriptions and prescriptions to generate new ones. The actual choice of which combinations should be generated would have to be based on the construction of a succession of partial, reorganized repre-

---

* In a series of more than two, the child must discover the associativity—i.e., that the order in which the blocks are chosen for comparison does not matter—through experience—Original editor's note.

sentations (structured models) of the relationships between prescriptions and descriptions, and of techniques for transcribing one into the other, thereby linking the structural and process descriptions. The selection of the adapted combinations would depend on an evaluation of their effects on the (external) problem environment, this evaluation being used to update the internal model and start a new recombination sequence.

This cyclic chaining of external observations and internal coordinations is emphasized in Piaget's recent reformulation of the equilibration model. By generating the extension of certain rules, new properties of the environment can be discovered. These new properties serve to invent new rules that can then be used to discover new properties. The cycle stops when nothing new is generated, under a given definition of the problem environment. The constructive interaction of rules and concepts through their extension is already very striking in the seriation experiments.

This type of analysis gave rise to a picture of cognitive development as a parallel evolution of cognitive categories, each composed of a neat filiation of progressively stronger structures. It has been recently complicated by the discovery that many different schemes and concepts may be applied by the child to the same problem, and that the different cognitive categories seem to evolve at slightly different rates. The net result is that lateral interactions between precursors appear at the decomposition and recombination level. These interactions (Piaget describes them as reciprocal assimilations between schemes, resulting in new coordinations) take place between elements that are heterogeneous in two ways: (1) they originate from different categories; and (2) their degrees of completion are not necessarily the same. Thus, Piaget's picture of development now incorporates *vertical* relations (intracategory filiations) *horizontal* ones (intercategory lateral interactions), and *oblique* ones (interactions between elements of different operatory levels).

Professor Inhelder's new line of experiments is partly responsible for this change in the model and will help to elucidate the following aspects of the problem at hand:

(1) Their initial diagnostic phase should produce an inventory of the possible precursor elements that the abstraction and coordination act upon. By repeating this analysis on the precursors themselves, and doing this on elements from different categories, we may find a set of elementary precursors that belong to the ancestry of a wide variety of structures. For instance, I believe some kind of elementary *contiguous composition* scheme is implemented throughout the various *groupments*. Its actualization on a given problem will depend on the coding of the problem's particular elements (e.g., logical, topologic) in a form acceptable by the composition routine. By *contiguous*, I mean the result of the first action must—in some way depending on the child's descriptors—resemble the initial conditions of the following one. For instance: $A \to B * C \to D$ is defined only if

there is some XY such that $(A \to B * X \to Y) = A \to C$. The converse decomposition scheme would also be a frequent common ancestor. An instance of this would be professor Inhelder's example of practice on inclusion of classes favoring acquisition of conservation. The common decomposition scheme being activated would be the commutative partition $A + A' = B = A' + A$ generalized to any partition of B, and extended to the assimilation of continuous objects.

(2) The actual learning experiments should allow us to observe not the coordination process itself, but a close series of snapshots of its effects—how the schemes are decomposed, what are the successive recombinations that are generated and tried out, what are the guiding constraints their generation is subjected to. This last aspect is already remarkably illustrated in Dr. Inhelder's paper by the conciliation solutions of the children who construct equal paths, but who break up their units to preserve numerical equality.

To sum up and conclude, I believe structural and process models are not just theoretically complementary descriptions of the same phenomena, but that they reflect—in a perhaps too stylized form—the constructive interplay of rules and concepts in actual thought. Children, or adults for that matter, use structured representations of their task environment to "compute out" on them possible courses of action. We call this process *thought*. It is not a random walk through a faceless maze, but more like the choice of a path through a somewhat uncharted one. Moreover, our rules of choice and the chart itself are constantly being updated by the discoveries we make not only on the maze, but also on our own methods of exploration. When we divest our representations of their contents, and our computations of their objects, we may, *a posteriori*, project thought on the two dimensions of structures and formal deduction systems.

Furthermore, I suspect the formative mechanisms Piaget defines, are not mere artifacts of the theory, but reflections of the processes that actually weave the two dimensions of our models into a functional performing system. I do not believe our representations are stored as permanently organized cognitive maps, but rather that we actively reconstruct the maps from sets of stored cues whenever we have a specific problem to solve in detail. When we do this, we integrate the relevant cues we may have accumulated since our last reconstruction. It is at this point that the final product—our cognitive maps—come closest to being models of the psychologist's structures. With practice, we may become better at the reconstruction of itself—that is, our rules for representation evolve. In this sense, structures are only *a posteriori* descriptions of the results of an evolving process.

In the same manner, schemes should not be conceptualized as fixed, stored programs or subroutines, but as being reinvented more or less completely whenever they are called in on a specific problem. There again

43

the final product may *a posteriori* be described as a formal system. In both cases, what we call *development* is the result of change in our reconstruction rules. How this change occurs is therefore the central problem in both structural and process theories. My conjecture is that it can only be solved by a synthetic approach describing a functional progressive reequilibration that would somehow avoid infinite regressions into metarules and metaconcepts by incorporating a cycle of alternating constructions of the metalanguage of one category in the language of the other.

Biology and Cognition

JEAN PIAGET

In order to compare cognitive and biologic mechanisms, we must first state that the former are an extension and utilization of organic autoregulations, of which they are a form of endproduct. To demonstrate this, one can begin by noting the close parallels between the major problems faced by biologists and those faced by theoreticians of the intelligence or of cognition. Secondly, one can analyze the functional analogies and especially the structural isomorphisms between organic life and the means of cognition: "nested" structures, structures of order, multiplicative correspondence, etc. One can also attempt a sort of comparative epistemology of the different levels of behavior (the "logic" of the instincts or of the learning processes, etc.). Finally, one can examine the explanations current among biologists to account for the formation of intelligence. But if these various analyses bring into relief the continuity between organic life and cognitive mechanisms, on the other hand it still remains to be seen that the latter constitute differentiated and specialized organs for reacting physiologically to the external world. Or in other words, that at the same time that they are an elaboration of organic structures in general, they fulfill particular functions, although still of a biologic nature. The following pages are based on this premise, but it should be understood that it is not a question of

Translated by Martin Faigel.

45

contrasting cognition with organic behavior but rather of placing the functions of the former within the framework of the latter.

THE FUNCTIONS SPECIFIC TO COGNITION

In studying the functional relationships and the partial structural isomorphisms between cognitive and organic functions, one notes the existence of a remarkable number of similarities but also a certain number of differences which show that cognition also has specific functions. Moreover the contrary would be unthinkable since if organisms were self-sufficient—without instincts, acquired ability, or intelligence—it would indicate a radical duality of kind between life and cognition, since cognitive mechanisms do in fact exist. This in turn would raise inextricable difficulties for an epistemology simply trying to explain how science is able to arrive at objective knowledge.

Behavior, the Extension of the Environment and the Closing of the "Open System"

To begin with the basic facts of ethology, the majority of perceptions characteristic of animals are of a utilitarian and practical kind. Instinct is always at the service of the three fundamental needs of nutrition, self-defense, and reproduction. If with migrations or different types of social organization it seems to pursue derivative ends, they are derivative only in the sense that these interests, grafted onto the three principal ones, are still based on them and are ultimately subordinate to the survival of the species and to the possible survival of the individual.

The elementary forms of perceptual or sensorimotor learning fall within a similar functional structure, and it is the same for a very large part of routine or sensorimotor intelligence. Nevertheless, in this latter area one must admit that with mammals and especially Anthropoids there is some development of activity which remains functional but involves comprehension for its own sake: we know that young mammals play and that this, despite K. Groos, is not just an exercise of the instincts, but a general exercise of the activities possible at a given level, without present utility or without being put into use. Now, play is but one pole of the functional processes operating in the course of individual development, the other pole being non-playful exercise, where the young subject "learns to learn" (Harlow) in a context of cognitive adaptation and not solely of play. One of our children, aged about one year, chanced to pass through the bars of his playpen a toy which he wanted but which, being too long, had to be placed vertically in order to make the passage possible. He was not satisfied by his chance success, but he put it outside again and repeated his efforts until he "understood." This beginning of disinterested knowledge is without doubt equally accessible to chimpanzees.

But whether exclusively utilitarian or involved in this transition from "know-how" to "understanding," animal cognition thus already quite clearly demonstrates a specific function, in comparison with survival, nutrition, or reproduction in their purely organic aspects: this is the function of extension of the environment. To search for food instead of drawing it from the earth or from the atmosphere like a plant, is already to enlarge the environment. To search for the female and to care for offspring is to assure to reproduction more spatiotemporal control than that of the purely physiologic function. And to explore for the sake of exploration (like the rats described by Blodgett), without immediate utility, to the point of learning for its own sake, as this already appears within the realm of sensorimotor intelligence, is to extend even further the part of the environment that is actually put to use.

It is clear that during later development the mere existence of instruments for intelligent cognition, even if it pursued only utilitarian ends at the start, creates a new functional situation, since every organ tends to develop and maintain itself for its own sake: from this stem the fundamental cognitive needs of comprehension and invention; but they in turn lead to an ever-growing extension of the environment, this time as an object of consciousness.

One can express biologically this slow extension, later to become more and more accelerated with man, of the accessible environment to needs at first biologic and later more specifically cognitive, by relating it to the fundamental traits of the living system. An organism, according to Bertalanffy, is an "open system" precisely in the sense that it retains its form only through a continuous flow of exchanges with the environment. Now, an open system is a constantly threatened system, and it is not for nothing that the basic concerns of survival, food, and reproduction lead to behavior which results in the extension of the usable environment. This extension must then be translated into terms which express its actual function: it is essentially an attempt to close the system and this precisely because it is too "open." From the point of view of probability (and it is the only one suitable here) the particular risk to the open system is that its immediate environment or its frontiers will not supply the necessary elements for its survival. To close the system would instead be to circumscribe an area capable of ensuring survival.

One sees at once that the closing of the system is a goal constantly pursued but never achieved. It is not that the initial needs of food, protection, or reproduction are infinite, far from it. Rather it is that, as soon as various actions serving to satisfy these needs are developed, thanks to a slight enlargement of the initial environment, the cognitive controls of these actions lead sooner or later to an unlimited extension of the system, and this for two reasons.

The first is related to the probability of encounter with desired elements (food and sex) or feared ones (protection). So long as a living creature does not have differentiated sensory organs, exterior events affect it only through immediate contacts and cease to exist as soon as the immediacy disappears. There exist then only momentary needs which disappear as soon as they are satisfied and reappear later, according to a periodic cycle of varying length. However, as soon as a cognitive control develops and olfactory or visual organs indicate food or danger some distance away, the needs are modified by this extension itself: even if the appetite is momentarily satisfied, the absence of visible nourishment or its odor becomes a disturbing modification of the possibilities of recurrence and creates a new need in the form of the need to search, although there may be no immediate desire to be satisfied. Similarly, awareness of enemies, even a safe distance away, engenders a new need for vigilance and watchfulness. In other words, the appearance of a cognitive control leads to its alteration as a consequence of function, and this change involves an enlargement of the environment without the possibility, on this elementary level, of ever closing the "open system." Moreover we should note that a similar general extension of the environment begins already on an organic scale previous to sensory controls. This is the dissemination of seed in the sexual reproduction of plants, a good example of spontaneous extension without cognitive control. What would happen if a cognitive control permitted the plant to be informed by feedback of the relative failure of this manner of propagation?

Behavior and Cognitive Controls

The second reason for the enlarging of the environment which aims at closing the "open system" but which constantly pushes back the limits of this closure is progress in the internal mechanisms of cognitive regulation. Here we reach an essential point about the nature of the cognitive process and the way it develops.

Let us take an ordinary physiologic cycle $(A \times A') \to (B \times B') \to \dots (Z \times Z') \to (A \times A') \to$, where $A, B \dots Z$ are the elements of the organism and $A', B' \dots Z'$ the elements of the milieu with which they are in basic interaction. One can then schematize the intervention of a developing cognitive mechanism as a control which reacts to the presence of some external element or other, A', informs the relevant organs, A, and thus participates in the process $A B$, facilitating its development.

From the beginning, therefore, cognitive response has a role of control and leads to compromise, intensification, change, compensation, or other regulation of the physiologic process. But it goes without saying that this elementary response, which can take the form of tropisms or of only slightly differentiated reflexes, precisely because it is a regulating mechanism involves the possibility of, and even requires, indefinite development, for it is in the nature of a regulating agency to be able to correct itself through the control of controls. In the case of our elementary scheme the chain or feedback leading from A' to A, which comprises a signal from A', or afference, and an effect on A, or effection, results in two kinds of possible improvements or controls of behavior to the second power, while internal or physiologic regulation affect the process $A \to B$: (1) there can be refinements in the recording of A' in the form of various conditionings which assimilate new signals or cues within the initial set of perceptive schemata and thus constantly enrich the perceptive keyboard with controls differentiating the initial total stimulus; (2) above all there will be refinements in the reactive systems affecting A, and it is here that new controls show their possibilities in an uninterrupted sequence, of which sensorimotor development in man's growth pattern gives a particularly striking example: on the basic reflex schemes such as suction, grasping, or oculomotor reflexes a succession of more and more complex behaviors is built, whose two general principles are the accommodation of assimilatory schemes leading to their differentiation, and above all the reciprocal assimilation of schemes (vision and touch, etc.), leading to their coordination. Now from the point of view which concerns us here, the double basic significance of this development, which produces sensorimotor intelligence, is (a) that the progress we have observed is due to a control of controls which results in the exercise of cognitive functions for their own sake, independently of utilitarian or strictly biologic basic needs (nutrition, etc.), and (b) that consequently this pushes further and further back the "closure" of a system open to the environment.

That this progress is due to a control of controls is evident, to begin with, in the differentiation by accommodation of the assimilatory systems. For on one hand this accommodation is carried out by trial and error, and this is typical of feedback systems where the action is corrected according to its results. But on the other hand, this trial and error control does not develop from nothing, but from within a previous framework of reflexes or acquired assimilatory schemes, and these initial schemes are the basic controls whose differentiation is elicited by a superimposed regulation.

The coordination of schemes by reciprocal assimilation also involves the control of previous regulations by new ones, and these secondary regulations are especially important since they are related to actions. For the coordination of schemes is a process which simultaneously moves forwards and backwards, since it arrives at a new synthesis which modifies in its turn the schemes thus coordinated.

The internal progression of the mechanism of cognitive control then implies its exercise, that is to say, the formation of a series of new interests no longer subject to the initial interests which are activated by the functioning *per se* of the system. These interests are the functional expression of the mechanism of cognitive assimilation itself but, again we see, as a direct extension of the initial sensory process. The resulting enlarged environment is therefore both the environment, in the biologic sense of all the stimuli which affect the organism in its physiologic cycle, and the cognitive milieu, considered as all the objects of interest to the consciousness.

But this new extension of the environment is unable to close the "open system" since it remains subject to probabilities of occurrence or, in other words, to the chance experiences of the subject. It is only with imagination or thought, which multiplies at an accelerating rate the spatiotemporal distances characterizing the field of action and comprehension of the subject, that the closing of the open system becomes a possibility. But this requires interindividual or social exchanges as well as individual exchanges with the environment, and we shall return to this problem later.

Organic Equilibrium and Cognitive Equilibrium

If the first essential function of cognitive mechanisms is thus the progressive closing of the "open system" of the organism thanks to an indefinite extension of the environment (and this function is indeed an essential part of the process even if, or above all if, it never reaches complete stability), this function leads to a series of others.

The second one to remember is of equally fundamental importance, for it relates to the system's mechanisms of equilibrium. Living systems are essentially self-regulating. If what we have discussed is correct, the development of cognitive functions is clearly, in accordance with our hypothesis, the creation of specialized organs of control for the regulation of exchanges with the exterior, at first of a physiologic type, directed at materials and forces, and later purely functional, that is to say, bearing essentially on the functioning of actions and of behavior. But once differentiated organs come into being, are their controls identical to those of the organism? Or in other words, are the forms of equilibrium the same?

The body of known facts leads to the reply, yes and no. They are the same regulations or the same forms of equilibrium in the sense that cognitive organization is an extension of living organization and therefore introduces an equilibrium in the sectors where the organic equilibrium is inadequate—in its particular sphere (as we have seen) and in its accomplishments. But the controls and the cognitive equilibrium differ from the organic equilibrium precisely in that they succeed where the latter is incomplete.

The evolution of organized life appears as an uninterrupted sequence of assimilations of the environment to more and more complex forms, but the very diversity of these forms shows that none of them has been able to put this assimilation in a state of lasting equilibrium. If each group or species is in equilibrium, their succession demonstrates a perpetual beginning anew. It is therefore first of all in the relationship between assimilation and adjustment that the cognitive functions introduce something new.

To begin with the development of knowledge, it seems at first sight that we are in the presence of a completely comparable phenomenon. Not to mention the diversity of instincts or of elementary learning processes, the evolution of the human sciences does not always give us a picture of coherent development easily able to introduce new adjustments required by experience into a permanent assimilatory framework by enlarging or simply differentiating it. But there is an exception, and this is the major one of logicomathematical structures, important enough by itself but notably increased in significance by the fact that these structures provide the principal assimilatory schemes used by the experimental sciences. In effect, logicomathematical structures present the unique example of a continuously evolving development, such that no new structurization has had to eliminate its predecessors. Of course these can be poorly adapted to an un foreseen situation but only in the sense that they are unable to resolve a new problem and not that they are contradicted by the very terms of this problem, as it can happen in physics.

Thus, in the relationship between assimilation and accommodation, logicomathematical structures involve a *sui generis* type of equilibrium. On one hand they can be viewed as the continuous construction of new schemes of assimilation—the assimilation of previous structures in a new, integrated one, and the assimilation of experimental data in the structures thus created. But on the other hand, they show a permanent accommodation in the sense that they are not modified by the newly created structures (except to be amplified) or by the experimental data which the latter are capable of assimilating. Certainly, new data on physical experience can pose unexpected problems for mathematicians and lead to the creation of theories which can absorb them; but the creation in this case is not drawn from an accommodation in the manner of the concepts of physics. On the contrary it is derived from previous structures or schemes at the same time that it is adapted to the new reality.

One can then propose an interpretation which might appear to be rash but which seems to have a true biologic foundation if one agrees, as everything seems to suggest, that the primary source for the coordination of actions, out of which come mathematics, can be found in the general laws of the system: it is that the equilibrium between assimilation and

51

accommodation reached by logicomathematical structures constitutes the simultaneously flexible, or dynamic, and stable state vainly sought after by the succession of forms, at least in the realm of behavior, during the evolution of organized life. While this evolution is marked by a continuous series of disequilibriums and equilibriums, logicomathematical structures achieve a permanent equilibrium despite the new additions which characterize their evolution.

This brings us to the problem of "vection" or of "progress" raised by many present-day biologists. Vection, which seems to be proved by organic evolution, is characterized by the remarkable union of two apparently antithetical qualities, whose cooperation is necessary for the major accomplishments of adaptation. One has been especially stressed by Schmalhausen: this is an increasing integration which makes the processes of development more and more autonomous with regard to the environment. The other, stressed by Rensch and by J. Huxley, is the increasing "widening" of possibilities for influencing the environment, and by consequence penetration into environments which become more and more extended.

It goes without saying that these two aspects in combination can be found in the development of the sciences. It is to the extent that human intelligence has found in logicomathematical structures an instrument of integration increasingly independent of experience that it has made a greater conquest of the experienced environment. But once again, because of the very nature of their equilibrium, the cognitive structures develop from the organic ones through extension. They have a similar nature but, as we have seen, in the case of cognition it has developed into forms which are inaccessible to the organic equilibrium. With regard to vection, the difference appears in the following way. The process of integration pointed out by Schmalhausen involves only a certain type of integration, which can be described as current or synchronous, and it therefore has to reconstitute itself in every new group without being able to integrate the entire phyletic past as a subsystem both retained and developed (to put it concretely, mammals have lost some of the characteristics of reptiles by becoming mammals, etc.). The unique character of the integration characteristic of cognitive evolution is, on the contrary, as we have seen, that it is more than temporary and integrates previous structures as subsystems of the current integration. This integration, surprisingly both diachronic and synchronous, occurs without conflict in mathematics (whose "crises" are only those of growth with but momentary contradictions); however, in the experimental sciences a new theory can contradict previous ones. It remains notable though that a new theory always aims at a *maximum* of integration of the past, so that the best theory is the one which integrates previous results, adding necessary retroactive corrections.

The Dissociation and Conservation of Forms

But this achievement is due to another specific character of the cognitive functions in contrast with organic life: this is the possible dissociation of form and content. An organic form is inseparable from the matter which it organizes, and in any particular case it is suited only to a limited and well-defined group of substances, whose modification necessitates a change in form. Once again we find a similar situation (given the continuity between the living system and the cognitive one) in elementary forms of consciousness such as sensorimotor or perceptual schemes, although they are already more generalized than the innumerable forms of biologic organization. But with the development of intelligence, operative systems become still more generalized, although at the level of concrete operations (classes and relations) they may still be related to their contents, just as structurization is to the structured matter when it can proceed only step by step without sufficient deductive mobility. Finally, with the hypothesizing-deductive activity which proportional combination permits, it becomes possible to elaborate a formal logic, in the sense of an organizing structure applicable to any kind of content whatever. This is what makes it possible to create "pure" mathematics, viewed as an ensemble of organized forms prepared to organize anything, but ceasing temporarily to act as it is dissociated from application. Once again we find a biologic situation impossible on an organic level, where microorganisms are capable of "transduction" of genetic messages from one species to another, but only as content or matter, and where genetic "transduction" of an organization understood as a form dissociated from all substance has not yet been observed!

But on the cognitive level, this refining of form leads to accomplishments constantly sought after, one might say, in the organic domain but never fully achieved. It is possible to establish certain analogies between the conservation of biologic forms (so evident in the regulatory self-conservation of the chromosome) and the exigencies of conservation characteristic of different forms of intelligence, from sensorimotor intelligence (a system for the permanency of objects) to operative conservation. In this respect it might seem that an artificial comparison is being made between quasi-physical systems on the one hand and normative or ideating ones on the other. But once one is aware of the basic nature of regulation characteristic of elementary cognitive functions and the sequence from regulation to action, the comparison becomes more natural, for organic conservation is in fact the outcome of regulatory mechanisms. But the analogies thus touched upon nonetheless run into an important difference, and this is what concerns us here: organic conservation is never more than approached. Moreover, this is also true for preliminary cognitive forms (perceptual constants), while only the operative conservations of intelligence are rigorous and "necessary," on account of the dissociation of form and content.

Conservation is closely related to operative reversibility, which is its source and which, in addition, demonstrates the particular form of equilibrium reached by logicomathematical structures. We must then be at the very heart of the difference which, deep within their similarity, distinguishes the constructive work of intelligence from that of organic transformations. The basic analogy is that both have to struggle incessantly against the irreversibility of events and the deterioration of energy and information. And both systems deal with the problem by elaborating organized and balanced systems whose principle is to compensate for deviation and error. Thus, beginning with controls of a homeostatic* nature—genetically as well as physiologically—there is a fundamental tendency toward reversibility of which the attempted conservation of the system is the result. Whatever may be the eventual explanations, still to be worked out, used to resolve the problem of the anti-chance function necessary to the organization and evolution of life (exceptions to Carnot's principle or various forms of conciliation) there remains however that an autoregulatory system involves actions oriented in two opposed directions and that it is this partial reversibility whose progress we can follow in the development of cognitive controls. But as we have pointed out above, the result of the general interplay of reflective abstractions and of reconstructions converging with this evolution, is that the evolution which marks the progress of each level with respect to the preceding one is based more on the regulation of regulations, and so on a reflexive refining of the system or on superimposed controls, rather than on a simple horizontal extension. This is why the mechanism of the "operations" of thought represents more than an extension of previous controls and constitutes a sort of limiting process toward the point where strict reversibility establishes itself as soon as the retroactive action of feedback becomes an "inverse operation," thus ensuring the exact functional equivalence of the two possible directions of the construction.

Social Life and the General Coordination of Action

But the most remarkable aspect of human knowledge in its mode of formation, as compared with the evolutionary transformations of organisms and the forms of knowledge achieved by animals, is its collective as well as individual nature. One can of course observe the outlines of a similar characteristic in a number of animal species, especially the

* According to Cannon, homeostasis means the regulatory mechanism which maintains equilibrium as a physiologic system, plus, as we have since discovered, the organic function which ensures hereditary transmission (genetic homeostasis).

chimpanzee. Nevertheless, the novelty with man is that external or educative transmission (as opposed to the hereditary or internal transmission of the instincts) has led to an organization capable of fathering civilizations.

We should first note that, if it is necessary to distinguish between two types of development, one organic (characteristic of a single organism) and the other genealogic (comprising lines of descent, whether social or genetic), the history of human science combines these two developments in a single whole: ideas, theories, and schools of thought develop genealogically, and one can construct for them genealogic trees representing the relationship of structures. But they are so well integrated into a single intellectual organism that the succession of thinkers is comparable, to quote Pascal, to a single man endlessly learning.

Now, human societies have been described, in turn, as the result of individual initiative propagating itself by imitation, as totalities acting from the outside on individuals, or as systems of complex interactions producing individual action, which is always in conjunction with a more or less important part of the group, as well as producing the entire group defined as the system of these interactions. In the area of cognition, it seems evident that the individual operations of intelligence and the operations that ensure the actual exchange in cognitive cooperation are one and the same thing, since the "general coordination of the actions," which is the source of logic, is an interindividual as well as intraindividual coordination, inasmuch as these "actions" are collective as well as individual. It is therefore a meaningless question to ask if logic or mathematics are essentially individual or social. The epistemic subject which creates them is both an individual, placed off-center with respect to his specific "me," and the sector of the social group, off-centered with respect to the constraining idols of the tribe; and these two types of displacement show the same intellectual interactions or general coordination of action which is constitutive of cognition.

The result is thus (and this is the final basic difference which we shall point out between biologic and cognitive organization) that the most general forms of thought, since they are capable of being dissociated from their content, are because of this the medium for cognitive exchange or interindividual regulation, at the same time that they arise out of common functions characteristic of all living systems. Certainly, from a psychogenetic point of view, these interindividual or social (and not hereditary) regulations form a new element with respect to individual thought, which if deprived of them is exposed to all kinds of egocentric deformation, and they are a necessary condition for the constitution of a decentralized, epistemic subject. But from a logical point of view, these higher controls are still dependent on the conditions of all general coordination of action and so have the same biologic origins.

ORGANIC REGULATION AND
COGNITIVE REGULATION

This collective reelaboration of forms already built out of elements pertaining to biologic organization also helps to locate the remaining observations within their true framework. Our hypothesis is thus that cognitive functions are a specialized organ for the regulation of exchanges with the external world, although they derive their instruments from biologic organization in its general forms.

Life and Truth

It might seem that the necessary existence of a differentiated organ is self-evident, since the specific character of knowledge is to attain truth, while it is specific of life only to seek its persistence. But if we do not know exactly what life consists of, we know even less about cognitive "truth." There is general agreement that it is something other than a faithful copy of reality, for the good reason that such a copy is impossible, since only the copy could provide the knowledge of the model to be copied and since this knowledge, on the other hand, is necessary for the copy! To attempt it leads to a simple phenomenism, where subjectivity constantly interferes with the perceived datum, which itself demonstrates an inextricable connection between subject and object.

If truth is not a copy, it is then an organization of reality. But organized by what subject? If we take the human subject, the risk in this case is expanding egocentrism into anthropocentrism—which will also be sociocentrism—and the gain is minimal. Consequently philosophers concerned with the absolute have had recourse to a transcendental subject which goes beyond man and especially "nature" so as to place truth outside spatiotemporal and physical contingencies and to make nature intelligible in a nontemporal or eternal perspective. But the question then is whether it is possible to leap over one's shadow and to reach the "Subject" *in se*, without his remaining, in spite of all, "human, too human," to quote Nietzsche. For the trouble is that from Plato to Husserl the transcendental subject has constantly changed shape, with no improvements other than those due to the progress of the sciences themselves, hence of the real model and not the transcendental one.

Our intention then is not to run away from nature, since no one escapes nature, but to investigate it step in step with the effort of science because, whatever the philosophers may think, it has still not given up all its secrets and because, before putting the absolute in the clouds, it may be useful to look at the inside of things. Consequently, if truth is an organization of reality, the first question is to understand how one organizes an organization, and this is a question for biology. In other words, since the epistemological problem is to know how science is possible, we should exhaust the possibilities of immanent organization before having recourse to the transcendental.

But if truth is not egocentric and should no longer be anthropocentric, is it then necessary to reduce it to a biocentric organization? If truth is more than man, is it necessary to look for it in protozoa, termites, or chimpanzees? If one defined it as a vision of the world shared in common by all living creatures, including man, the result would be a meager one. But the character of life is to surpass itself constantly, and if one seeks the secret of rational organization in the living system, *including its own mechanisms of progress*, the method then consists of trying to understand knowledge by its very construction, which is not the least bit absurd, since it is *essentially construction*.

The Deficiencies of the Organism

From a cognitive point of view, these progressive evolutions, which are just as essential as the initial state, seem inherent to the living system itself. Its organization is that of the system of all exchanges with the environment; it tends then to spread out into the entire environment but it never completely succeeds. This is where cognition comes in to assimilate functionally the whole universe without being limited to material physiologic assimilation. The living system creates forms and it tends to conserve them in as much stability as possible, but without success. And this again is where cognition comes in to extend material forms into forms of action or of operation which are then capable of conservation under their applications to the various contents from which they are dissociated. This living system is a source of homeostasis at every step; its regulations ensure equilibrium by the evolution of quasi-reversible mechanisms. However, this equilibrium remains fragile and resists the surrounding irreversibility during but transient stages, so that evolution appears to be a series of disequilibriums and of returns to equilibrium, partially giving way to a mode of structuring that comprises the integrations and reversible mobility which cognitive mechanisms only are able to accomplish completely by integrating control into the construction itself in the form of "operations."

In short, the need for differentiated organs to regulate exchanges with the external world results from the inability of the living system to carry out it own program, implicit in the very laws of its organization. For on one hand, it involves genetic mechanisms which are formative and not merely transmittive; but their method of formation (as it is now understood) founded on the recombination of genes, ensures only a limited construction, bounded by the needs of hereditary programming which is necessarily restricted, as it is unable to conciliate construction and conservation within a single coherent dynamic (as cognition will do), and as it lacks sufficiently flexible information on the environment. On the other hand, phenotypes (by phenotypes we mean the form which individual organisms take with relation to the milieu, as opposed to the "genotype" or hereditary form), that achieve a certain amount of interaction with the environment, fall within a norm of reactions in itself bounded; but above all their individual achievements remain both limited and without influence on the whole (for want of the social or external interactions which are made possible for man by cognitive exchanges) except through genetic recombinations, with their afore-mentioned limitations.

This double deficiency of organisms in their material exchanges with the environment is partly compensated by the constitution of structured behaviors, created by the system as an extension of its internal program. For behavior is nothing more than the very organization of life, but applied or generalized to a larger sector of material and energy exchanges than those which are already ensured by the physiologic organization. And functional implies that the emphasis is on the actions and forms or schemes of action that extend organic forms. Nonetheless, these new exchanges, like all the others, consist in adaptations to the environment that take into account its events and their sequence; but above all they consist of assimilations which use the environment and often even impose shapes upon it through constructions or arrangements of objects satisfying the needs of the organism.

Like all organization, this behavior involves regulations, whose function is to control constructive adaptations and assimilations by acting on information on the results received in the course of action or by the elaboration of anticipations which allow the forecasting of favorable events or of obstacles and the preparation of the necessary compensations. These regulations, which are differentiated with regard to the internal control of the organism (since we are concerned here with behavior) constitute the cognitive functions. And the problem then is to understand how they widen the scope of organic regulation to the point where they can carry out the internal program of the system without being subject to the deficiencies we mentioned.

Instinct, Learning, and Logicomathematical Structures

The basic facts here are in the first place, that cognitive controls begin by using only the instruments of organic adaptation in general, that is to say, heredity with its limited variations and phenotypic accommodation: from these stem the hereditary modes of cognition such as those that appear in instinctive behavior. But subsequently the deficiencies of the initial system that are corrected only slightly on the new behavioral level turn up at the level of this innate cognition. This is what causes, but only during the later stages of evolution, the final break-up of instinct and the separation of its two components, internal organization and phenotypic adaptation. What results then (and this is not immediately upon dissociation, but as an effect of complementary reconstructions in two opposite directions), is the double emergence of logicomathematical structures and of experimental science, still undifferentiated in the practical intelligence of Anthropoids, who are geometers* as much as they are technicians, and in the technical intelligence of the beginnings of humanity.

The three fundamental types of knowledge are innate skill, whose prototype is instinct, knowledge of the physical world, which extends the learning process as a function of the environment, and logicomathematical knowledge; and the connection between the first and the latter two seems essential to an understanding of the way in which higher forms are indeed an organ for controlling interchanges. We shall return to this point in conclusion.

Instinct indeed already includes some cognitive controls as may be observed, for example, in the feedback system formed by· Grassé's "stigmergies."† But these controls remain limited and rigid, precisely because they develop within a framework of hereditary programming, and programmed controls are not capable of invention. Certainly it happens that animals are able to deal with unforeseen situations through readjustments which foretoken intelligence. The coordination of schemes that occurs on this occasion can be compared with the innate coordinations of the instinctual, transindividual cycle, which gives an important indication of the possible functional relationship between instinct and intelligence, despite the difference of epigenotypic (the epigenotype is a structure using the definition suggested by the work of Waddington which includes both genotypic and epigenotypic structures, that is, related to an embryonic development interacting with the environment), and phenotypic levels which characterizes them. But the phenotypic developments of instinct remain very limited and its deficiency thus remains tied to its nature, which demonstrates that a form of cognition that remains linked to the simple mechanisms of organic adaptation, despite some traces of cognitive regulation, scarcely approaches the achievements of intelligence.

Though the area of learning *stricto sensu*, that which lies beyond the innate, begins with protozoa, it grows only very slowly until the cerebralization of the higher vertebrates, and however remarkable the exceptions that begin to appear with insects, it shows no systematic development until the primates.

* See the interesting experiments of I. Meyerson and P. Guillaume.

† Grassé calls "stigmergies" certain hereditary behavioral regulations of termites. They form small pellets of matter in building their homes, and when these reach a specific volume, the pellets then become used as supports, floors, etc., in accordance with a new set of laws, but without a particular order of succession.

The Break-up of Instinct

The fundamental phenomenon of this scission, or in other words, the almost total disappearance in the Anthropoids and man, of a cognitive organization which remained dominant throughout the entire evolution of animal behavior, is thus highly significant. This is not, as it is generally said, because a new mode of cognition, that is to say, intelligence considered en bloc, replaces a superseded one. More deeply, it is because a still quasi-organic form of cognition develops into new forms of control which take the place of the preceding form but do not replace it. Properly speaking, they inherit it, dissociating it and using its components in two complementary directions.

What disappears with the dismemberment of instinct is hereditary programming, and this benefits two new types of cognitive self-regulation, that are both flexible and constructive. One might then say that this is in fact a replacement, and indeed a complete one. But one then forgets two essential factors. Instinct does not consist exclusively of hereditary mechanisms—such a concept is an extreme one, as Viaud has properly pointed out. On the one hand, instinct derives its programs and above all its "logic" from an organized activity which originates in the most general forms of the living system. On the other hand, it extends this programming by individual or phenotypic actions that contain an important element of adaptation and even of assimilation, in part learned and in certain cases almost intelligent.

Now, what vanishes with the disappearance of instinct is only the central or median part, that is to say, programmed control, while the other two components—the origins of organization and the results of individual or phenotypic adjustment—remain. Intelligence therefore inherits instinct while it rejects the methods of programmed regulation in favor of constructive self-regulation. What it retains allows it to follow the two complementary directions of interiorization, toward sources, and of exteriorization, toward learned or experienced adjustments.

The condition for this double evolution is naturally the construction of a new mode of control, and this must be remembered to begin with. These controls, which are no longer programmed but from now on are flexible, begin with the usual corrective activity, carried out as a function of the results of actions and of anticipations. But as participants in the construction of schemes of assimilation and in their coordination, under the combined influence of progressive and retroactive effects they end up moving in the direction taken by operations themselves, inasmuch as these are viewed as controls for precorrection and not just correction, and as the inverse operation is viewed as an action ensuring complete and not simply approximate reversibility.

It is thanks to this new kind of control, that constitutes a differentiated organ for deductive verification as well as for construction, that intelligence can evolve simultaneously in the two directions of reflexive interiorization and experimental exteriorization we have just discussed. It is clear that this double orientation does not involve, and in fact has nothing in common with a sharing of the spoils of instinctual cognition. On the contrary, what remains of instinct is only its sources of organization and its end-products such as exploration and individual research. For intelligence to use the former and extend the latter, it must therefore turn to new constructions, of which some release the preconditions for general coordination of action through the use of reflective abstraction, and others absorb the experimental data into the operatory systems thus constructed. But it remains no less true that these two directions carry on the functions of two of the previous components of instinct.

After the break-up of instinct, a new cognitive evolution begins and in fact it starts from scratch since the innate mechanisms of instinct have disappeared and, no matter how hereditary the cerebral nervous system and intelligence, seen as an ability to learn and invent, may be, the work to be done henceforth is phenotypic. Moreover, it is because this intellectual evolution starts from scratch that one generally finds it so difficult to relate it to the living system or above all to the structures, remarkable in their own right, of instinct.

This is a good example of what one might call "convergent evolving reconstructions." In the case of human intelligence, this reconstruction is in fact so complete that hardly any theoreticians of logicomathematical knowledge have thought to explain it in the clearly necessary framework of biologic organization. This was true at least before mechanophysiology showed the connection between logic, cybernetic models and the neurophysiologic activity of the brain, or before McCulloch described the logic of neurons.

Knowledge and Society

But if such complete reconstruction is possible, it is because intelligence, by discarding the prop provided by hereditary structures and moving toward constructed and phenotypic controls, turns away from the transindividual cycles of instinct only in order to engage in interindividual and social interaction. There does not seem to be any discontinuity here, since we already find group action in chimpanzees.

One might say in this connection that from a cognitive point of view the social group plays the same role that "population" does from the point of view of genetics and therefore from that of instinct. In this sense society is the supreme unit, and the individual succeeds in inventing or in creating intellectual structures only to the degree that he is the seat of collective interactions whose level and value naturally depend on that of the society in general. The great man who seems to initiate new trends is only a point of intersection or of synthesis, of ideas elaborated by continuous cooperation, and even when he dissents from majority opinion he is responding to underlying needs of which he is not the source. This is why the social environment actually does for intelligence what genetic recombinations in the entire population did for evolutionary variation or the transindividual cycle of the instincts.

But society, however external and educative its methods of transmission and interaction may be in comparison with those of hereditary transmission or combination, is no less than the latter a product of life. And "collective representations," as Durkheim called them, still presuppose the existence of a nervous system in the members of the group. This is why the important question is not to weigh the merits of the individual versus the group (like asking which came first, the chicken or the egg): it is to distinguish between logic, whether in the course of solitary reflection or cooperation, and errors or insanities in collective opinion or in the individual consciousness. For, despite Tarde, there are not two logics, one serving the group and the other, the individual. There is only one way of coordinating actions A and B in a nested relationship or in one of order, etc., regardless of whether these are the actions of various individuals, one or some for A and another or others for B, or the actions of the same person (who did not after all invent them alone, since he is a member of the whole society). It is in this sense that cognitive controls or operations are the same whether in a single brain or in a system of cooperations (which is the meaning in French of the word *coopération*).

In sum, and however banal the thesis might seem, it is worth stressing that cognitive functions are extensions of organic controls and that they constitute a differentiated organ for regulating exchanges with the external world, for this hypothesis implies far more than these few pages can suggest.

5

The Affective Unconscious and the Cognitive Unconscious

JEAN PIAGET

I would like to thank first the American Psychoanalytic Association for having invited me to speak at this congress. It is a great honor and I am very flattered. This invitation has a scientific importance that I would like to underline. There was a time when no contact existed between psychoanalysts and "academic psychologists." Since then, scientific psychologists—who have an advantage over you in that they don't belong to a particular school—have understood the importance of Freudian psychoanalysis and have incorporated, more or less prudently and successfully, its central ideas into their theories of behavior. But apart from some famous exceptions (D. Rapaport, P. Wolff, Spitz, Cobliner, and Anthony) psychoanalysts have seldom made use of their experimental results. You have invited me to speak to you today about the possible links between psychoanalytic and cognitive theories. Although I have always been rather heretical as regards dogmas, I did at one time undertake a didactic psychoanalysis in order to more fully understand the theory, and I therefore appreciate your invitation all the more, and thank you for it once again.

I would like to talk about the role of conscious and unconscious processes in the study of intelligence, representation, and cognitive functioning, because I believe that questions concerning the cognitive uncon-

Translated by Anne Sinclair.

scious are similar to questions concerning the affective unconscious. I shall not try to criticize psychoanalytic theories, nor to introduce new ideas, but I am convinced that one day cognitive psychology and psychoanalysis must merge and form a general theory, which will improve and correct both cognitive psychology and psychoanalysis. We can make a start by discussing the possible links between these two theories.

THE PROBLEM OF STRUCTURES

On the one hand, affectivity is characterized by the distribution of positive and negative object cathexes. On the other hand, the cognitive aspects of behavior are characterized by their structure, be they elementary action schemes, concrete operations (seriation, classification), or propositional logic. The results of affective processes are relatively conscious; that is, they are feelings that subjects experience more or less consciously. But their mechanism remains unconscious. The subject does not know where his feelings come from nor why. He makes no link between them and his past and does not understand why their intensity varies. Psychoanalysis endeavors to reveal these hidden mechanisms. As you all know, the content of the affective unconscious is very rich and its dynamics extremely complex.

I would like to show that the situation is very similar for cognitive structures. The results of cognitive functioning are relatively conscious but the internal mechanisms are entirely, or almost entirely, unconscious. For example, the subject knows more or less what he thinks about a problem or an object; he is relatively sure of his beliefs. But though this is true for the results of his thinking, the subject is usually unconscious of the structures that guide his thinking. The structures determine what he can or cannot "do," and what he "must do," in the sense that certain logical relations are necessary for his thinking. Cognitive structures are not the conscious content of thinking, but impose one form of thinking rather than another. These forms depend on the subject's developmental level, which derives ultimately from early organic coordinations. Binet, when he wittily said "thinking is an unconscious activity of the mind," was quite justified because the cognitive unconscious consists in a set of structures and functions; the subject is only conscious of their results. Binet meant that even though the subject is conscious of the content of his thought, he ignores the functional and structural reasons that constrain his thinking. In other words, he has no access to the internal mechanisms that direct his thinking.

I believe that this phenomenon is not limited to children's thinking but also exists in the adult and even in the development of scientific thought. For example, mathematical thinking has always unconsciously obeyed certain structural laws. The most important of these, i.e., the laws of mathematical groups, were not explicitly stated until the nineteenth century (by Galois), but their presence is easily detectable in Euclid's Elements. Today, group structures are recognized as fundamental. Aristotle, by examining the way he and his contemporaries reasoned, became aware of some of the simple class structures and syllogisms. But he did not become aware of the structures of relational logic (subsequently stated by Morgan in the nineteenth century) even though he obviously used them himself.

If the cognitive unconscious operates in the field of scientific thought (one of its aims being the study of cognitive structures) it is clear that it will be even more evident in all other types of thinking, for example, in the "natural" thinking of the adult, and of course, in the spontaneous, creative thinking characteristic of the child.

Let us give one example. A 5- or 6-year-old child is shown two sticks: A and B (B being longer than A). He is then shown stick B with stick C (C being longer than B). The child often cannot conclude that C is longer than A as long as he does not see A and C together. When he has acquired the structure of transitivity (around the age of six) he can apply it successfully to many different types of problems: causal, logical, and mathematical. But the child does not realize that he has constructed the structure of transitivity and he believes he always reasoned in the same way. He knows nothing about the foundations of this structure, that is, the "grouping" of relations. He does not know how or why this transitivity structure has become necessary to his thinking. He does not know that his thinking has been transformed by internal mechanisms, and he is unconscious of the structure of his thought; only the results are clear to him. By cognitive unconscious, I mean the structure and function of these internal mechanisms.

ACTION AWARENESS AND
COGNITIVE REPRESSION

Let us now examine the subject's actions, not as actions dependent on underlying structures, but as actions the content of which is manifest. These are the results of the functioning of the mind, and not part of the functioning itself, and therefore the subject should be aware of them. But even in this area awareness is sometimes inhibited by a mechanism comparable to affective repression.

For example, becoming aware of the action of throwing a ball into a box is relatively easy. Children of four say they stood opposite the box and explain, that even if they were told to stand sideways, they turned around so as to be facing it again. In another experiment the child is given a very simple type of sling: a ball attached to a string that he rotates at arm's length and then releases in the direction of a goal (This experiment was conducted with M. Fluckiger.) To start with, no goal is set, and the child simply swings the ball around and releases it. He notices that the ball goes off sideways and usually he even notices that the trajectory of the ball continues the rotatory movement. The child is then asked to make the ball go into a box. He is quickly able (often from the age of five) to succeed. If the rotation is thought of as describing the circumference of a disc parallel to the floor, the string has to be released at what, on the face of a clock, would be 9 o'clock, the box being placed in a straight line from 12 o'clock. We congratulate the child, and he repeats the action several times. We then ask him at what point he released the ball.

Strangely enough, the youngest subjects maintain that they released the ball directly in front of them (6 o'clock) and that the ball traveled in a straight line, from there to the box. The 7- and 8-year-old subjects say they let the ball go opposite the box, that is, at 12 o'clock. Nine- or ten-year-old children often give compromise solutions. They say they released the ball at 11 o'clock or between 10 ond 11 o'clock. Only the 10- or 11-year-old children immediately answer that they released the ball at 9 o'clock, that is, that the ball was released at a point tangential to the box and not opposite it. Thus we find that at an early age the child can perform the action correctly but years pass before his apprehension of the action is correct. It is as if something repressed this apprehension and kept unconscious certain movements or certain parts of otherwise successful and intentional behavior.

It is easy to unearth this inhibitory factor. The child sees his action as divided into two parts: first, swing the ball, and second, throw it into the box. But, as far as the child is concerned, the fact that the ball went into the box means that the ball followed a trajectory perpendicular to the box, and therefore the ball's departure point was directly opposite the box. When we ask the child to describe his action he reconstitutes it logically according to this preconceived idea, and he does not realize that in fact he did something different. The child deforms or even ignores the observable facts in favor of his idea (which to him seems the only correct one).

There are many other similar examples. When the child manages (on his own, or by imitating someone else) to roll a ping-pong ball on a horizontal plane in such a way that the ping-pong ball comes back, he does not realize that he pushed the ball forward and rotated it backwards at the same time. He thinks that the ball rolled forward and then changed direction all by itself. Another example: when the child pushes an object forward by pushing one side with a stick he does not realize that he is simultaneously applying two movements to the object, rotation and translation. It is tempting to explain these distortions and lacks of apprehension by simply saying that the child does not understand what he has done and only remembers what is intelligible to him. But this interpretation is clearly insufficient. The child *has* understood his successful action (tangential movement of the ball when released; inverse rotation of the ping-pong ball, etc.) but has understood it in action and not in thought: he uses sensorimotor schemes rather than representational schemes. In other words, children know how to perform such actions; this knowledge is acquired perceptually and by motoractivity and is certainly not innate. Consequently, the problem can be formulated as follows: why do certain sensorimotor schemes become conscious (i.e., take a representational, particularly verbal form) whereas others remain unconscious? The reason would appear to be that certain action schemes contradict ideas that the subject has already consciously formulated. These rank higher than action schemes, and therefore block their integration into conscious thought. The situation is comparable to affective repression: when a feeling or drive contradicts an emotion or tendency of a higher rank (coming from the superego, for example) it is eliminated by conscious suppression or unconscious repression. Thus, in cognition, a mechanism analogous to unconscious repression can be observed. The child does not first formulate a conscious hypothesis and then discard it. On the contrary, he represses a scheme before it later appears in concept form. Later, we shall see that schemes cannot become explicit in any but a conceptualized form because even a mental image refers to a concept.

This mechanism of cognitive repression is undoubtedly not only limited to becoming aware of actions (that is, sensorimotor schemes). Even at the neurologic level, Pribram has demonstrated that a cortical regulation mechanism operates selectively on inputs; some are retained and become stimuli; others are rejected and thereby rendered inactive.

BECOMING AWARE

Becoming aware is commonly thought of as a process that simply illuminates hidden facts without otherwise changing them, like a flashlight which lights up a dark corner without modifying the positions of the objects revealed or the relations between them. However, this conception of becoming aware is insufficient, not to say false. Becoming aware is far more complex than this: some elements at the unconscious level are raised to the conscious level. These two levels are very different, otherwise the transition would be easy; there would be no problem. Becoming aware is thus a reconstruction on a superior, conscious level of elements already organized in a different way on an inferior, unconscious level. Two questions remain to be answered: what is the structure of the process of becoming aware, and what is its function?

As to the functional aspect, Claparède noticed that awareness occurs when the subject encounters difficulties; when the subject is well adapted and functioning adequately he does not need to consciously analyze the mechanism of his behavior. For example, it is easier to go quickly down the stairs without analyzing the foot and leg movements involved. A. Papert asked children to crawl; then she asked them to describe how they moved their hands and feet. Younger subjects give an unrealistic description of their action. They say, for example, that they first moved both hands forward, and then both feet. Older subjects still do not correctly describe what they actually did, but their descriptions are slightly more realistic. They say, for example, that they first moved their left arm and leg forward, and then their right arm and leg. Even at the ages of 10 and 11 only two-thirds of the subjects describe the action correctly. Before presenting her results at one of our symposia, A. Papert asked those present to crawl and then to describe the movements involved. The psychologists and physicists correctly analyzed their movements, while the mathematicians and logicians deduced that they had first moved their left limbs forward, and then their right limbs!

Indeed, one does not need to be aware of well adapted actions because they are directed by sensorimotor regulations that have become automatic. By contrast, when there is a need to adjust actions consciously (which presupposes choosing between two or more possibilities) there exists a beginning awareness of this need itself.

As to the structural process, awareness is a conceptual reconstruction. There are no concepts in representational form in the cognitive unconscious. The idea of "unconscious representation" seems contradictory to me. The cognitive unconscious is made up of sensorimotor or operatory schemes already organized into structures. The schemes express what the subject can "do" but not what he thinks. The subject also has affective and personality schemes, i.e., tendencies, drives, etc.

When the conceptual reconstruction is not inhibited by contradictions, awareness can be immediately adequate. Otherwise awareness is at first faulty and distorted and is completed later, but by bit, by new conceptual systems that allow hitherto incompatible facts to be incorporated and contradictions to be resolved.

CATHARSIS AND MEMORY

Cognitive awareness reminds one of what psychoanalysts have called catharsis. Catharsis consists in becoming aware of affective conflicts and reorganizing them in order to resolve them. Although I am not competent in psychoanalysis, it seems to me that catharsis is not at all the same thing as a simple clarification; otherwise it would be difficult to understand its therapeutic value. Rather, catharsis must be a reintegration and a reorganization allowing conflicts to be resolved. But where does this reorganization come from?

Erikson's ideas concerning this problem are very interesting: present affective experience is determined by past experience, as Freud has shown; but the past is constantly being restructured by the present. The same is true of cognitive systems. Becoming aware is thus always partly a reorganization and not only a simple evocation or translation.

Erikson's ideas imply that there are two possible interpretations of memory and that one must opt for the second interpretation. The first possible interpretation is that memories are stored in the unconscious and can be evoked at will without being modified or reorganized. The second interpretation, on the other hand, is that remembering always involves a reorganization. In other words, memory works in the same way as a historian works, when he reconstructs the past deductively from incomplete historical records.

The fact that inaccurate memories exist and that they seem as vivid and real as accurate memories is clear evidence for the second interpretation. For example, I have a very precise, detailed, visual memory of having almost been kidnapped when I was a baby in my pram. I can still visualize the scene of the crime, the fight between my nurse and the kidnapper, the arrival of the police and passers-by, etc. When I was 15 the nurse wrote to my parents telling them that she had made the whole story up and that the scratches on her face had been self-inflicted, etc. When I was five or six I must have heard my parents telling this story, which they believed at the time, and fabricated a durable, visual memory of the event. This is a clear case of false reconstruction. However, as infant memory can only recognize and not evoke, even if the attempted kidnapping had really taken place, I probably would have reconstructed the event in the same way.

In collaboration with B. Inhelder and H. Sinclair we conducted a developmental study of child memory. The results clearly support the idea that memory is a reconstruction. We showed the child a series of 10 sticks arranged in decreasing order of length. A week later we asked him what he had seen the week before. What the child remembered can be classified into stages:

Fig. 5.1   a)
         b)
         c)
         d)
         e) (correct)

It is clear that, in this case, what the child remembers does not correspond (except in stage e) to what was objectively perceived, but to the child's idea about what he had seen. Six months later we conducted a posttest (without showing the series of sticks again) and 74% of the subjects showed some improvement in remembering what they had seen. Some stage a subjects attained stage b, and some stage b subjects attained stage c, etc. Our subjects' progress can be explained in the following way: a memory image is a symbol representing a scheme (in this case, a seriation scheme). In six months the scheme has made some progress and the symbolic image that represents it must necessarily conform to the new form of the scheme.

Obviously not all memories improve in this way; in most cases memories deteriorate. In every case there is some schematization and this can help resolve certain cognitive conflicts. For example, when a young child is shown

Fig. 5.2

he perceives that there are the same number of elements in each line and so he concludes that the lines must be of the same length. But, for him, two lines of equal length must have extremities that coincide. So, when the child remembers the two lines, he often extends the W and adds extra elements to it so that its extremities coincide with those of the straight line. This is a striking example of reconstruction in memory.

Clearly we must be very prudent when considering childhood memories, because if memory on a cognitive level is only an approximate reconstruction, it goes without saying that once affective processes (conflicts, etc.) come into play, this reconstruction will be even more complex. Comparative studies of affective and cognitive transformations of memory would therefore be of great interest.

THE PROBLEM OF STAGES

The relations between our analysis of cognitive development during the sensorimotor period and the stages Freud described during the same period have been discussed by several authors [cf. D. Rapaport, Wolff, and Cobliner in the appendix in Spitz (1968)].

T. Gouin-Décarie (Montreal) studied the relationship between the cognitive development of object permanency and the development of object relations. I once demonstrated that an object that disappears from a baby's perceptual field is not conceived of as being permanent. When the object is hidden behind a screen, the baby will not look for it; it is as if the object is reabsorbed instead of continuing to exist. At the end of the first year of life, the baby begins looking for the object while taking into account its successive movements. T. Gouin-Décarie has shown that this reaction is related to the development of object relations. Thus, generally speaking, these two forms of development correspond. T. Gouin-Décarie verified my hypothesis (which was based on the observation of one subject) that the first cognitively permanent object is a person and not an inanimate object.

There are other correlations between cognitive and affective stages. For example, when the child is 7 or 8 years old, new logical relations of reciprocity develop in connection with the formation of reversible operations. At the same age moral judgment becomes less dependent on the superego and authority; fairness and other aspects of reciprocity become more important. Similiar links exist between cognitive and affective transformations at the time when adolescents become part of the adult world.

These parallels do not, of course, allow one to conclude that it is cognitive constructions that cause affective modifications. But I do not believe that the latter determine the former as certain psychoanalysts might be tempted to believe (cf. Odier's research on the subject). Obviously, affective factors play a role in accelerating or retarding cognitive development, as Spitz has shown. However, this does not mean that affectivity engenders or modifies cognitive structures. Affective and cognitive mechanisms are inseparable, although distinct: the former depend on energy, and the latter depend on structure.

In conclusion, many problems remain to be solved; we look forward to the foundation of a general theory of psychology that integrates the discoveries of cognitive psychology and psychoanalysis. The remarks I made today are but a small step in this direction.

The Development of the Concepts of Chance and Probability in Children

BÄRBEL INHELDER

INTRODUCTION

It is both stimulating and gratifying to see great physicists and mathematicians interested in the developmental psychology of certain basic concepts of their topic. Einstein was the first to suggest to Piaget the analysis of the relation between the concepts of speed and time in children. Now it is particularly Rosenfeld, in the Niels Bohr Institute in Copenhagen, who through his original insights as theoretician and historian of physics is giving new incentives to the Genevan research in the genetic epistemology of causality. We feel honored by this current interest in our past studies on the concept of random events in children. This research was done by Piaget and myself with a team of colleagues some time age [the complete body of research may be found in Piaget and Inhelder (1951)]. If we had to do it today with all the knowledge we have acquired on cognitive development in general, we could do so from a more sophisticated conceptual and methodological standpoint. In any case, a specialist on probability theory generated our research on random situations by asking us whether in every "normal" person (i.e., neither a scientist nor mental patient) there is an intuition of probability just as there is an intuition of primary numbers.

In epistemological terms this problem may be expressed as follows: are the concepts of chance and probability the result of mere registering of everyday observation, and therefore essentially empirical in origin? At first, one might be tempted to say that this is the case. Indeed, most of our actions imply a spontaneous estimation of the more or less probable nature of the expected or perhaps dreaded events. An observer watching an adult crossing a road will see that he behaves as if he is continuously evaluating the probability of an encounter in terms of the frequency and speed of the traffic; young children appear to have become practically adapted to such a situation, although the psychologic mechanisms behind this adaptation are still unknown. In everyday life we are continually involved in an inextricable mixture of causal factors and sequences. Objectively, daily life consists mainly of complex situations and events: the fanciful trajectory of a falling leaf is a more common observation than a rectilinear movement. Subjectively, of course, our interpretation of these situations and events can either simplify or complicate them. During our life we are forced to guess or to make our decisions on the basis of empirical frequencies and stochastic functions. For the young child also, life is full of unexpected events, frustrated expectations, and whims.

It is necessary, however, to distinguish between adaptive behavior at the practical level and systems of conceptualization. This distinction is essential not only for probabilistic behavior, but also for other aspects of the development of knowledge. The current research of Piaget and his team on children's solution of problems of practical intelligence confirms the existence of a very clear gap between two developmental levels: the elementary level of the action itself and the growing awareness of this action as an expression of its conceptualization. One of our collaborators asked logicians, physicists, and mathematicians to walk on all fours and then to recall the movements they had made. While the eminent physicists were quite successful at this, the no less eminent logicians and mathematicians were not.

Concerning the topic of this discussion, we can state the hypothesis that reasoning about frequency, probability, and concepts of random situations are distinct from forms of practical behavior without conceptual awareness and do not simply reflect or duplicate the observable events. They require as a frame of reference the construction of logicomathematical operations which are then attributed to physical events in terms of causal explanations. If this hypothesis turns out to be true, probability and chance thinking would occur relatively late in cognitive development.

The general trend that has emerged from our work in Geneva indicates that the operations of thought (logical, mathematical, spatial, temporal operations) have their origin in the child's sensorimotor activity and end up as closed systems. In the psychology of knowledge we consider a system of operations to be closed when the outcomes of these operations (singly or in combinations) remain elements within the original system. These systems as Piaget has shown, are isomorphic first with semilattices and then later on in development with lattices, group structures, and Boolean algebra. The outstanding feature of this constructive process is the progressive reversibility of interiorized actions which, through self-regulating mechanisms, can compensate for disturbances. These disturbances result from the continual confrontation between the subject's schemes of interiorized actions and the resistance of physical reality. This process of progressive construction reaches two levels of equilibration which Piaget defines as maximal stability with low entropy. The first level of equilibration is formed by the structures of so-called "concrete" operations; we call them "concrete" since their application is restricted to objects actually present in the field of the subject's action. These operations may be found in class relations and number systems and in our culture are attained around the age of seven. The second level is constituted by the structures of formal logic, such as propositional logic, implying the existence of combinatorial systems.

Recent research of the Genevan Epistemological Center has shown that causal explanations develop in close connection with the operations of thought and consist in attributing the subjects' operations to physical reality. But the problem of how the developing child assimilates and understands that which at first glance appears to resist physical causality (including random phenomena) remains open. This problem was the subject of the research about which I am going to talk today.

THE INTUITION OF AN INCREASING MIXTURE IN A COLLECTION OF DISCRETE ELEMENTS

Problem

The notion of a progressive and decreasingly reversible mixing is perhaps the starting point of a naive intuition of the concept of random collections. A mixing of elements seems to provide a good illustration of Cournot's definition of random collections as: "Causal series both interfering and initially independent." The developmental problem is therefore to find out whether, when confronted with an observable mixing of elements, the child imagines that this will result in an increasing mixture of the elements, or whether, on the other hand, he thinks these are interconnected by invisible forces. In other words, does the intuition of mixture (as an expression of the concept of random collections) occur at an early developmental stage or is it brought about by a specific developmental process, the steps of which we must discover?

Method

The child is presented with an open rectangular box (a cigar box) resting along its width axis on a device which enables it to be titled back and forth. From this stationary position, the box is tilted towards one of its short sides along which there are aligned eight red beads and eight white beads, separated from each other by a short midline separator. Each time the box is tilted and then returned to its original position, the beads run to the opposite short side and then return to their starting point, having undergone a certain number of possible permutations. Thus one creates a progressive mixture: at first two or three red beads join the white beads and vice versa, and slowly this number increases. Initially, before any tilting, the child is asked to forecast in what order the beads will return to their original places, and whether each color will remain on its original side, or if not, how they will mix. The box is then tilted for the first time and the child notes the changed positions of a few beads. He is then asked to predict the result of a second tilt of the box, which is then carried out, and so on. Next, he is asked to predict the result of a large number of such tilts so that we can see whether he expects a progressive mixture, a to-and-fro pattern (i.e., an exchange pattern in which the red and the white beads gradually change places), or a return to the original alignments. In addition the child is asked to draw his ideas of the final situation and of the various stages leading to it. These drawings were very revealing.

The Developmental Pattern

During a first stage, between 4 and 7 years of age, the child neither predicts a progressive mixture nor shows signs of an intuition of the concept of random collections. His behavior reveals a very significant conflict between his observation of the progressive mixing and the inability of his thought processes to accept this. The child cannot but see the mixing of the beads, but he refuses to acknowledge the random nature of the mixture and above all he predicts a return to their original places—a sort of "unmixing." He thinks the beads will "go back to their own places" and therefore seems to consider the mixing unnatural. Thus, initially, the children predict a straightforward return of the beads to their original positions. Those few who say that the beads will mix are clearly not convinced and it seems that the idea that the beads should return to their proper places remains predominant. When questioned about progressive steps in the mixing, these children think that "it can't mix more, it will remain the same." Some expect a to-and-fro, red taking the place of white and vice versa, until, as they say, "the beads go back to their own places." The mixing seems to be interpreted as the result of a temporary disorder of which the elements seek to free themselves. The apparent reversibility which the children thus attribute to the mixing is in fact the very opposite of operational reversibility.

The second stage is characterized by a first intuition of the concept of random collections, as is shown by the child's own scepticism: "You can't tell, each bead can go to either side." The child predicts that "the beads will mix little by little, they go to a different place" and thinks that the to-and-fro exchange pattern is very unlikely: "It's difficult for that to happen." The child now starts to understand the random character of the beads' trajectories. The concept of mixing is therefore acquired without being clearly analyzed. But because he cannot imagine the multiple possibilities resulting from the interference of the trajectories (collisions) and does not understand permutations, the child has difficulty deciding what the final state will be.

During the third stage, the final positions of the beads after mixing are pictured on the basis of an exchange system: initially, the child imagines the path of each bead according to a general and regular pattern of movement, as if the beads never collided. Subsequently, however, he regards the final mixture as the chance result of a number of different possible random encounters. Instead of ascribing to the mixture an unpredictable and incomprehensible nature, preadolescent thinking translates this phenomenon into thought operations that are realized even without regularity. The mixture seems at last to be understood as being due to the interference of independent causal sequences, a concept which corresponds to Cournot's definition.

THE NOTION OF A RANDOM DISTRIBUTION AND
OF THE EXPERIMENTAL METHOD

Problem

In order to analyze the formation of the concept of random distribution in a concrete situation, we have to find out how the child becomes able to dissociate what is due to chance and what can be determined and predicted by simple applications of deterministic laws. We have chosen a situation where the elements are distributed uniformly or concentrated for reasons unknown to the child. For it is a grasp of this distinction between what is random and what is not, that constitutes the most important intuition of probabilities.

Method

The experiment was conducted in a most simple form: a pin is put into a central hole in a brass disk and then fixed onto a board which is divided into equal segments (there is a reference point marked on the rim of the disk). Each segment of the board is painted a different color. The disk is made to rotate continuously and the child is asked several questions, for example: "Can you tell where the disk will stop, on which color the little marker will stop, and could it stop on a different color?" Each time the disk stops the child puts a match on the spot. "If we continue to rotate the disk a great number of times, ten times, twenty times, will there be more, less or the same number of matches on each segment, or will there be many on one segment and none on the others?" This first part of the experiment was devised only to examine the development of the concepts of random distribution. Once a child has noted the regular and random distribution, the experimenter introduces a constant relation by placing small magnets capable of attracting an iron bar on the bottom of the disk. On each segment is placed a box of matches, two (of different color) weighing 20 gm (a, a'); two weighing 50 gm and containing a magnet (b, b'); also two weighing 50 gm without a magnet (c, c'); and two weighing 100 gm (d, d'). We wanted to know what the child's reaction would be. Would he be struck by the miracle? By which mental operations of exclusive disjunction would be confirm or refute this hypothesis?

The Developmental Pattern

At the first stage the children did not grasp the idea either of chance in terms of random distribution or of a constant nonrandom relation. They thought they could foresee and explain it all. If they were wrong, then they thought this was a whim of nature: "The disk stopped, it's a little tired." For many years the child thinks one can aim for a particular color, the one not yet hit. No doubt he has the idea that something like moral justice underlies the physical phenomenon. The impossibility of conceiving of either random or lawful processes corresponds, from the logical point of view, to the child's incapacity to comprehend the disjunction "A *or* B." At this stage, everything is constituted as a mixture of whim and moral determination. Hence the child is impervious to any experimental evidence to the contrary. Some children attribute the stopping of the disk to the weight of the box. It is quite fruitless to show them that the disk never stops opposite the heaviest boxes. The child simply answers: "It's the middle weight that attracts," without thinking of verifying that of the two boxes with equal weights, one but not the other stops the disk.

During the second stage, one can see the beginnings of a grasp of the concept of random distribution and the gradual interrelating of the successive random results. The child puts forward several possibilities which indicate a trace of doubt and he begins to dissociate *certainty* from *possibility*. To the question, "Can you tell where the disk will stop?," a child answers: "It turns and the speed becomes smaller, smaller, and you can't tell where it's going to stop." However, he thinks that it will stop on a different color each time: "It's more just," meaning correct and fairer, "as it cannot stop each time on the same." But he does not take a stand on the increasingly regular distribution as the number of trials increases, and to the question, "If you play a great number of times, is there a chance that the disk will have stopped on each color?," the child replies: "I can't say in advance, we'll see." Nevertheless, he thinks it is more probable "that it's more regular (both in the moral and statistical senses) when you do it less often," adding, "I can't explain, but I understand it well." So it seems as if the child is capable of anticipating possible compensations between successive trials, but this only for small numbers, what a Genevan physicist called "the law of small and large numbers." It is clear that the child is amazed at the constant stopping due to the magnet and thinks that "it isn't natural, there's a trick" without, on the other hand, being as yet able to proceed systematically to the exclusion of the different possible factors which could cause the constant stopping. Later research on the inductive reasoning processes and experimental strategies has shown that these methods imply formal logical operations.

During the third stage, the preadolescent discovers formal operations of exclusive disjunction, and starts thinking in terms of relative frequencies in long-run sequences of trials. He says, for instance, "The greater the number of trials, the greater the chance of it being regular; the more you do, the more it evens out, because it stops once here, once there, and after a certain number of trials they're all equal." Underlying these still clumsy explanations lies the growing understanding of compensation between series of successive events. At the same time he can draw up a set of formal operations of exclusive disjunction and in this experiment says: "Why does the disk always stop on this same segment? If there was nothing to stop it, it would be as likely to stop on another segment, let's have a look. It stops either because of the boxes or because of something else. I take off the boxes, the disk stops somewhere else. If that happens only once, it doesn't mean anything, it may be due to chance." He repeats the experiment. "Without the boxes, it doesn't stop, therefore there's something in the boxes making it stop. I'll see whether all the boxes do the same thing." He eliminates all save b and b'. "Here we are, it may be due to the weight of the boxes." He compares b and b' to c and c'. "These two stop the disk, the other two have the same weight, it's therefore something else that makes it stop, etc., etc. . . ." To avoid misunderstandings, we must stress that even in this third stage the child does not grasp the idea of the expected frequencies that would be obtained in a long-run sequence of trials. We see from this example that the progress in probabilistic reasoning is closely connected to progress in formal thought operations, which underlies the experimental method of systematically varying the various factors involved.

CHANCE AND MIRACLE IN THE GAME OF "HEADS OR TAILS"

Problem

Having studied the development of the concept of random distribution in terms of physical events, it seemed equally important to analyze this same concept in the games of chance that children know so well. These games, as it is well known, were at the basis of Pascal's early probability theories long before their discovery in the realm of physics. Of course, these games of "heads or tails" or drawing of beads out of a bag imply a physical aspect; but it is essential here that the player himself intervenes (rather than being a mere observer of a random distribution) by actually doing the drawing and placing the bets. It is precisely these operations effected by the subject himself that create the emotive appeal of games based on chance and were the basis of the mathematization of probability. As the Genevan studies on number and geometry have shown, mathematical concepts are acquired by means of a special process of abstraction, applied not only to the objects, but primarily to coordinations of actions. It is thus to be expected that when the subject's action intervenes in a random event or situation, he is more likely to grasp the concept earlier. In order to understand better the contribution of this operational concept of random situations, we introduced into the game a sort of miracle in the form of a series of exclusively heads or tails, in contrast to the random distribution of either type in the normal game.

Chance is indeed, for the subject, the negation of miracle. To understand the nature of a random distribution is for the child, as for us, to admit the very low probability of a long sequence of either heads or tails. So we occasionally introduced a trick into the chance game in order to find out whether children or different ages are in any way aware of this low probability, surprised at this astonishing fact or miracle, or even realize the impossibility of the situation which then leads them to discover the trick.

Method

One of the experiments proceeded as follows: about 20 white counters showing on one side a cross and on the other a circle were used. Heads or tails was played and the child was asked to observe 20 tosses. Then without the child's knowledge, 20 loaded counters having a cross on each side were substituted. The experiment was repeated and the trick explained should the child not have discovered it for himself. Then, one further experiment was conducted. Again without the child's knowledge of whether or not they were marked with crosses on both sides, the counters were tossed one by one in order to observe the child's reasoning underlying his assessment of whether or not the counters were loaded.

The Developmental Pattern

At the first stage, the child was sometimes surprised by the exclusive appearance of the crosses but he did not deem this impossible in terms of probability. Even after he had been shown the "trick" he thought he could achieve the same result, i.e., the miracle with counters that were not loaded. Three types of responses can be noted. The first may be called phenomenistic: the child thinks that "if you haven't seen them you can't tell." Here everything is considered perfectly natural and reality is not dissociated from appearances. There is therefore no miracle, only new facts. The case of the trick counters seems quite natural or simply amusing because rare. As one child said: "They turn upwards."

A second response is compensatory in nature. The child seems half-way between a feeling of justice and of sufficient reason. He thinks "that next time there will be more crosses because last time there were more circles."

The third response is one of "personal power." As a child said, "It's a trick you did with your hands. You throw them like that," and he thinks he himself can recreate the phenomenon with the nonloaded counters. The child can see that shaking-up of the counters and their spinning during their fall, he says, "They're spinning and falling," yet he still feels one needs only to throw them in a certain way in order to obtain only crosses.

The second stage is characterized more by the appearance of a qualitative notion of randomness coupled with a lack of understanding of long-run frequencies. The most striking fact is the refusal to accept a miracle. We ask, "How will they fall?" "Face-up and face-down," says the child, and when he uses the trick counters, he ponders for a moment and discovers that "they're on both sides (the crosses)." "Could that happen with the other counters?" "No, because they fall on one side or the other, they can't all fall on the same side because they spin while falling." Or "could one have all the counters fall on the side with crosses?" "No, because there are too many, they are too well mixed." However, the children still refuse to estimate the relative frequencies of the crosses and the circles in terms of probability and they clearly think that in order to know whether or not the game is tricked, one is no more certain after one hundred than after ten trials.

A true estimation of probabilities is characteristic of the third stage. As a child 12 years old says: "For one counter it is chance that is the deciding factor, but the more there are, the more one is likely to know whether they are mixed." "With the ordinary games and many counters, there will be a good half on each side" (he means exactly half).

Finally, to find out if the game is rigged, the child reasons, "If you go on throwing them, you can become more and more sure. With five counters, all the crosses would turn up say once out of twenty-five tosses, but with six counters you would need forty tosses, and with seven counters, it's impossible." However arbitrary these estimates may be, they show a remarkable and growing awareness of probability as a function of long-run frequencies. The most likely result is half and half and it becomes even more likely as the number of tosses is increased (the same child thinks that with a million tosses one can be sure). Similarly, the same child understands that the least likely situation is either all crosses or all circles, an outcome that becomes increasingly unlikely as the number of tosses increases.

RANDOM SELECTION OF PAIRS

Problem

The quantification of probabilities and random selections is founded on combinatorial operations and in certain cases on the results of combination and permutation.

Method

The child is shown 40 marbles, 20 red and 20 blue, which are all put into a bag. He is then asked to draw out pairs of marbles in succession. We wondered in particular if the child would understand that the most likely distribution would yield 5 red pairs, 5 blue pairs, and 10 mixed pairs according to the laws of distribution a–a, a–b, b–a, b–b. In other words, would he have an intuition of probability corresponding to Mendel's law?

The Developmental Pattern

The developmental trend can rapidly be outlined: during a first stage, the child does not foresee the appearance of any mixed pairs, and he refuses to make any estimate of frequency. "I don't know anything, I'm guessing, there will be both red and blue ones." "Which will come out easiest?" The child answers: "Perhaps the red because they're not as mixed," but after a few draws he changes his mind and thinks that "the red and the blue together go quicker, because the marbles are mixed better." "And what if we keep on starting all over again? Will there be the same number of marbles of one color or of mixed marbles, or more of any one kind?" The child answers: "You can't tell, it's luck, maybe it will be the same."

During the second stage he predicts quite well the three types of pairs but only during the third stage does the preadolescent think there will be more mixed pairs than pairs of one particular color. When the experimenter says: "If we play a great number of times?" he thinks that there will be 10 mixed draws, 5 all red draws and 5 all blue. At this point in their development the children are able to draw up a table of all possible two-element pairings.

THE QUANTIFICATION OF PROBABILITIES

Problem

Progress in the interpretation of the concept of chance depends both on the child's capacity to perform combinatorial operations and on his gradual interrelating of individual cases with the expected general distribution. This interrelating itself requires the performance of logical operations (class inclusion and disjunction) and mathematical quantifications. It was therefore important to study those underlying operations. We thus devised a lottery game.

Method

We used two series of white counters, of which some had a cross on the back. The child examined the composition of each series: the crosses represent what we call favorable cases, while the total number of counters in each series constitutes the number of possible cases. Both series are then laid on the table and the child was asked to evaluate in which of the two series he was more likely to find a cross on the first draw. The composition of the two series can be as following: same number of favorable and possible cases in each series; same number of favorable, but not possible cases in each; a different number of favorable, but the same number of possible cases, etc.

An easier version of the problem of relating favorable to possible outcomes can be studied with a simple sequence: if two black and one white counter are mixed in the palm of a closed hand, which color is more likely to be drawn?

The Developmental Pattern

Let us note only the particularly interesting fact about the first stage, namely, that the children think they will draw the single white counter more often. This, we think, is explained by the lack of understanding of the logical relation between part and whole. The children are incapable of executing the inclusive addition $A + A' = B$, and never say that B could be either A or A' and that A' is more probable in this case because it stands for two units against only one for A. It is quite clear, therefore, that there can be no probabilistic reasoning at this point since the child cannot as yet conceive the relation between favorable and possible cases.

During the second stage, however, the children begin to be able to quantify these probabilities thanks to a grasp of the relation between disjunctive and inclusive operations. The child understands that if the unknown "x" $= B$, then it must be either A or A' but it is just as likely to be A as A'. The disjunction operation thus reveals the dependency of probabilistic quantification on the basic logical operations. Finally, during the third stage, the preadolescent is able to link favorable draws with the total number of possible draws, and henceforth interprets probability as a degree of rational expectation that can be mathematically assessed.

THE CONCEPT OF RANDOM SITUATIONS IN PSYCHOTIC CHILDREN

We thought it would be interesting to examine a group of psychotic children, between 10 to 15 years of age, at different levels of operational development and deterioration. It is well known that the reasoning processes of such children are more or less deeply disturbed. All of them, even those who were still functioning on a high intellectual level, betrayed an incapacity to understand and assimilate random phenomena and refused to reason in probabilistic terms. They judged all events as though the universe were perfectly rational and predictable or as if it were governed by magical causes. In the experiment with magnetic disks a typical but very gifted and intellectually oriented psychotic boy of 13 said, despite repeatedly unsuccessful predictions: "It will always stop on the same color, you can do that very easily if you've got speed in your fingers; if you haven't got it, you give it again each time. There will always be the same braking strength, it stops at the same place, only you've got to start from the same place." When I objected that this precision in the fingers is very difficult to obtain, he insisted: "You start learning in the fingers, if you get the red once, you always get it . . . it depends what you want." For as soon as physical reality resists and cannot be fitted into clear causal sequences, the psychotic children object to predicting or judging in probabilistic terms. We have seen that it is not the capacity to perform the underlying logical and mathematical operations that is lacking. The psychotic child of this type cannot consider chance phenomena, because he attributes to these phenomena hidden causes of external interventions in the form of tricks. He regards the world as animistic and his thinking often betrays forms of primitive adualism. The general reason seems to be, on the one hand, his systematic attribution of meanings to everything and, on the other, the feeling that his own reasoning powers are unlimited. These are two reasons for refusing to admit that anything is beyond his comprehension and for minimizing the chance factor which can be upsetting both intellectually and emotionally.

CONCLUSIONS

Our psychologic experiments of which we have been able to mention only a few examples leave no doubt as to the fact that the first qualitative notion of randomness, even when limited to concrete contexts, only appears around the age of 6 or 7, and is dependent upon the ability to perform concrete logical operations. Furthermore, the gradual nature of the elaboration of reasoning about probability could account for its late acquisition. In order to interpret these results, we must situate them within the larger framework of our knowledge of the development of the child's mental operations.

Logical and mathematical operations are structured systems of interconnected operations resulting in total reversibility and rigorous deduction. However, where the most probable composition of forces favors random events, each single random event is irreversible. Between these two extremes, we see the inductive procedures of the child as he seeks to sort out in any given event what is random and what is deductible.

During a first period from about 4 to 7 years of age, a child's reasoning does not distinguish between possible and necessary events, and evolves within a sphere of activity as remote from the idea of chance as it is from operational deductions. In fact, the child's thinking often oscillates between the predictable and the unpredictable, but nothing is predictable or unpredictable in principle. One might therefore say that it is the lack of a system of reference consisting of a series of deductive operations which prevents the child of this stage from understanding the true nature of random events. The strangest fact is certainly the children's difficulty in grasping the irreversibility underlying the random process of progressive intermixture (at a given moment) when their thought processes are still dominated by preoperational irreversibility (not being able in one's thinking to cancel or mentally compensate a perceived transformation). It is precisely the lack of this system of reference that explains why the child at this stage cannot apprehend the irreversibility inherent in random events.

It is also because of lack of operational reasoning that the child, like some of his famous historical predecessors, accepts miracles as natural, and this because he cannot conceive of the rare event with a very low probability relative to both natural regularities and random fluctuations.

During the second period from about 7 to 11 years of age, the child discovers random events in their most unsophisticated form, i.e., conceiving undetermined events as unpredictable, which contrasts with that which is determined or predictable in the domain of facts that can be organized by means of concrete logical operations. This discovery takes place at a time when the concrete operations on classes, relations, number, as well as causal and spatiotemporal operations are being progressively elaborated. In consequence, the child reacts very skeptically: "You can't tell, this might happen or that might happen." During this period, children become aware of random situations by antithesis to deductive necessity, as they are now capable of deductive reasoning and therefore can note the distinction between what is deductive and what is not.

During the third period, when he elaborates formal, and more particularly combinatorial operations, the preadolescent becomes capable of assessing the total number of possibilities, and of conceiving of the relation between those cases selected as favorable and the whole, seen as the sum of the combination of all possible cases. The assessment of probability is thus the product of a comparison between combinable and reversible events and irreversible random events, since only a small fraction of the totality of possible events is actualized.

The discovery of the random distribution as a function of "large numbers in the long run" is, psychologically speaking, the true basis of probability. During the preceding second period, the child reflects only on particular events and behaves as if he were naively applying Joseph Bertrand's dictum: "chance has neither conscience nor memory." He now seems to behave in accordance with the principle that "frequency of occurrence tends toward probability." It is therefore clearly within the framework of an operational system, that the concepts of randomness and probabilistic reasoning are developed. Rational operations gradually confer their degree of intelligibility on random events.

I hope that our research may help to shed light on the psychologic and developmental mechanisms at work in the elaboration of the most elementary forms of probabilistic thinking.

TWO

Experiments in Cognitive Development

7

Identity and Conservation

JEAN PIAGET

For several years, we have been studying the development of the concept and perception of identity, and the relationship between the concept of identity and notions of conservation. I know that J. Bruner (Bruner *et al.*, 1966) and other psychologists are looking into the same problem. This is an interesting convergence between bodies of research which are in fact independent; but it is a natural convergence, since it is normal to study identity sooner or later if we are concerned with conservation.

INTRODUCTION, DEFINITIONS AND STATEMENT OF THE PROBLEMS

The obvious fact for all of us is that the concept of identity is much more precocious than conservation. But even to accept this statement we must agree on some definitions, because the concept of identity changes with development (as it does throughout the history of science and mathematics), and nothing remains less identical than the concept or the notion of identity.

We shall use the term "conservation" for notions which appear at about 7 or 8 years of age, and which affirm the existence of *quantitative* invariants. The conservation of substance, of weight, etc., thus deal with quantities of matter or weight. The conservation of a group, in the logical or mathematical sense, when the distribution of the parts or the subgroups has been modified, deals with the "extension" of the group, that is, with the quantity of individual objects which make up the group. The conservation of number is surely quantitative, and so is that of weight, volume, etc.

But on the other hand, precisely because they are quantitative, notions of conservation always deal with invariants which are based on the *composition* of certain transformations, so that we can say that where there is no transformation we cannot speak of conservation. For example, when we pour water from a wide glass to a narrow glass, the shape of the water is changed both in height and in width, and observation shows that either the subject only notices one (usually the height) or he notices both, but only as covariations, and not as compensations. Conservation is possible only when there is composition of quantitative variations, which can take the form of a compensation of relations (higher $\times$ thinner = the same amount), or simply of an additive composition (nothing added, nothing taken away = the same amount).

The essential characteristic of preoperational (that is, preconservational) identity, on the other hand, is that it deals with simple qualitative invariants, without any quantitative composition. For example, in the pouring of liquids, even a 4 or 5 year old, who maintains that the amount of water has changed, will admit that it is "the same water," in the sense that the nature of the matter "water" has not changed even if the quantity of that matter has changed. Similarly, if the draws his own body as he was when he was little and again as he is now, he will recognize that it is still the same individual, even if he is bigger in size ("It's still me"). In this case, the invariant is obtained without quantitative composition; there is simply a *dissociation* between a permanent quality (the same water, the same me) and the variable qualities (the shape or size), but there is no composition of these variations.

Thus defined, the first conservations appear around the age of 6½ or 7 years, and others continue to appear at 9–10 years, or as late as 11–12 years, because they are tied to the elaboration of quantitative notions which are very complex, and which require a transition from purely ordinal judgments (for instance, longer = goes farther) to extensive, numerical, or metric judgments. On the other hand, there are very early examples of qualitative identity, as early as the end of the sensorimotor period, because it does not necessitate quantification.

One might say that there is one notable exception to what I have just said, namely, the appearance between 9 and 12 months of the scheme of the object permanency, which I myself have often considered to be the first form of conservation. In fact, that is a misuse of language; if we wish to conform to the preceding definitions, then the scheme of the permanent object is a case of identity, and not of quantitative conservation. It is the identity of an object which does not vary quantitatively but remains the same while changing its position, or being hidden behind a screen.

Given these definitions, identity raises three general problems, each of which we shall treat briefly: (1) What is the nature of the notion of identity, compared with the nature of reversible operations? (2) What are the stages in its development, and the reasons for its early appearance? (3) How is it related to conservation? As far as the third question is concerned, the most interesting one to our way of thinking, identity can be seen, as J. Bruner sees it, as one of the stages in the formation of conservations, with direct continuity between them; or it can be seen, as we shall try to show, not as the source of conservations, but as one of its conditions. According to this second alternative, the roots of conservation would be found in the system of reversible operations, which alone permit quantification (or the coherent elaboration of various types of quantities). In this case, we could understand that identity is more precocious than conservations, and we could understand that later identity would be integrated into the systems of conservations, as one operation among many, while the conservations would depend on the whole system, and not only on identity.

THE NATURE OF IDENTITY

If we agree to call "operations" any actions which have been interiorized, which are reversible (addition and subtraction, for example), and which are coordinated into systems (groupings, groups, lattices, etc.), then we can admit that identity can become at some point an operation among others, but only relatively late, at a rather advanced level, and as a part of a system of operations. For example, in an additive classification, where $A + A^1 = B$; $B + B^1 = C$, etc., we do have $A = A$, $B = B$, etc., but only on condition that $A - A = 0$ and $A + 0 = A$. The identity, $A = A$ depends on a regulator, the "identical operation" of a grouping, that is ± 0; from this point of view, identity has become operational only because it has been integrated into a system of operations.

But this is a late development (7 or 8 years) and there exist preoperational identities long before these systems of operations have been established. Preoperational qualitative identities can very well exist in situations where there is no sign of any of the fundamental rules of operations, such as reversibility and transitivity. For example, in one experiment which we carried out with G. Voyat, 3 to 5 year olds who took apart a necklace and spread out the beads in a box, said that the beads were "still the same necklace," calling on a notion of identity by assimilation to their own action; but if they started from the separate beads, without having made the necklace, they naturally did not say that the beads were the same as the necklace: identity here thus depends on the chronological order of the actions, and is not reversible. Similarly (in another experiment with Voyat to which we shall return), if the children draw several steps in the growth of a plant, calling them A, B, C, etc., they will admit the identity of A with B, B with C, C with D, but before 7 years of age they will not admit the identity of A with D (saying, "it's not the same plant any more"); here the identity is not transitive.

However, well before it becomes operational, identity is already a logical instrument. I have often maintained that preoperational structures were prelogical, but drawing attention all the while to what I have called "articulated intuitions," that is, partial coordinations which sketch out future operations. Now we have found that there is indeed a sort of preoperational logic, much broader than the notion of identity, which makes up in a way the first half of operational logic, that is, an oriented system which is sufficient as long as it is oriented in the right direction, but which lacks the inverse orientation, or in other words, reversibility. This preoperational logic is the logic of functions, that is, of ordered couples, one-way "applications," etc., and it leads to the discovery of coproperties, of covariations, and other *functional relationships* of the form $y = f(x)$.

Now preoperational identity is one aspect of these elementary functions. Let us take as an example a string, pulled down by a weight at end b (Fig. 7.1). The child discovers easily the covariation involved: if the segment a becomes shorter, then the segment b becomes longer. He discovers just as easily the coproperty, which is even an identity: "it's the same string," which gets shorter in the segment a and longer in the segment b. And, significantly, he discovers this well before arriving at the conservation of length a + b. This conservation, no matter how long the segment b or a may be, is reached at about 7 or 8 years of age, while the covariation and identity are affirmed at 4 or 5 years of age. Here, then, is an example of the absence of operational quantification and conservation, since the quantities remain ordinal: "longer" and "shorter" are still judged in terms of "farther" and "not as far," based simply on the endpoints, but that in no way precludes the use of functions or qualitative identity.

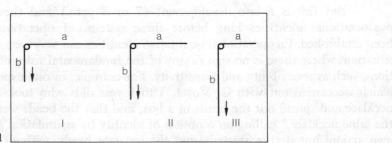

Fig. 7.1

We might say, then, that this logic of functions and of qualitative identity is just half of the logic of reversible operations, because it is based on directed actions, or, in other words, the concept of order, which appears so fundamental, and which plays such an important role (sometimes correctly, sometimes with error) in preoperational intuitions where topologic and ordinal notions of boundaries remain so long predominant. In general terms, we can say that the essential instrument of this semilogic is that of *correspondence*, but of one-way correspondence which lacks the reciprocity which alone guarantees equivalences and conservations. For example, a 5 or 6 year old will use *"applications"* of the type "many-to-one," which are already truly functions, in the mathematical sense, but usually they will lack the inverse correspondence, "one-to-many," which is no longer a simple "application," and which is necessary for the construction of equivalence classes and their inclusions. Even in the case of one-to-one correspondence they often lack reciprocity. A Belgian mathematician did the following experiment at our Center in Geneva. A little truck takes a random route through a collection of houses, A, B, C, etc., picking up a colored token in front of each house (there is a different color for each house, while a little man of the same color stays in front of the house, to establish a color–house correspondence). These tokens are placed in the truck in the order in which they are picked up, and at the end of the trip the child is asked why the tokens are in that order. From the age of 5, children are easily able to show that the tokens correspond to the order in which they were picked up in front of the houses. But if we then ask them to retrace the truck's route, it is only at 7 or 8 years of age that they are able to reconstitute the sequence of stops in front of the houses, as if the reciprocal correspondence were more difficult than the direct correspondence. (For the details of this experiment, see Van den Bogaerts-Rombouts, 1966.)

In a word, preoperational identity is one aspect of a partial logic, the logic of functions which translates the sense of direction of actions themselves; but this logic lacks the general reversibility which would be necessary for the elaboration of quantities and the instruments of quantification.

PRECOCITY AND DEVELOPMENT OF THE NOTION OF IDENTITY

First of all, let us recall that identity progresses during development; it progresses a good deal, in fact. Nothing remains identical during normal mental evolution, not even identity, in spite of its very function; and this is precisely because it changes its function from one stage to another. There are a certain number of experiments which we have done, with G. Voyat and M. Bovet in the area of concepts, and with Vinh-Bang and R. Droz in the area of perception. We shall deal only with concepts here.

One of these experiments consists of presenting the child with a wire which can be made into an arc, or a straight line, and asking in each case if it is the same piece of wire, the same object, etc. We find four successive levels, which no doubt correspond to stages of a sort. At the first level (3 or 4 years) the children do not question the identity and base it essentially on the assimilation of the object to their possible actions: we can make an arc with a straight line or vice versa, so it is still the same object, with which we can do many things. At the second level (4–5 years), the child starts to take an interest in the object itself, as well as in the action which can modify it; or more precisely, to take an interest in the objective modifications themselves, as well as in their ability to produce them. So he often concludes (although this second level may not be very general) that the object is no longer the same object because it changed its form. At the third level, the child makes still more progress toward objective analysis, and begins to dissociate the permanent qualities from the variable qualities. It is, then, "the same object" since it is still the same piece of wire, but it has changed shape. But this qualitative identity does not yet imply conservation. The child thinks that in changing its form, the wire changes its length; the straight line is longer than the arc since it goes beyond it. He still lacks metric quantifications, for judging intervals, and he still bases his idea of length on an ordinal judgment comparing the endpoints. Finally, at the fourth level, the child attains the conservation of length as well as the identity of the object. But the conservation is not directly derived from the identity. It requires a new composition, based on the intervals between the endpoints, and thus on a system of additive inclusions, within which identity is integrated, without constituting the source.

Similarly, with G. Voyat, we studied the identity of water as it was poured from one glass to another, or of a piece of modeling clay as it was given different shapes. Is it "the same water," "the same clay," etc? The stages are the same, except that the second is often shortened, according to the type or the magnitude of the differences.

But now let us look at the analysis of an irreversible process, that is, a process which takes place in time, without any possibility for operational reversibility or even for a physical, empirical return to the point of departure. Growth is such a process.

Voyat first used the growth of a bean, but it was too slow! Then he used a solution of copper sulphate in water, in which he "planted" a grain of potassium ferrocyanide; in a few minutes this gives an arborescent growth something like a seaweed. The child watched this phenomenon, and then we asked him to make some drawings of steps in the growth of this "seaweed," and we had him order them. Then we asked whether his drawings, A, B, C, . . . N, represented "the same seaweed" (or "the same plant," etc., according to the term he uses). Then he was asked to draw himself during his own growth, when he was a little baby, a little bigger, etc., and we questioned him about the identity of his own body, or of himself. Finally, we had him do the same with the experimenter. In the cases where the child did not assert the identity of the seaweed during its growth, we came back again to this question to see whether the identity of the child's own body during its growth brought out the identity of the seaweed.

We find at least three levels in the children's responses. In the first one, the child accepts easily the identity of his own body, in spite of the differences in size ("It's still me"), and the identity of the experimenter is accepted also. But in the case of the plant, he accepts certain identities (A = B or G = H), but he refuses to accept the identity if the difference is too great (A to H, for instance): "it grew, but it isn't the same any more; here it's a little plant and there it's a big plant, it's not the same plant." Once they have accepted the identity of their own body, and we return to the question of the "seaweed," they continue to deny this latter identity. At a second level, the initial reactions are the same, but when we come back to the question of the "seaweed," the child modifies his position, and accepts the identity of the plant. Finally, after about 7 or 8 years of age, the three types of identity are accepted without any problem.

This experiment is instructive in that it shows us at one and the same time both the difficulties presented by the notion of identity during growth, and the precocity of this notion in the case of the child's own body. At first glance, the origins of identity would seem to be bipolar, if we go back as far as the sensorimotor level: the permanent object on the one hand and one's own body on the other. But we must bear in mind that one's own body is discovered and known only in relation to other human bodies, as J. M. Baldwin has emphasized in his essays on the role of imitation. In addition, Th. Gouin-Décarie has demonstrated the synchronization and the correlation between the discovery of object permanency (as we have outlined it) and the establishment of object relations (in the Freudian sense) which includes a more and more systematic interest in other human bodies (cf. Gouin-Décarie, 1966a). Finally, as I had hypothesized on the basis of observation, and as Gouin-Décarie (1966b) has verified experimentally, the first object to become permanent is another human body. It would seem, then, that the roots of identity are to be found in the complex involving "own body × body of another × permanent object." This complex is not bipolar, but derives from the functional unity of the exchanges between the subject and his physical and interpersonal surroundings, and is reinforced by the interplay of all the subject's objectivized actions, and particularly his instrumental actions.

In light of this, G. Voyat questioned subjects on the identity of the movement itself in an instrumental action: the subject A throws a ball B to hit another ball C, and the question is whether it is the "same movement" which is transmitted from A to C; in another situation, the subject A is replaced by a release mechanism A^1. We found three levels of reaction. At the first level, the identity is affirmed in both cases, because of assimilation to action. At the second level, the subject takes an interest in the objective conditions of the movement (loss of speed, etc.) and reacts differently to the two conditions: when he himself throws the ball, he says it is "just one throw," it is "my throw" which is transmitted to C; but if the mechanism throws it, he does not see it as the same movement through B to C. There is a clear analogy between these results and the results of the plant and the child's own body.

IDENTITY AND CONSERVATION

The facts presented so far show how much the notion of identity progresses during a child's development. It appears early as a preoperational notion, and even a sensorimotor scheme, as a qualitative identity and as a projection of relations between the child's body and other objects, as he acts upon them. Later, it takes the form of an "identical operation," integrated into operational structures which make possible quantification and conservation.

In a recent book which he was so kind as to dedicate to me, Bruner (Bruner *et al.*, 1966) hypothesizes that conservations are simply identities, generalized through language, etc. He thinks that conservation does not result from reversibility since, according to him, one can find cases of reversibility without conservation. Similarly, conservation does not result from compensation, since once again he claims that there are cases of compensation without conservation. Conservation, then, would simply be a generalization of the notion of identity, due to development of the symbolic instruments of thought.

Before approaching the heart of this discussion, which is the central problem of our discussion, I should like to note that the dialogue with Bruner is rather difficult, since there are certain elementary distinctions which he does not make and, from my point of view, the absence of these distinctions necessarily gives rise to a certain confusion. I should like to mention three of these distinctions:

(1) First, we must distinguish *covariations* (which are functional) from compensations (which are operational). For example, when we asked

5 to 6 year olds to predict where the water level would be in a thin glass when the water was poured from a wider glass, 23% anticipated that the water would rise higher in the thin glass, but once it was done, they denied the conservation (cf. Piaget and Inhelder, 1966a, p. 310). Bruner would say that this is a case of compensation without conservation, but in fact it is not compensation: it is simply the prediction of a covariation, due to previous experience (a child may have noticed this covariation already when he has seen liquids poured, but this is a simple function, and not an operation); the subject does not understand that what is gained in height is lost in width, which alone constitutes compensation and leads to conservation.

(2) Secondly, we must distinguish true conservation from pseudo-conservation, which is easy enough with certain control experiments. For example, in the liquid-pouring experiment done behind a screen, which we ourselves did some time ago (Piaget and Inhelder, 1966a, Chap. VIII), we often find 5 year olds who say that there will be "as much to drink" in the thin glass as in the wide glass (it is even the general rule, with the exception of the 23% mentioned above). But this is a pseudoconservation, because they also predict that the water level will stay the same in the thinner glass. The control experiment then is to present the child with two empty glasses, one wide and one thin, and ask him to pour the same amount into each glass (so that it's fair, etc.). Pseudoconservation subjects pour the water *to the same level* in each glass, without seeing that one contains much more than the other (this is an example of ordinal evaluation, based on the endpoint, without any metric evaluation). Bruner did not do this control experiment, so that many of the "conservations" he cites are simply pseudoconservations.

(3) In the third place, Bruner does not distinguish reversibility, which is a logical and operational notion, from an empirical return, which is a physical notion (we have referred to it for many years as "an empirical return to the point of departure"). I am not convinced by his examples of reversibility without conservation: they are simply cases of empirical return, as an elastic band comes back to its original size if it is stretched and released.

(4) I should like to make one more point before continuing. Bruner constantly attributes to language a role which has in no way been verified. The work of Sinclair-de Zwart (1967a) gives clear evidence to the effect that a child's language is subordinated to his operational level, and does not constitute the formative mechanism of the operations.

Now let us come back to the problem of the relations between identity and conservation. Our hypothesis is that conservation is not simply a generalization of identity, and we base this hypothesis on the two following reasons. First, the identity of an object is derived simply by *dissociating the permanent qualities* from its variable qualities—and that is why it appears so early. Second, conservation necessitates a composition of quantitative transformations, according to the rules of operational composition—which is why it appears so late. (Note that I said the rules of operational composition, and not linguistic composition, for reasons which I mentioned above.)

The whole question, then, becomes that of establishing whether *quantities* are discovered in the same was as *qualities*, or if they necessitate a real construction, that is, a more complex process of elaboration. Now it is clear that qualities that can be identified simply through perception: color, shape, etc., are apprehended without any particular construction, and without going beyond the laws of perception. But the only quantitative relations apprehended by this means at the preoperational levels are ordinal and local evaluations. So expressions like "darker," "bigger," "wider," "heavier," etc., are at first understood only as comparisons which imply a partial, one-way order, and not a complete seriation with ordered ranks and inclusions which can run in either direction. For example, "longer" is understood in the sense of "going farther," with the arrival point being a privileged center of attention, and the departure point or the interval between the two being neglected.

Quantity in the true sense requires much more, whether it be numerical or metric, or even relative to the extension of classes ($A < B$ if $B = A + A^1$) or to the inclusion of order positions ("distance" $A - B$ is smaller than "distance" $A - C$ if B falls between A and C). Quantity is necessarily based on a system of inclusions, which takes into account the intervals, or the complementary classes. Now such an inclusion is not a perceptual given, but must be constructed operationally, which is why quantitative conservations are so late appearing. If language alone imposed these structures, as J. Bruner believes, then of course the evolution would be much faster, since there would be no need for the child to build the structures himself, and he would receive ready-made, through linguistic training, all the instruments he needed. Unfortunately, the facts reveal the opposite situation, and we all know that, even at our age, we succeed in talking well only if we begin thinking well. But thinking means structuring reality by means of operations. I know that Bruner does not believe, or declares that he does not believe, in operations, but this is true only in appearance, since he locates them implicitly in language, and above all since he uses "identity" or identification as if it were a real operation, even according it much more power than it actually has.

Quantification is then the product of operational structures of increasing complexity, spreading over classification (with inclusion of extensions), and seriation as well as numerical "groups" and spatial measurement. Identity does not disappear with the onset of operations, but it is integrated into structures which go far beyond it, and which encompass it as one operation among many. This process is clearly visible in the very arguments which a 7 or 8 year old uses to justify the conservations which these structures make possible.

In fact, in all forms of conservation, these arguments come down to three, one of which is identity, which has become operational, and is tightly linked to the two others. The first of these arguments is reversibility by inversion: you have changed A to B, but you could change it back again from B to A and you would have the same A again. The second argument is reversibility through reciprocity or compensation: in changing A to B, you changed aspect x of A to x^1, greater than x, and aspect y of A to y^1, less than y, so that the two compensate each other, $x^1 y^1 = xy$. The third argument seems to be a simple identity: you didn't add anything or take anything away, so it's still the same amount. But in fact this identity raises a curious problem. The young subjects who deny conservation also know very well that nothing has been added or taken away, but this knowledge does not lead them to conservation. So it is not identity as such which is new in the reasoning of the 7–8 year olds; what is new is that now it has become an argument in favor of conservation whereas until that point it in no way implied conservation. What has happened to give identity this power which it did not have before? The point is that this is no longer the same identity. The qualitative identity "it's the same water" does not lead to the same thing at all. But the notion of "nothing added" is the quantitative and operational identity "$+ 0$," and the notion of "nothing taken away" is the quantitative and operational identity "$- 0$." The composition "$+ 0 - 0 = 0$" is the "identity operation" of an operational grouping, and this operation can only take form in conjunction with the other operations, and as a part of their total system (the additive system, etc.). It is in this sense that we believe that the structure of a "grouping" of operations as such has a profound psychologic meaning, and not only a logical one.

It is, then, the total system or grouping which is responsible for the formation of the conservations, and not identity. Identity is but one element of the system, and an element which has been transformed by the system itself, rather than being the source of the system.

Memory and Intelligence
in the Child

BÄRBEL INHELDER

PRELIMINARY CONSIDERATIONS

Since the days of Ebbinghaus, a long tradition of research has been devoted to the laws of memory. Against this background our manner of approaching the study of memory may appear somewhat unusual. However, in some respects our work harks back to Bartlett, about whose theories we shall have more to say later on.

In contrast to the strict behavioristic tradition, we were mainly interested in the internal mechanisms of transformations between stimulus and response. We did not follow the experimental tradition of varying the spatiotemporal and meaning constellations of the stimuli to discover new laws or the optimal conditions for memory performance. Instead, we attempted to state hypotheses concerning the transformations within the "black box" and focused our attention upon unobservable events. However, we hope we avoided falling into subjective mentalism, for indeed unobservable transformations can be objectively studied as a function of factors that depend on general development. Perhaps, after the manner of G. Miller, we should label ourselves "subjective behaviorists." Our previous studies on the genesis of the operations of thought have demonstrated that it is possible to study the results of thinking activities in an objective fashion. From the progressive and coherent modifications of these activities as a function of age, laws of internal transformations can be inferred.

These internal mechanisms seem closely linked to what one usually calls the processes of encoding and decoding. We were particularly interested in the code as such. If the structure of the code remains the same, one would expect memory to stay intact or to deteriorate in proportion to its complexity and especially to the passage of time. Such assumptions seem to be implied by those who hold that memory in general, and memory images in particular, are copies of reality. If on the contrary the structure of the code changes in the course of, and perhaps as a function of, the development of thought operations, some initial hypotheses about the functioning of the internal mechanism of transformation become possible.

If we are right in supposing that the structure of the mnemonic code varies with the passage of time, it remains to be seen whether this modification is dependent on specific mnemonic laws or rather on the developmental changes in the cognitive structures. The laws of development proper to the cognitive structures were known to us from previous research. This approach to the problem naturally influenced the choice of experimental situations.

We presented children between the ages of 3 and 12 years with a great variety of configurations that they were asked to memorize. Most of the configurations were the (static) end result of operatory transformations (classifications, seriations, numerical and metric correspondence, and so on). There were also spatial configurations, the product of spatial operatory activity. Finally, some configurations were presented that embodied the outsome of a physical process: understanding the causal sequence of these processes follows readily analyzable developmental lines. A number of situations involved random elements. Our purpose was to observe qualitative differences of behavior according to age levels and to throw some light onto the process of memory organization.

Even if, in these processes of mnemonic organization, we discovered many regularities dependent on the development of operativity, we had no intention of equating memory with intelligence as a whole. In a broad sense, memory is the apprehension of that which has been experienced or acquired in the past and implies the conservation of schemes of intelligence as well as conservation of biologic mechanisms. But we proposed to study memory in the strict sense and this memory is limited to types of behavior such as recognition, reconstruction, and particularly evocation of particular events located in the past. It is clear that mnemonic evocation, which is our particular concern, is possible only by means of memory images or of recall based on figurative or semiotic mechanisms. It should be noted that the memory image in the mnemonic evocation is distinct from the reproductive or anticipatory image in general. The former is accompanied by a localization in the past that manifests itself through an impression of something that has already been experienced or perceived, and not of something that is merely known.

In this connection it is useful to recall the distinction introduced by Piaget between the operative and figurative aspects of cognitive functions. Operative aspects (actions or operations) bear on transformations of reality, and consequently, action schemes depend on the operative aspects. Figurative aspects on the other hand (perception, imitation, image) are limited to the representation of states without reference to the transformations that result in those states. This distinction will be frequently used as we describe some of the surprising results of our experiments. If one presents the child with such simple configurations as, for instance, a series of lengths to be memorized, the memory performance seems to be determined not merely by the figurative presentation but equally by the operative schemes that influence the way in which the child understands the configuration. The distinction between operative and figurative is essential for understanding the distinction between a *scheme* and a *schema*. A *scheme* indicates the general structure of actions and operations (e.g., the scheme that permits one to arrange elements in an ordered series). A *schema*, by contrast, is merely a simplified imagined representation of the result of a specific action; this term can therefore be applied suitably in the figurative field. A model can unite the two: it is a schema insofar as it is a simplified representation, but it is a scheme as a means of generalization.

Our general problem is that of the relations between memory and schemes of intelligence, thus between memory in the strict sense and in the broad sense since memory in the broad sense includes schemes. More specifically, is the conservation of memory images possible without the functioning and the support of schemes? Some examples of our memory experiments may clarify this question.

MEMORY OF A SERIAL CONFIGURATION

This particularly simple experiment will exemplify our preliminary working hypotheses and the general procedure of most of our studies.

Children of 3 to 8 years of age were shown a configuration consisting of ten sticks of 9 to 15 cm in length. The sticks were arranged in a series from the shortest to the longest. The children were told merely to look carefully at the sticks in free vision to remember them later. There was no particular time limit. After a week they were asked first to indicate by gesture what they remembered and then to make a drawing. On this and the following occasion there was no new presentation of the model. Six to eight months later the children were asked to draw again from memory what they had seen previously. A special group was also asked to describe the series verbally.

A series of coordinated experiments with comparable groups of subjects allowed us to draw conclusions with regard to the level of memory organization and the level of operational and linguistic development. In a modification of the experiment, to be described later, we arranged the sticks in the form of the letter "M" and compared mnemonic evocation with recognition.

After the children finished their memory drawings, they were given sticks and asked to make the seriation themselves so that their level of operativity could be determined. On the basis of their performance and the criteria established previously (Piaget and Inhelder, 1964), the children were assigned to one of the four groups in Table 8.1. At the third stage the child uses an empirical trial-and-error method, whereas at the fourth he is clearly operatory.

With regard to memory performance, while there was no clear-cut separation without overlap, the drawings could be divided reasonably into a sequence of types of organization (Fig. 8.1). (1) The youngest subjects, 3 to 4 years of age, drew a number of sticks lined up, but the length of the sticks was more or less equal. (2) The drawings of children in the next age group, 4 to 5 years, showed one or other of the following features: (a) the sticks were paired, a large one with a small one; (b) all the sticks were divided into two classes, one big, one small; (c) sticks were arranged in threes or fours, in groups of small-, big-, and middle-sized sticks; and (d) starting with 5 years of age, the children generally succeeded in drawing a correct seriation but which comprised only a few elements. (3) Starting with 6 to 7 years, correct serial configurations were frequently drawn.

These types of drawings correspond closely to what the children did when they were asked to make a series with the sticks. The drawings are also similar to what children drew when they had not seen a series

Table 8.1 *Seriation: Distribution of Subjects*
(in Percentages) by
Memory Types and Operational Stages

OPERATIONAL STAGES	MEMORY TYPES		
	1	2(a–d)	3
Preoperational	83	17	0
Transitional	0	65	35
Empirical seriation	0	27	73
Operatory seriation	0	0	100

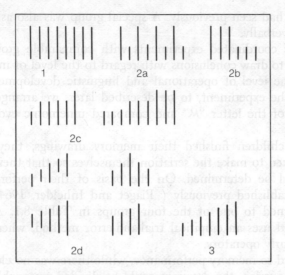

Fig. 8.1 *Three types of memory reproduction of a size graded seriation.*

beforehand and were asked to imagine what a number of sticks would look like when put into order.

The drawings relate also to the manner in which children describe the seriation verbally (Sinclair, 1967a). In fact, the verbal descriptions also fall into four distinct patterns: (1) only two descriptive terms are used, the adjectives *long* and *short* (or equivalent words). The children say either: "This one is short, this one is short, this one too, this one too, this one is long, this one is long," dividing the sticks into two groups, short sticks and long sticks. Or they say: "This one is short, this one is long, this one is short, this one is long," describing successive pairs of sticks.

(2) Three or more terms are used, and sometimes a different label is attached to each of the sticks: "Tiny, very short, a bit short, middling long, long, very long."

(3) Only two terms are used, but with the addition of one comparative: "short, longer, longer, longer." The characteristic of this pattern is that when the child is asked to immediately give a second description, starting at the other end of the series, he is incapable of describing the sticks he has just called *longer* as *shorter*; and he falls back into pattern 2.

(4) The description of the series from the shortest to the longest is the same as in pattern 3, but now the child can also reverse his pattern and use a second comparative: "short, longer," "long, shorter." It seems that memory images are linked to operatory schemes and that schemes control the images and dominate the model perceived. Table 8.1 sum-

marizes the distribution of subjects by memory types and operatory stages.

A second result is even more striking. After an interval of six to eight months, most of the children (74% of the group as a whole and 90% of children between 5 and 8 years) made drawings that showed progress relative to the first drawing. This progress was always gradual; that is to say, subjects progressed from one substage to the next.

How can these results be interpreted? It is clear that the memory image is not a simple residue of the perception of the model, but rather a symbol that corresponds to the schemes of the child. What seems to happen is that the child interprets the seriation as a possible result of his own actions. During the interval between the first and the second evocation, the schemes themselves develop because of their own inherent functioning through the spontaneous experiences and actions of the child. According to our hypothesis, the action schemes—in this particular case, the schemes of seriation—constitute the code for memorizing: this code is modified during the interval and the modified version is used as a new code for the next evocation. At each stage, the memory image is symbolized according to the constraints of the corresponding code.

The first results of this experiment seemed too good to be true. We therefore attempted to check our hypothesis about the transformations of the code by means of a more complex configurational situation.

Here we used a double seriation in the shape of the letter "M" of sticks placed vertically in symmetrical order (Fig. 8.2). The children were to draw the configuration from memory after one week and again after two and one-half months. Once more, the results were found to be in good agreement with the operatory activity of the subjects and there was progress in the type of mnemonic representation in gradual fashion, from one substage to the next (Fig. 8.3 a, b, c). When the children were presented with a set of drawings corresponding to the various substages (and the correct model), recognition was better than evocation, but was still far from perfect, especially among the younger children. Here also there apparently was assimilation to schemes according to the operatory level of the subject. The progress from the first evocation to the second was less marked than in the case of the simple seriation (38% as against 74%). But this difference seems to confirm our hypothesis of a development of the code in accord with operatory development. If the code were fixed, one

Fig. 8.2 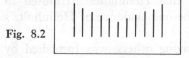 "M" *variation of a size graded seriation used as a standard for memory reproduction.*

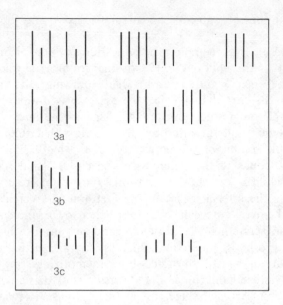

Fig. 8.3 *Three types of memory reproductions of the "M"
variation of a size graded seriation.*

might suppose that the memory would show greater deterioration the
greater the interval of time. On the contrary, progress was more evident
after the longer delay and this can be interpreted as being due to a
further development of schemes. It can also be suggested that the improvement of memory is in direct proportion to the simplicity of the underlying operatory activity. A more difficult model, as in the case of the
"M," would then give results that are qualitatively similar but quantitatively less marked. The essential fact is that for the configuration "M" too,
the code changed in the course of the retention period.

MEMORY OF HORIZONTAL LEVELS OF LIQUID

In most memory experiments with children, one does not deal
with modifications of a single scheme but with a whole group of converging
schemes. For example, there might be present preoperatory schemes
and empirical regularities that would lead to solutions that are close to the
preinferences (or unconscious reasonings) that Helmholtz attributed to
perception. Pavlov considered this idea to be one evidence of Helmholtz's
genius.

A particularly striking example, among others, was furnished by
the memory of the horizontal level of water in an inclined decanter. Our

previous research on the representation of space (Piaget and Inhelder, 1956) had shown that the notion of horizontality is acquired relatively late (around 9 years of age). This was observed in situations where the child was required to anticipate the direction of the water level in a decanter that was presented first vertical, then lying down, then turned upside down, and finally inclined at 45°. The decanter was covered with a cloth so that the water level was not visible. Before the child succeeds in utilizing natural systems of reference and constructing coordinates that permit him to establish interfigural relations, he does not draw horizontal water levels but levels that are inclined or parallel to the base or the side of the decanter or that adhere to the angles of the decanter. At this stage, the child obviously cannot establish interfigural relations.

For the memory experiment, two situations were presented. In one situation, children were shown the drawing of a bottle inclined at 45°, one-quarter of which was filled with colored water. The horizontal water level was parallel to an external line of reference (Fig. 8.4). After one hour, after one week, and after six months the children were asked to draw what they remembered of the presentations.

On the occasion of the first and second evocations, several memory types were found which shows once more that memory does not conform to the perceptual configuration of the model but rather to the manner in which the model was assimilated to the preoperatory schemes of the child. In fact, the series of memory types corresponds to a compromise between a symbolization of schemes and empirical inferences. Memory types as a function of age and operatory level can be characterized as follows. At the lowest level, between 5 and 7 years of age, there was a preponderance of drawings (71% to 87%) that depicted straight or inclined bottles with the liquid placed either against the side or parallel to the inclined base (Fig. 8.5). Then there were solutions of a somewhat superior type: bottles were inclined and water levels were still not horizontal, but no longer parallel to the base or to the side. Next, there was a series of characteristic compromises such as drawings of a vertical bottle

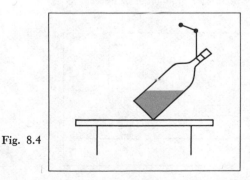

Fig. 8.4

Figure used as standard for memory reproduction of water level orientation.

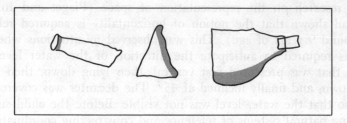

Fig. 8.5 *Memory reproductions of water orientation standard (Fig. 8-4).*

with an inclined surface of water, or of an inclined bottle that was completely filled with water. Finally, the model was correctly represented.

After one week's interval the children reproduced with very little deviation the drawing they had made after one hour. After six months there were some modifications: 30% of children progressed, 12% regressed, and 58% remained stationary. In general, correct drawings after one week remained correct after six months.

While the first experimental situation reflected mainly preoperatory schemes, the second situation revealed compromise solutions in which preinferences based on empirical probabilities were evident.

The drawing to be memorized depicted three objects (Fig. 8.6). One of these was a bottle, partially filled with colored liquid, lying on its side, another was of a car in a normal position, and the third was another bottle turned upside down and partially filled with liquid. The water level could thus be related not only to a base line but also to the car which moreover had a horizontal colored strip along the lower part of the body.

We wanted to know whether the children would recall the prone bottle as it was in the model, or whether the fact that in real situations bottles are seldom lying on their sides or standing upside down would

Fig. 8.6 *Figures used as standards for memory reproduction of water level orientation.*

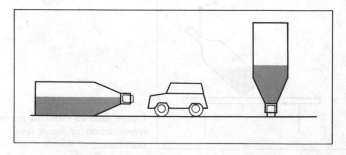

interfere with the memory image of the model as it was perceived. It should again be noted that we simply took only the children's drawings as data and did not ask any questions. If the child modified the position of the bottles, would he nevertheless recall the horizontal water level? A horizontal level was of course strongly suggested by the little car with its horizontal colored strip: a car is seen only exceptionally in any but a horizontal position.

The memory drawings of the children of 5 to 6 years of age appeared at first sight rather fantastic (Fig. 8.7). Nonetheless their spontaneous commentaries indicated that they really believed they had seen what they drew and that they did not think their drawings of the water level unrealistic. "That is easy," said a 6-year-old child, "I should draw some bottles and a car; I remember because I've been thinking." Some children remembered the upside-down bottle correctly and failed only with the water level of the bottle on its side, but others turned the upside-down bottle right-side up which in itself is perhaps not very surprising, but they also drew the liquid as if it were sticking to the side. The reason for such a performance seems obvious. First, they drew the bottle in an upright, i.e., its most probable position; second, they drew the water parallel to the side since they remembered the side as close to the water level; and, third, from these premises, they made the inference that a vertical wall required a vertical orientation of the water level.

MEMORY FOR NUMERICAL AND SPATIAL CORRESPONDENCES

As operativity develops, modifications of the memory code may lead to surprising, though not fortuitous, deformations. When two or more schemes are in active conflict because of nonsynchronous development, interesting memory types emerge. Such conflict can be brought about, for example, by the following situation. The child was shown four matches placed in a horizontal broken line and another four matches directly underneath, arranged in a flattened "W" so as to avoid suggesting the letter

Fig. 8.7   *Memory reproductions of water orientation standards (Fig.8-6).*

Fig. 8.8

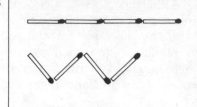

Figures used as standards for memory reproduction of length and number.

of the alphabet (Fig. 8.8). This configuration of matches could be assimilated by the child either as the result of a numerical or as that of a spatial relationship.

Previous research on the spontaneous development of geometric notions indicated that these two systems, numerical as against spatial, produce antagonistic results before becoming coordinated in the thinking of the other child (Piaget *et al.*, 1960). In fact, when the child establishes numerical equivalences by a one-to-one correspondence, he is still at a level at which he estimates the equality of spatial extensions by the coincidence or noncoincidence of the extremities of lines, so that "to pass" or "to go beyond" means to the child "to be longer." This characteristic of preoperatory thinking is moreover reinforced by the particulars of the mental image at this level. We have noted in our study of mental images (Piaget and Inhelder, 1966a) that boundaries play a predominant role in the formation of such structures.

An analysis of memory drawings of the matches as a function of age and operativity suggested five successive types. Type 1: a double line-up of a great number of matches without any numerical or figural correspondence. In type 2 (an interesting intermediate form): the coincidence of extremities dominates over numerical correspondence; the child draws one horizontal line-up of matches and another one in a zigzag fashion, several times repeated, such that the extremities of the line-ups coincide. Type 3 shows the conflict at its height in a false solution that respects the numerical correspondence but in which the length of the matches in the second line is exaggerated so as to achieve a topologic coincidence with those in the first. In type 4 the conflict is attenuated; the matches in the straight line go beyond the matches in zigzag, but the number of the segments in the two lines is not the same. Finally, type 5 achieves the correct solution (Fig. 8.9).

The evocation of the matches six months later shows considerable deterioration. The drawings, far from being faithful to the model, were organized by the dominating tendency to equalize the extremities. Apparently the developing schemes accentuated the conflict between the numerical and the spatial systems before the schemes were sufficiently developed to overcome the conflict.

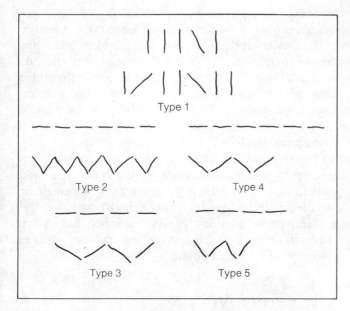

Fig. 8.9 *Types of memory reproductions of lengths and numbers*
(Fig. 8.8).

It is noteworthy that the conflict does not reside in the configurations as such, but in the assimilatory schemes with which the child responds to the configurations. In fact, the memory drawings of a figure using continuous lines, resulted in hardly any deformations and then only with the youngest subjects. Yet the same figure, arranged in broken lines by means of matches, produced types of deformations similar to those of the main experiment (Fig. 8.10).

Fig. 8.10 *Figures used as standards for memory reproduction of*
length and number.

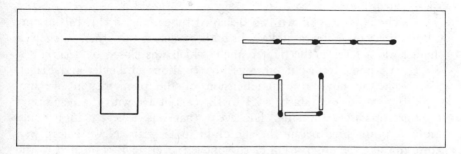

As with previous experiments, one may assume that in the memory performance preinferential processes intervened that are midway between perception and conceptual elaboration. It seems that children of a pre-operatory level apprehend that numerical correspondence. But they do not yet possess the scheme of spatial conservation that would enable them to understand that a line twisted into a zigzag remains of the same metrical length as it was before transformation. It was as if the children made a memory preinference as follows: if the two lines are equal by numerical correspondence of their elements, their extremities must coincide.

It is difficult to state exactly at which moment such preinferences are made. We have frequently noticed immediate quasi-deformations, and are accordingly inclined to believe that there occurs a kind of deforming conceptual assimilation already in the presence of the model, and that this deformation becomes manifest in memory. Previous research has shown that the image represents an object by means of its "concept" as much as or even more than by means of its "perception."

MEMORY OF A SITUATION INVOLVING CAUSAL RELATIONSHIPS

We have so far discussed memory situations related to configurations that are apt to activate the subjects' operatory schemes; other experiments concerned the evocation of a sequence of events or states that become comprehensible only when they are seen as the result of a causal process. In fact, causality can be considered as a system of actions and operations that are attributed to the objects themselves. One could therefore expect that, just as before, the schemes of the child would intervene in memory according to his level of comprehension.

We used models that permitted the child to notice a causal process, for instance, the transmission of movement by means of balls rolling down an inclined plane, or the movement of objects through a system of levers. There were also some static situations that could be encoded either as spatial configurations or as the result of causal processes. The following experiment is an example.

The child was shown two U-shaped tubes (Fig. 8.11). In the one, A, the water was at the same level in both branches, the other, B, showed a higher water level in the right branch, which was closed by a cork.

We knew from our previous investigations (Inhelder and Piaget, 1958) that the physical comprehension of the phenomenon of communicating vessels only starts at 11 to 12 years of age with the beginnings of formal operatory thinking. The event that was indicated in B could hardly be understood before the age of 14 to 15 years. Nevertheless, well before this age the observation of the uneven levels in B compared to the

Fig. 8.11

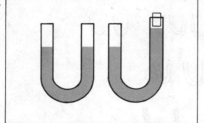

Figure used as standard for memory reproductions of water levels.

even levels in A could suggest an interesting problem situation to the child and the cork in B could indicate a causal influence.

We used an essentially similar procedure as before with some slight modifications. The child was first told to look carefully at what he was going to see so as to remember it afterwards. Then the actual physical model was shown to him for 45 seconds. Immediately afterwards the child was asked to draw what he could remember and to accompany the drawing with a verbal description. No questions of any sort were asked and no mention was made of any further memorization. One week later, and again six months later, the child was asked to draw what he remembered. Finally, one week after his last memory performance, a recognition procedure was used. For this purpose we utilized drawings representing different ways in which children of various ages had represented the model. One of the drawings was of course the correct one. In the course of this experiment we realized that the drawing furnished by the children corresponded more closely to the manner in which they became aware of the existence of a problem than to the manner in which they solved the problem. Subsequently we worked with some control groups with whom we attempted to modify the memory performance through situations and questions that facilitated awareness of the problem. These children would first watch the tubes being filled from cups that obviously contained equal amounts of liquid, and they would be asked such anticipatory questions as: "What would happen if I remove the cork in B?" "What would happen if I put a cork in A?"

The overall results of this experiment provided many interesting insights into the types and modifications of the schemes as a function of the development of the child and of the child's discovery that there *was* a problem. With a group of children mainly between 4 and 9 years of age, we distinguished five types of memory performance (Fig. 8.12): (1) no differentiation between the container and its content; (2) differentiation between container and content, with four even water levels but no indication of the cork; (3) tube A is drawn just like tube B with the water levels in the two branches of both tubes clearly differentiated; (4) differentiation between the drawing of the water in A and B but the water level

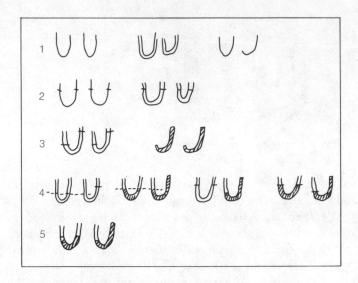

Fig. 8.12 *Types of memory reproductions of water levels (Fig.8-11).*

in the right branch of B does not reach the top, nor is the cork indicated; hence one cannot assume that there is a causal comprehension of the situation; and (5) a correct memory drawing.

Table 8.2 summarizes the percentage distribution of memory types after one week as related to age. It is particularly striking that even at the age of 8 and beyond, a correct drawing of such a simple constellation as two U-shaped tubes is provided by no more than 25% of the children. Analysis of the changes of memory from one evocation to another indicated an uneven progress, depending on level of development and memory type. In fact, after the immediate memory and the evocation after one week, 17% of the group improved, whereas at age 6 to 7 as many as 39% improved. The difference seems to be related to the fact that children of this age group begin to be intrigued by the phenomenon that they assimilate to a problem of physical causality. Here, by way of illustration, is what a 6-year-old child whose memory became better with time said during immediate evocation: "This water level is funny because it is not like the other. It must be because of the cork." A week later he said: "I still don't understand that." Probably he became aware of a problem at the occasion of the evocation rather than at the moment when he perceived the model.

When a child recognizes that his drawing does not quite meet the model, he often will verbally express his dissatisfaction with the drawing. Recognition implies some rather elementary sensorimotor schemes and develops long before the formation of representational images. Moreover,

Table 8.2 *U-Shaped Tubes: Distribution of Subjects*
(in Percentages) by
Memory Types and Age Groups

AGE	MEMORY TYPES				
	1	2	3	4	5
4–5	45	36	9	9	0
6–7	11	27	11	33	16
8 and beyond	0	5	10	60	25

schemes of recognition are more faithful than schemes of evocation. Even a partial recognition could therefore be sufficient to create the impression that "something is not quite right." This would motivate the child to improve his evocation. If the child in the interval between successive memory performances acquires schemes that enable him to understand the phenomenon better, then one can expect progress.

We observed that progress after six months was marked particularly by an increase of type 3 memories. Children at that stage recall that there are unequal water levels, but they easily forget the difference between tubes A and B. At the same time we observed some deterioration of memory in children who initially had made fairly adequate drawings. The deterioration was probably due to the child's lack of causal comprehension. Interestingly enough, the conditions that were introduced to help the child notice the problem facilitated the second recall, so that we obtained about 80% correct solutions.

There is, therefore, no justification for postulating a memory of a previous memory as a simple, automatic preservation of the first memory within the second. Rather, the memorizing of a previous memory is modified according to what the child has learned and understood during the interval.

MEMORY OF A CONFIGURATION INVOLVING ARBITRARY COMBINATIONS

Traditionally, studies of memory have been conducted in such a manner as to maximize the singular, the fortuitous, if possible the senseless, e.g., nonsense syllables. It was argued that memory would reveal itself the purer the more completely it is deprived of any significance. In actual fact, memory is never like this in real life. Yet it seemed of interest to investigate the memory of a configuration that is in part arbitrary. Strictly speaking, each configuration is always the outcome of some previous action, hence the result of a transformation. However, the transformations correspond only rarely to simple operations. The models that were used in the present experiments provided a mixture of elements some of which lent themselves readily to a reasoning process, whereas others did not.

In one of these experiments children were presented with a model of eight regular (cut-out) figures in the sequence triangle, circle, square, oval, triangle, circle, square, oval. On these figures were pasted black strips in a rather irregular fashion from an operatory viewpoint yet with some figural regularities (Fig. 8.13). For each pair of identical figures there was a short interior strip on one of them and a long one continuing beyond the frontiers of the figure on the other. The strips were vertical in four cases and horizontal in four cases. But there was no relation between the length of the strips and the directions from one element in the series to the next. Consequently there were three regular features to be noted: (1) pairs of figures; (2) contrast of short and long strips; and (3) contrast of horizontal and vertical strips.

How would children of different operatory levels retain the figures? Would they use methods of perceptual encoding or conceptual schematizations? The children were divided into two groups. One group, but not the other, was led toward some general conceptual organizing activity by being asked during the presentation session to classify the figures. What effect would this activity have on memory? In other respects the procedure was as before with evocations after one week and after six months. We also investigated memory reconstruction from the choice of a variety of figures and strips. Furthermore, after the second evocation, we proceeded to a new presentation of the model and asked for a third evocation and reconstruction one week later. This was a kind of mnemonic relearning.

From a great variety of suggestive results we here select two for discussion. First, when the model includes an inextricable mixture of elements some of which can and some cannot be readily assimilated to schemes of classification, the child appears to proceed as follows: for the first elements he will utilize schematizations that correspond to his operatory level of classification and he will simplify, often in a deforming man-

Fig. 8.13   *Figures used as standards for memory reproduction of enclosed and overlapping lines.*

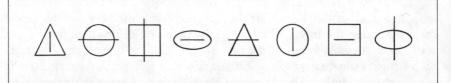

Fig. 8.14

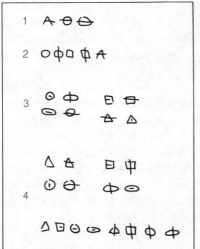

Four *types of memory reproductions of enclosed and overlapping lines* (Fig. 8.13).

ner, or leave out the second elements. An illustration of these procedures is furnished by the developmental sequence of memory behavior that we can present here only in a summary fashion.

For the total group of children between 4 and 9 years of age, we could distinguish four types of memory performance (Fig. 8.14).

1. The youngest children retained only some isolated forms without any obvious systematization; no pairing or contrasting of shapes or strips was evident.

2. There was a beginning of schematization that became manifest by some pairing, which however was not systematic. For example, one or two pairs would be noted based on a simple contrast between the length or the orientation of the strips.

3. In this group there was the beginning of a coordination between the contrasting attributes within a pair. For example, there were at least two pairs each with a single contrasting attribute or at least one pair with double contrasting features.

4. This last class showed a generalization of pairs together with the double contrasting features.

When memory levels were compared with levels of classification we noticed a convergence, but there was no direct influence on memory drawings of the previous classifying activity. In fact, while there were some striking correspondences in the manner of general schematizations, the particular content in which schematization was expressed was not identical in detail. The behavior of children at superior levels who can take account of all the three regular attributes at the same time constitutes an exception. The schematization of the nonclassifying children was similar to that of the classifying children except that in the former it occurred at a somewhat more advanced age level. Hence the previous classifying activity seems to have less to do with establishing classifying schemes in memory than with activating a schematization inherent in the spontaneous development of the child.

A second noteworthy result relates to the clear advance of reconstructions over evocation, as noted also in many other experiments. In fact, for the total population we observed improvement for 50% of the subjects, and on relearning even in 70%. This raises an interesting question. Why is reconstruction so clearly better than evocation in a situation that is rather close to those that were employed in traditional investigations of rote memory? Obviously it is not sufficient merely to have figures and strips some of which are identical to the perceived model to remember the combination originally presented. It should be noted that reconstruction is an action and, according to our working hypothesis, an action presupposes the utilization of schemes. Moreover, the conservation of an operatory scheme is easier than the conservation of a figurative schema since a scheme is conserved by its own functioning. But why during the reconstruction of an action are schemes progressively more easily organized than during evocation as an image or a drawing? Various experiments, the above-mentioned especially, indicate that during encoding, the perceived input is assimilated to a totality of schemes. In memorizing the particular figures and strips, schemes of similarities and differences of length and direction were involved. In the case of a simple evocation, these schemes probably are present but are not always actively applied. The quite fragmentary memory image of these elements is not sufficient to make the schemes active. On the other hand, reconstruction through manipulation of the elements activates the schemes directly and they in turn determine the emergence of the memory image.

FINAL REMARKS

Admittedly, it is rather ambitious to want to contribute something new in a field that has been so extensively worked over as has memory. It should be emphasized again that our investigations of memory were limited to the relations between memory and the general structure of intelligence. We hope to have clarified some points that have general implications for memory and thinking behavior.

Thus the developmental study of memory in its relation to intelligence, of which we have here sketched some characteristic results, seems through a converging number of facts to support the initial hypothesis. We hypothesized that the mnemonic code, far from being fixed and unchangeable, is structured and restructured along with general cognitive development. Such a restructuring of the code takes place in close dependence on the schemes of intelligence. The clearest indications of this is the observation of different types of memory organization in accordance with the age level of a child so that a longer interval of retention without any new presentation, far from causing a deterioration of memory, may actually improve it. In fact, such progress is due to and makes evident the general progress of intelligence during the interval concerned.

This hypothesis should not be taken to mean that any kind of memory encoding in situations related to operativity will lead to progress with a sufficient interval of time. The progress observed occurred in relatively simple memory situations in which quite general schemes sufficed as a support for the child's memory. In addition, these schemes were in a state of active development during the ages under study. When conflicting schemes exist side by side, as is frequently the case in everyday situations, and especially when the situations are fortuitous, the schemes of the subjects, as we have seen, can play a twofold role. They can bring about deformations or adaptive simplifications. Hence we are far from asserting that memory is always making progress. Our main assumption is that the figurative schemas of memory—from perceptual recognition to image evocation—are not by themselves sufficient to explain memory. They need the support of operatory schemes, on which the element of comprehension—which is nearly always present in memory behavior—depends.

At this point, we would again like to emphasize that our work in memory is in the tradition of the famous Bartlett (1932). In fact, our terminology, and, at a deeper level, the ideas that have directed our research are no doubt reminiscent of his highly original approach to these problems. Bartlett used the term "schema" proposed by Head, though he expressed his dislike for the word. According to him a more dynamic term, such as active developing patterns, or organized setting, would be more appropriate. Such schemata or patterns are always active in well-adapted reactions of the organism according to Bartlett. Head's schemata were primarily conceived as applying to functions of afferent sensibility; Bartlett went much further and saw in the schemata the explanation of many facts of memory. It is hardly necessary to emphasize in this context that Bartlett's term 'schema' is coextensive neither with our term *scheme* nor with our *schema*, though it is nearer to *scheme*. Bartlett encounters a difficulty in the fact that each of these schemata possesses its own natural and essential time order, in which the "last preceding member" of a series dominates. The iterative and circular character of motor habits poses no problem here; but it is obvious that in many facets of memory, especially those of the kind we have explored, the individual succeeds in "breaking up" the temporal order. As an explanation of this "breaking up" Bartlett very tentatively proposes a kind of general attitude of the subject toward new experiences, this attitude being determined by the schemata. Perhaps we have contributed in some measure to the solving of Bartlett's problem.

To sum up, memory cannot be dissociated as a separate ability from the functioning of intelligence as a whole. The problem of the relation of memory and intelligence remains to be analyzed in greater depth and with greater precision than in our preliminary investigations.

The observed developmental dependence of memory on the encompassing structures of the child suggests two rather general implications. First, our results reconfirm the importance of operatory structures. These structures not only control strictly logical behavior but also become manifest as determining factors in many different fields; this has been shown in experiments on perception, on mental image, on learning, and now also on memory. Second, even in the field of biologic memory it seems that it is no longer appropriate merely to speak of traces or engrams. There is always an underlying structure that contributes to the integration of memory acquisition. These structures may well depend on the integrity of RNA or DNA or on some other factor. But whatever role may in the future be assigned to such biochemical factors, a process of structuration will no doubt always be present in mnemonic organization.

Information Processing
Tendencies in
Recent Experiments
in Cognitive Learning
—Empirical Studies

BÄRBEL INHELDER

Piaget's theory concerns cognitive development and developmental epistemology. It is therefore not surprising that such a theory is itself constantly developing. New problems are being raised, new methods are applied to deal with these problems, and explanatory models are refined and readjusted to account for new findings. Piaget showed that cognitive development has a direction, and proceeds toward increasingly better adaptation of the knowing subject to the reality that is the object of his knowledge. Through intensive and detailed study of the acquisition of various concepts (number, weight, volume, space, time, causality, probability, and others) it was possible to determine the underlying structures of thought that allow attainment of these concepts. Subsequently, it was possible to establish a hierarchy within these structures and to hypothesize their possible filiation. These structures have been formalized in algebraic form, as grouplike structures and semilattices for the preformal stages of thought, and as lattices and groups for the formal stage. The structures are atemporal and reflect the possibilities of a total system, but to locate the formative mechanisms that can explain the transition from one stage to another, we have to go beyond such structural models. Piaget and his collaborators have become increasingly interested in dynamic models, more specifically in self-regulatory mechanisms.

From a biologic viewpoint, all regulations during development go

121

beyond the mere maintenance of equilibrium. They originate through compensation for perturbations arising either in the organism or its environment, and result in new constructions. Similarly, in psychologic development, incomplete systems or partial systems that conflict with one another are enlarged or integrated through regulatory mechanisms. An important aspect of such mechanisms resides in *post hoc* corrections that modify action schemes.

Piaget calls his developmental epistemology "naturalist, but not positivist." Cognitive behavior is an outward sign of the assimilatory and accommodatory capacities of a living organism. The biologic aspect of Piaget's theory is often difficult to grasp for those psychologists who believe that mental development is infinitely malleable (under favorable conditions and with adequate teaching methods) and who are convinced that what they think of as errors of growth can easily be corrected.

A biologically inspired theory that uses such concepts as assimilation, accommodation, and action schemes is very different from a learning theory that tries to account for cognitive development in terms of associations, connections, and conditioning. These latter types of mechanisms always suppose that two events are linked in the subject's mind because he has passively submitted to an outside pressure connecting the two. The concept of assimilation, by contrast, supposes that the subject actively assimilates a new event to existing structures. It is not a question of the subject's knowledge merely reflecting outside events, but of his own activity on the outside world, plus the feedback from this action which allows him to construct new concepts and action schemes.

Therefore, there is an interaction between the knowing subject and the objects that are to be known. It is true that Piaget has, until recently, emphasized the constructive role of the subject, and that comparatively little attention has been given to features of the objects favoring the attainment of knowledge. Objects can only be known, in closer and closer approximation, through the activity of the subject himself. The subject never attains complete knowledge of these objects; objectivity is the limit of these convergent processes. As knowledge of objects proceeds, the subject's activity becomes better and better organized. In a sense, this justifies Piaget's theoretical distinction between two types of knowledge—*logicomathematical knowledge* and the *knowledge of the physical world*. From the Piagetian viewpoint, these types of knowledge result, on the one hand, from the organization of the subject's activities (logicomathematical knowledge resulting from reflective abstraction) and, on the other hand, from the knowledge the subject gains about the object's properties (knowledge of the physical world resulting from physical abstraction).

From the viewpoint of developmental psychology, the relations between the two abstraction processes and their reciprocal influence have not yet been sufficiently studied. Among our ambitions is to explore these relations through learning experiments. We suppose that what the child learns about objects influences the way he organizes his own activity (and vice versa) and that in this link resides one of the dynamic factors of development. Learning experiments seem particularly apt to help us observe transition mechanisms at work. By inducing the elaboration of a concept, and by working with the child in several (sometimes as many as six) sessions during 2 or 3 weeks, we may observe, or even induce, some of the crucial instances where "something happens." Evidently, we can never observe the mechanisms, but only the behavior that is their result.

We hope that with new facts obtained from the learning experiments, we will be able to get some ideas as to the possible form of a dynamic model of transition mechanisms. In order to study as closely as possible the mechanisms at work in the transition of one substage to another, we chose to conduct learning experiments on well-explored problems in conservation and class inclusion (just to give these two examples among many others). As I have already said, developmental psychology aimed first of all at establishing a hierarchy of underlying structures. Conservation principles and class inclusion operations are important indicators of the existence of a grouplike structure. Logically speaking, an operation transforms a state A into a state B, while its inverse transforms B back into A. Through these transformations some quantitative property is kept constant, and this invariance can exist only in a coherent system of operations. It is for his reason that when a child understands that (for instance) the weight of a plasticine ball does not change when the ball is transformed into a sausage or a pancake, we can interpret his understanding as an indicator of the existence of a coherent system of operations. Though the underlying structure of operations may be the same in many concepts of conservation, it is well known that in development they do not all appear at the same time, but become established successively over a number of years. One of the very first, attained by most children around the age of six, is that of numerical quantity. At that age, children know that a change in the disposition of a set of discontinuous elements does not change its number. Younger children, when presented with two linear arrangements of discontinuous elements in optical one-to-one correspondence, of which one is then spread out, think that the spread out elements, because they go *further than* the other elements, are *more* in number.

One of the questions we hoped to elucidate by learning experiments was how do children construct more difficult conservation concepts once the conservation of numerical quantity is attained? Since the different conservation concepts have been extensively studied, both cross-sectionally and longitudinally, they appeared to constitute a priviliged case in which we might be able to observe supposedly general transition mechanisms in action.

In one of our experiments designed by M. Bovet (Inhelder *et al.,* 1967), we tried to lead children who showed (in pretests) an incipient notion of numerical conservation to a grasp of the conservation of continuous quantities (normally acquired some 3 years later).

The children had to succeed in a test of numerical conservation, consisting of the following items:

(a) Two identical glasses, A and B, are filled with large beads (where the experimenter and the child simultaneously drop beads, one or two at a time into the glasses). Glass B then is emptied into a narrower glass (N), or into a larger glass (L). The conservation question is asked. The beads in glass N (or L) are then poured back into B.

(b) The beads in glass A are poured into L, and those in B are poured into N at the same time. The conservation question is asked again.

Children who passed the pretest then participated in the experiment. Without going into the details of the procedure, the following types of situations were used. In a preliminary situation, toy houses glued onto matchsticks are first set out in two rows, in one-to-one-correspondence. Then houses in the second row are displaced (see Fig. 9.1).

Questions are asked, first on conservation of the number of houses ("Are there as many green houses as red houses? or more? or less? How do you know?") and then on the length of the paths ("Is one of the paths just as long as the other?").

In other situations, the child himself has to construct paths with

Fig. 9.1 *Toy houses, glued to matchsticks, used in conservation experiment.*

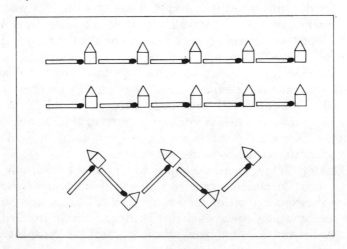

Fig. 9.2

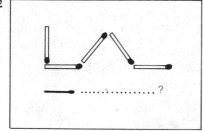

The first problem situation: child must construct a straight line equal in length to the zigzag line.

matchsticks. Both experimenter and child have a number of matches at their disposal, but the child's matches are shorter than those of the experimenter and a different color (seven of the child's red matches add up to the same length as five of the experimenter's black matches). The experimenter constructs either a straight or a broken line (a "path") and asks the child to construct a line of the same length ("just as long a path"; "just as far to walk," etc.). Three such problems are presented.

1. The first problem situation is the most complex: the experimenter constructs a sort of zigzag line and the child has to construct a straight line of the same length directly underneath (Fig. 9.2).

2. In the second situation, the child again has to construct a straight line of the same length as the experimenter's zigzag line, but no longer directly underneath (Fig. 9.3).

3. The third situation is the easiest, since the experimenter's line is straight and the child is asked to construct a straight line directly underneath it (Fig 9.4).

The experimenter uses the same number of matches (five) as in problem situations 1 and 2, so that this third situation (seven of the child's matches are needed to make a straight line of the same length) suggests a correct solution to situations 1 and 2 by transitivity.

The three problem situations remain in front of the child. After he has given his first three solutions, he is asked to give explanations

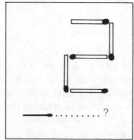

Fig. 9.3

The second problem situation.

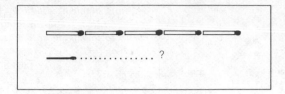

Fig. 9.4 *The third problem situation.*

and eventually to reconsider his constructions, while the experimenter draws his attention to one situation after another.

In this experiment, we interviewed a group of children (mean age, 6 years) who without having the concept of conservation of length had to succeed in a test of numerical conservation (Piaget and Szeminska, 1952). Of course, not only must the subjects give consistent numerical conservation answers, but they must also be able to justify their answers. Some typical examples of solutions to problems 1, 2, and 3 are as follows.

In problem situation 1, the most elementary solution is to construct a straight line with its extremities in coincidence with those of the experimenter's zigzag line. The child is convinced that the two lines are the same length, although his line is made up of four short matches, and the experimenter's line of five long matches.

In situation 2, the child finds no ordinal point of reference, since he has to construct his line at some distance from the experimenter's line, and so he uses the numerical reference: he constructs his line with the same number of matches the experimenter has used, regardless of the fact that his matches are shorter. When the experimenter now goes back to the problem situation 1, the child will notice—with some embarrassment—that there he has constructed a line, which he judged to be of equal length, that does not have the same number of elements as the model line. At this point, we often see amusing and original compromise solutions. For instance, in situation 1, the child may break one of his matches in two, thus creating a line with the same number of elements without destroying the ordinal correspondence (see Fig. 9.5).

Fig. 9.5

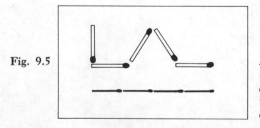

A *child's attempt to integrate ordinal and numerical references by breaking a match. (Inhelder later describes this as the third stage of the construction process.—E.)*

Fig. 9.6

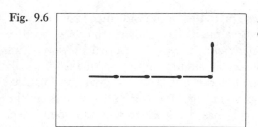

Another attempt to integrate ordinal and numerical references.

Another solution, again clearly indicating the conflict between ordinal and numerical references, consists of adding one match, but placing it vertically instead of horizontally (Fig. 9.6).

When the child then is asked to construct his line in situation 3, he starts by using the same number of matches (five) as the experimenter has used for his line. Since this time both lines are straight and the child's line is directly under the model, line, he sees immediately that this does not give the right solution. Because his matches are shorter, his line is not as long as the model line (Fig. 9.7).

It is not the purpose of this chapter to discuss in detail the purely psychologic results of these learning sessions. We intend to use this experiment as one of the many examples of the intricate coordinations and differentiations that take place when a new concept is formed, and of the nature of the processes that make this progress possible. In fact, in many other experiments we observed the same type of progress, and we feel justified in generalizing from this particularly clear instance.

We were able to observe that our subjects not only made considerable progress, but that there were qualitative differences in this progress, dependent upon their developmental level at the beginning of the learning sessions. A good proportion had clearly mastered conservation of length at the end of the sessions. Another group went part of the way. Some subjects progressed only a little or not at all, thereby making

Fig. 9.7 *In the third problem situation, the child may discover the inadequacy of his counting solution.*

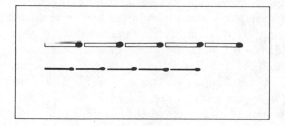

explicit a number of obstacles that the more advanced or brighter children overcame so quickly that we might have missed their significance.

At the outset of the experiment, as was mentioned previously, all our subjects were capable of conserving simple numerical quantity, which implies they had already coordinated the initial way of judging quantity by an ordinal relation ("going beyond" or "starting and finishing at the same point") with a way of judging based on one-to-one correspondence. It could therefore be supposed that the attainment of conservation of continuous length is a simple result of what, in associationist theories, is called *generalization*. Nonconservation of length shows that the obstacle is, again, an ordinal or topologic way of judging by "going just as far" or "going further than." By presenting lengths constructed from separate, but contiguous elements, a "transfer" would take place and the problem of transition mechanisms would have been solved in a simple, but, for our purpose, uninteresting way. A first result of our analysis of the subjects' behavior showed clearly that this was not the way in which the transition took place.

Essentially, it was possible to distinguish four successive steps in the construction process. Those subjects that made hardly any progress at all showed us the importance of the *first step*. In the preliminary situation with the toy houses glued to matchsticks (all of equal length) one asks questions of the number of houses and the length of the path. These children answered correctly the number of houses question. They counted the houses, and did not talk about one set of houses "going further" than the other. However, as soon as they were asked a question about the respective lengths of the paths, they did not think of counting the elements, or of going back to the one-to-one correspondence. They answered incorrectly, judging according to the going-beyond criterion. In this way, it became clear that one or another of two (or more) different systems of evaluation could be solicited, both being, in a sense, pertinent to the question, but neither were sufficiently developed to allow their integration. There was successive activation of two separate systems, and no contradiction was felt by the subject.

A *second step* in the construction process follows very soon afterward. Instead of the two evaluation schemes arising separately, according to the question asked, both seem to be present practically simultaneously. For example, when the subjects had to construct a path "just as long" as, and parallel to, the experimenter's, but with shorter matches, they would start off by counting the elements [scheme activated by problem situation (2)] and build their path with the same number of elements. However, no sooner had they finished their construction, than they noticed that one path "went further" and they found their solution no longer acceptable. They could then turn to the other solution, but on noticing that despite the coincidence there were more small matches in the one path than long matches in the other, they went back to their first solution. Neither could satisfy them and they could not conceive of a new solution taking both the preceding ones into account, though they were aware of the contradiction.

The *third step* did not appear in all the different experiments, but it is perhaps the most significant one. It consists of an inadequate effort at integration, and is visible in what we have called compromise solutions. As we have already mentioned, the child will break one of his matches in several pieces and thus obtain the same number of matches and still not have a path that "goes beyond." Either that, or he will ignore the instruction that he has to make a straight path and put one of his matches vertically instead of horizontally. In this way, he fulfills both his demands in a solution that, at least temporarily, satisfies him.

From here, the *fourth step* in the construction process follows for many subjects. Instead of one scheme operating a *post hoc* correction on the other, we now see a *reciprocal adjustment* whereby the criterion of coincidence (sufficient provided the two paths are parallel) and that of numerical equality (sufficient provided all matches are of equal length) are successfully integrated into a coherent system which allows the child to solve problems of length in all generality, and no longer only in special cases. Now the different schemes can be integrated, which gives a new impetus to the search for necessary and sufficient conditions for equality of length. This results in a complete understanding of the compensation involved. The children explain, "You need more matches when they are smaller" and "The path goes less far but it has zigzags."

Development takes place in a very similar way in all the processes that have come to light during our training experiments. There is, however, one essential difference, namely: with logical operations (in the strict sense of the term), the regulatory mechanisms which sooner or later lead to an awareness of contradiction are not followed by compromise solutions in the form of partial compensations, but are immediately followed by complete logical compensations which later result in correct solutions. A particularly striking example is that of the acquisition of logical quantification (Piaget and Szeminska, 1952; Inhelder and Piaget, 1965).

The problem of class inclusion concerns additive compositions. For instance, if B is the general class and A and A' the subclasses, the following operations obtain: $A + A' = B$; $B - A' = A$ and $B - A = A'$. From this it can be deduced that if both A and A' are nonempty classes, B is larger than A'. The inclusion of class A in class B provides the relationship which proves the statements "all A's are some B's" and "A is smaller than B." Certain subjects can agree with the first statement even though they do not understand the second. Complete understanding of the concept of inclusion implies the understanding of the link between the operation $A + A' = B$; and the operation $B - A' = A$. This link takes the form of logical compensation. It is only at the level of concrete operations that the child becomes capable of working simultaneously on a general class defined by a general property (e.g., flowers), and on sub-classes of this general class that are defined by a more restrictive property (e.g., roses). At the preoperatory level, the child does not conserve the whole when he has to compare it to one of the parts. His mistake is that, when he begins by mentally evaluating A, he isolates it from the whole B and can only compare it with A' and not with B. When faced with a bunch of flowers containing a great many roses and a few tulips, and asked if there are more roses or more flowers, the child replies that there are more roses. If he is then asked "more than what?" he often answers "than tulips." The main difficulty lies in the fact that the child is asked to compare within only one collection the logical extension of a subclass A with the logical extension of the total class B.

H. Sinclair constructed a learning procedure in which the children had to construct by themselves two collections within which the sub-classes varied in comparative size while the total collection was kept constant (Inhelder and Sinclair, 1969).

The experimenter gives to one girl doll six pieces of fruit, for example four peaches and two apples (PPPPAA). The child is asked to give the other (the boy doll) "just as many pieces of fruit, so that they have just as much to eat but more apples, because he likes them better than peaches." The instruction is repeated as often as necessary, in different forms. The situation can be varied, made easier, or more difficult.

Let me just mention one typical example. At the beginning of the learning sessions, a child asserts that the experimenter's instructions cannot be complied with: "It can't be done." He finally gives the other doll an identical collection: four peaches and two apples.—"Can you remember what I just said?"—"*He is to have the same thing as the girl.*" —"The same thing as what?"—"*The same thing of the other fruit.*" He thus refers to A' and not to B in classes $A + A' = B$, which corresponds to the second step in the construction process in the preceding experiment.

The experimenter's instructions: "Give the other doll more apples, but just as many pieces of fruit" contains two conditions: *more apples*, referring to the subclass; *just as many*, referring to the total class. In his interpretation of these instructions, the child seems to be in-capable of simultaneously taking into account the four components, namely: the *same, more, total class, subclass*. At first he mentions only the condition referring to the total class ("*the same thing as the girl*"), but when the experimenter asks him about the first part of the instruc-tions he disconnects this condition from the total class and applies it to the subclass ("*the same thing of the other fruit*"). When the other condition is stressed (more apples) the child applies it correctly, but then neglects the first one. He says *"We've got to add some then"* and proceeds to add two apples to the whole collection (four peaches and four apples). When he is asked if he is satisfied with his solution, he says *"No."* When we repeat the instructions, he takes away all the fruit he had given the boy doll, ponders, and then seems to make a real discovery. *"We've got to give just apples then?"* and gives six apples. This solution actually does solve the conflict among the conditions. It does satisfy all the conditions, but vacuously. That is, he solves the problem of including one class in another by identifying the total class with one subclass. He identifies the part and the whole without going through the trouble of having to make compensations for the members of the complementary subclasses. (Compensation means: taking away one A' whenever one A is added.)

This kind of solution is functionally similar to the *third step* in the construction process in the preceding experiment: the compromise solution between ordinal and numerical schemes, but here the compensation is immediately complete because it happens to be a special case of the solution. It is specific to logical problems in the strict sense where the ordinal and extensional aspects of quantification are nondifferentiated.

That this is a special case and not a general logical solution is clearly demonstrated by the fact that when the experimenter's questions reintroduce the two aspects, the child again decomposes his solution into his former disconnected categories.—*"Now he's got more apples than the girl."*—"Right. Do they have the same number of pieces of fruit?" —*"No, one's got more: the boy. I gave him two extra apples."*—"How many pieces of fruit has he got then?" (Without counting)—*"He's got eight."*—"Count them carefully." (Surprised)—*"He's got six too!"*

This particular child, who started at the lowest operatory level was not able to go further. However, children who were more advanced at the beginning of the learning sessions resolved the contradiction by a very adequate, complete compensation of logical operations and acquired full understanding of class inclusion, not only in situations involving two collections, but also in the more difficult one-collection situation. Finally, for all these children, training in class inclusion had a unexpected positive effect on progress in conservation problems.

These two examples among many of our learning studies seem to lead to the following conclusions. Instead of a more or less straightforward type of development, with differentiations becoming more and more refined (in the form of a treelike diagram), the interactions between different subsystems appear of the greatest importance. As the first example has shown, interactions between numerical and ordinal ways of dealing with problems of judging or constructing lengths lead to a conflict. It is this conflict which will trigger the process leading to the final resolution, through reciprocal assimilation of the two different sub-systems that do not necessarily belong to the same developmental level. The emergence of conflicts can explain the frequently occurring regressions in the subject's overt reasoning—they are only apparent regressions. In fact, they are observable symptoms of an internal event announcing the beginning of a structuration of a higher order.

It now seems necessary to relate such a dynamic model to the classic Piagetian structural model. In the first place, the different systems of judging or constructing are internalized schemes. As to their appearance and their possibilities of being integrated into others, these schemes are determined by the general structure of the corresponding level of development.

In the second place, the hierarchical structures are in part common to both types of knowledge—logicomathematical on the one hand, and knowledge of the physical world on the other. During the four successive steps in the construction process exemplified in the preceding experiments, either the apprehension of the properties of the subject's own actions, or the apprehension of the actual properties or features of the objects may be preponderant at one time. The epistemological nature of their interplay only becomes clear in the structural model.

From our point of view, it is illusory to try to establish process models which are not closely linked to structural ones. Since we are concerned with the specific Piagetian perspective, it would appear that the structural model, since it is based on a developmental hierarchy of structures, can absorb the process one. In fact, if we want to find the components that are common to both, we should think of the all-important concept of *compensation*.

The structural model uses, for each different level of development, specific types of compensation—for instance, the cancellation of a direct operation, or reciprocity in the case of the logic of relations. Psychologically and even biologically speaking, disturbances always give rise to a reaction on the part of the organism, but this reaction is not a passive submission to the environment. On the contrary, it leads to recombination of already existing capacities, in order to reestablish the destroyed equilibrium. In this sense, the reestablishment of an equilibrium involving a novel construction is also a compensation. The process model would therefore comprise compensations in the psychological sense. We have seen the example of first *juxtaposition*, then an *opposition*, then a *compromise*, and finally an *integration* of different schemes. The final integration, as we have also shown, gives rise to a new set of compensations.

In biology, new combinations only take place inside what are called *reaction-norms*. Similarly, we propose that in cognitive development, these new combinations can only occur inside what may be called narrow zones of assimilating capacities. The structural levels are at the root of the generation of new combinations, but simultaneously they impose limits on the novelties that can be produced. The compensations in the structural model would thus find their dynamic explanation in the process model; and the way these new combinations act will find their explanation in the structural model.

10

Operational Thought and Symbolic Imagery

BÄRBEL INHELDER

It may seem otiose to try to revive the old problem of imagery in thinking since Binet, Marbe, and Külpe have shown that thought without images is possible, and especially since certain opponents of associationism have gone so far as to deny the very existence of mental imagery. However, contemporary psychology, on the basis of data obtained by neurophysiologic and other experimental methods, has broken with the tradition, according to which the image is a residue of perceptions, and has raised imagery to the rank of a signifier. Thus, the genesis of symbolic imagery is seen in a new light.

WHAT ROLE SHOULD BE ATTRIBUTED TO SYMBOLIC IMAGERY AS AN AUXILIARY OF THOUGHT?

It may be asked whether language—without doubt the vehicle of choice for thought—is not sufficient to serve all the needs of symbolic function. Its affective scope apart, language essentially indicates concepts. Yet it seems that there is a large domain that language is not competent

---

I am grateful to H. and M. Sinclair for their kind assistance in translating this paper.

to describe except in devious and complex ways, that is, the domain of everything that is perceived (as opposed to conceived). Sometimes it is useful to communicate things perceived, but, above all, it is necessary to retain a large part of them in the memory if future action is to be possible. Recourse to symbolic imagery would thus be necessary every time that past perceptions are to be evoked or future perceptions anticipated.

The importance of symbolic imagery varies according to the type of operation it is called upon to support. It is inadequate for symbolizing logical and arithmetical operations, which, at the higher level, rely on arbitrary sign systems; nevertheless, it provides an important adjunct for the so-called geometric intuitions, since in these there is partial isomorphism between signifiers and signified, the former consisting of spatial figures, themselves imagined, and the latter consisting of spatial relations on which geometric operations are performed.

EXPERIMENTAL TECHNIQUES AND SUMMARY OF RESULTS

The techniques and results to be set forth in this paper are part of a larger study on the development of mental imagery carried out in Geneva under the leadership of Jean Piaget and in cooperation with a group of assistants: M. Bobel, F. Frank, E. Siotis, and S. Taponier. Experiments involving reproductive, evocative, and anticipatory images were carried out. It is the intention here to concentrate especially on the last group, which bears more particularly on our problem: the relation between the development of operativity and the development of symbolic imagery. In the first set of experiments, children were asked to anticipate the results of the displacement of one figure in respect to another and to imagine successive transformations of one and the same figure. A second set concerned kinetic anticipations in relation to a frame of reference, and a third concerned the part played by anticipation in the development of the concept of conservation.

Methods

The development of symbolic imagery can, of course, never be grasped directly but must be approached through actualizations, such as drawings, gestures, selections from among a series of drawings representing both correct solutions and typical errors of children of different ages, and verbal comments. Along these lines, starting from consonant or contradictory indices, we tried to make inferences about the various kinds of anticipatory imagery. Following our genetic method, we put the same problem to children of different ages, and, from comparisons and the hierarchial arrangements of their ways of symbolization, as well as from the increasing frequency of successful solutions, we tried to extract the laws governing the development and modification of symbolic representation.

DISPLACEMENT AND TRANSFORMATION OF FIGURES

Translation of a Square in Relation to Another Square which is Kept Immobile

(a) The children (aged 4 to 9 years) were shown two square pieces of cardboard (5 cm square). The upper edge of the immobile square was parallel to and contiguous with the lower edge of the square that was to be laterally displaced (see Fig. 10.1).

First we made sure that the child could actually draw the configurations. Then he was asked to anticipate the result of displacing the upper square from left to right. In terms comprehensible to the child we might say, "If I push the upper square a little bit to the right, can you do a drawing to show me what the two squares will be like?" The experimenter made a gesture to suggest the lateral displacement and requested the child (1) to draw the result of the displacement without seeing the actual displacement, that is, to anticipate the result; (2) to choose from a set of drawings the one that seemed best to represent the actual displacement; and (3) to draw the result of the displacement, but this time after actually seeing the displacement and the two squares in the new position. We asked the child to comment on his trials and errors in order to gain insight into his special difficulties and into the beginning of representative imagery.

From a qualitative analysis of how young children try to arrive at figurative symbols (see Fig. 10.1) one may deduce that the symbol long remains static even in as simple a case as the displacement of one figure in relation to another. The child did indeed indicate clearly by gesture the direction followed by the upper square, but this was only a global, all-encompassing image. When he tried to represent details, however, he sometimes drew the upper square as if it was detached from the lower one, or else—and this was more frequent from 4 to 7 years—he refused to go beyond one of the two frontiers. Thus, instead of con-

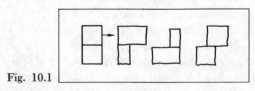

Fig. 10.1

Fig. 10.2

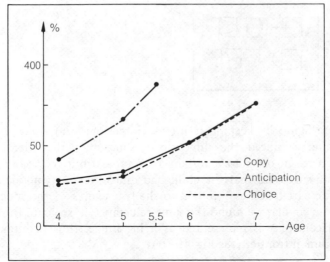

serving the surface sizes, he "conserved" a frontier, that is to say, he rigidly maintained its original position. This kind of "pseudoconservation," which we encountered several times, was not caused simply by difficulties of drawing. This is shown by the fact that in choosing a drawing from among those presented to him the child picked the one that was like his own drawing of the anticipated result. In this experiment, the curves representing the gradual increase in the number of correct solutions in the two procedures practically overlapped (see Fig. 10.2). The drawings of the final configuration, after the experimenter had actually performed the displacement, presented no difficulties from about 5½ years onward, although among 4-year-old children the drawings showed the same peculiarities as those of the anticipated results among children of 5 to 7 years.

(b) A complementary experiment also provided some interesting results. It consisted of superimposing two framed transparent squares of the same dimensions (5 cm square) and asking the child to imagine the lateral displacement of the superimposed square (see Fig. 10.3a). This time, young children succeeded in going beyond the outer frontier, but they failed to indicate the inner frontier, thus, in a way, "conserving"

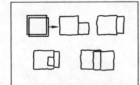

Fig. 10.3a

Fig. 10.3b

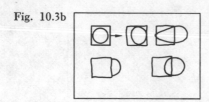

the square figure by keeping it intact. Sometimes they drew juxtaposed squares and sacrificed the dimensions; sometimes they deformed one of the squares in order to maintain a common frontier (see Fig. 10.3a). Everything suggested that the child had difficulties in symbolically representing the part that was common to the two figures. If the superimposed figures were circular we found the same reluctance to separate the frontiers; the displacement was represented as a big bulge, thus maintaining part of the common frontier (see Fig. 10.3b).

Folds: Rotating a Figure through 180°

(*a*) The child was presented with a transparent sheet to be folded along its vertical axis. On the left side, which was to remain stationary, a 5 cm square was drawn adjacent to the axis. On the right side, which was to be rotated through 180°, a small round figure (or square) was placed successively at different distances from the axis in such a way that, after folding, the small figure would appear outside, or inside, or on the frontier of the larger figure (see Fig. 10.4). The child was requested to draw what he expected would be the result of the folding. He was asked, for example, "Where will the little circle be when the book is closed?"

(*b*) The same experiment was done with a square frame placed on a background surface.

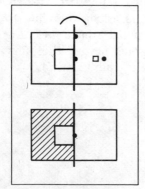

Fig. 10.4

Fig. 10.5

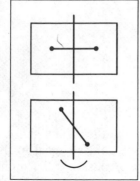

(c) The child was asked to imagine the paper being folded in a straight line at an angle of 45° or 90°, etc., to the vertical folding axis (see Fig. 10.5).

Two results struck us as particularly interesting.

1. Children from 5 to 7 years showed considerable reluctance to place the small figure inside or on the frontier of the larger one, but the problem became much easier to solve if the large square had an opening (a hole), thus depriving it of the figural quality manifested in the small circles or squares.

2. The representative imagery of topologic relations of interiority or exteriority came long before the imagery of the transformation of Euclidian figures, such as changes of direction of straight lines in relation to a frame of reference. The latter form of representation did not become general until fairly late, that is for children between 9 and 11 years. The figurative symbolism seemed to be closely related to the corresponding geometric operations.

Transformations of Arcs into Straight Lines and Vice Versa

A supple piece of wire in the shape of an arc (10, 13, or 24 cm long) was presented to children aged 5 to 9 or 10 years, and they were asked

(a) to draw a straight line showing the length of the wire if it were straightened out (by gesture, the experimenter suggested the action of pulling the wire straight by its extremities); to cut lengths of wire equal to the result of straightening the arc; and

(b) to draw successive intermediate stages of the transformation.

The drawings by the young children (see Fig. 10.6), as well as the cutting of the lengths of wire, were evidence of an initial difficulty of representing the result of a transformation and of a much more persistent inability to symbolize successive stages of the transformation.

Fig. 10.6

Centering his attention on the extremities of the figure, the child first behaved as if the result of the straightening would be equal to the chord of the arc, in other words, as if he had to "conserve" the ordinal relations of the figure's frontiers. Only very gradually, along with the development of operativity, did older children succeed in more or less correctly imagining the straight lines resulting from arcs. When this first obstacle was overcome, there remained the difficulty of representing intermediate stages of the transformation. This symbolization required an operatory understanding of the ordinal change of the extremities, the seriation of intermediate stages, and the conservation of length. With progress in operatory thinking, it would seem that a new form of imagery developed which captured successive moments of a continuous transformation (like the frames of a film) in order, as it were, to represent the continuity of the transformation in a schematic way.

Comparison of Inscribed Segments (in Open or Closed Figures)

The children were presented with a large variety of closed figures, partially or totally inscribed within one another (see Fig. 10.7) so that their frontiers coincided in one or more points (e.g., a square inscribed in a circle). They were also shown fragments of these same figures as open figures (for example, a semicircle with half the inscribed square, i.e., two chords forming an angle of 90°). The child was to judge whether the total length of the one figure (e.g., the sides of the square) was equal to the total length of the other (e.g., the circumference of the circle). To make it easier for the child to dissociate length and shape, the experimenter suggested, for example, two ants traveling along the two paths.

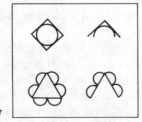

Fig. 10.7

From a large number of modes of evaluation, which can be linked to development, two extreme cases may be mentioned here. Small children, in accordance with their fixation on the frontiers of the figures, frequently judged the total length of the open figures according to whether their extremities coincided or not, and, thus, considered the straight segments and associated curves to be of equal length. Again, the importance of the frontiers induced the child to judge the length by the inclosure so that any figure on the inside was considered to have a shorter perimeter than the one that enveloped it. The answers thus arrived at were, or were not, correct depending on the shape of the figures. Older children, however, succeeded in anticipating the possible transformations of the figures, which enabled them, for example, to imagine the lines as overlapping when they tried to judge the lengths of the various parts.

KINETIC ANTICIPATION OF TRAJECTORY TRANSFORMATION

The Somersault

A tube with its extremities painted different colors was placed on a horizontal support in such a way that part of the tube projected beyond the support. By striking it on the projecting end, the tube could be made to perform a somersault (translation as well as rotation through 180°), so that it arrived in the inverse position on a lower support. After having rapidly performed this movement before the child, the experimenter removed the tube and asked the child to reproduce very slowly the same movement and then to draw the tube in its initial position, in its final position, and in intermediate positions. Finally, the child was asked to draw the trajectories traveled by the two extremities of the tube during the somersault.

From observing the rich variety of symbolic images provided by children aged 4 to 9 years, we would have concluded that, generally, the symbolic representation of the result of a transformation preceded the symbolic representation of the transformation itself. This seemed to command the overall development of imagery. The drawings (see Fig. 10.8) show the clumsy way that the children tried to represent the ordinal change of the extremities resulting from this movement. The lag between symbolization of results and symbolization of transformations would seem to be explained by the fact that the child needs to understand what happens during the transformation before he can symbolize it in detail; the transformation image thus seems to be subordinate to operatory activities.

141

Fig. 10.8

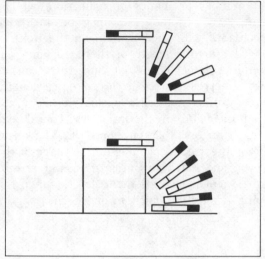

*Anticipation of the Trajectories of Three Fixed Beads on a
Rigid Stem Rotating through 180° (the Axis of Rotation
Coinciding with the Middle Bead)*

The results obtained in this experiment (Fig. 10.9), while con-
firming previous results, provided a remarkable example of the relation
between the development of imagery and the development of operativity.
Ordinal operations (change of order), which were acquired relatively
early (in this particular case at the age of 5), went with representative
images, also acquired early, of results of changes of order. Displacement
operations, which were arrived at later, went with figurative symbolizations of the trajectories of the beads, which were also acquired later.
There were, in fact, 3 to 4 years difference between the image of positions
and the image of movements. It would, thus, seem permissible to conclude that the anticipatory images relating to movement transformation
do not arise of themselves independent of operatory thinking.

THE ROLE OF ANTICIPATORY IMAGERY IN THE
DEVELOPMENT OF THE IDEAS OF CONSERVATION

In order to make a deeper analysis of the relation between the
development of anticipatory images and the development of operativity,
we repeated a series of earlier experiments on the development of conservation of numerical, geometric, and physical quantity, and compared
the child's level of operativity with his capacity to anticipate the transformations and their results. We give here only two examples.

Fig. 10.9

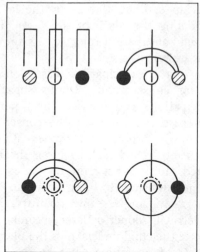

Liquids Poured into Vessels of Different Dimensions

In the experiment on the conservation of liquids, colored water was poured from a cylindrical vessel into another of the same height but a different diameter, and the children were asked whether the quantity of liquid remained the same. The children were also asked to anticipate the level of the liquid which was poured from a transparent vessel into six other opaque vessels of equal height but of different diameters. Finally, the children were asked to pour equal quantities of liquid into vessels of different shapes.

Comparing the various procedures was very interesting. On the one hand, it was noted that for the younger children a rough anticipation was easier than operatory conservation, but for the older children the reverse was true: they found operatory solutions easier than correct anticipation of levels. On the other hand, it was noted that, of all the children from 4 to 8 years of age, 30% could neither anticipate the levels correctly nor solve the problem of conservation; 22.5% anticipated correctly but without discovering conservation; and 5%, without being able to anticipate correctly, answered correctly the question of conservation; 42.5% showed both correct anticipation and conservation of quantities.

How, first of all, can the failure to anticipate changes of level be explained? While conservation does not force itself upon the child, the younger ones, by their previous experience, as well as by a kind of perseverance, moved toward what might be called "pseudoconservations." As long as they did not see the level of the liquids in the experiment, they considered that the quantities were the same; but when they noted a difference in level, they lapsed into nonconservation. The children, thus, mostly evaluated quantity by its upper limit, that is, by the level of the column of liquid, without considering the width of the vessel. It was as if the children judged more by rigid and partial rules (e.g., same quantity = same level) than by previous experience.

Second, what were the correct anticipations based on and did they constitute a preparation for conservation? Results suggested the hypothesis that a correct anticipation, as a consequence, perhaps, of experience, did not in itself prepare the child for the conservation of quantities; for the same child, called upon to pour two equal quantities into two vessels of different diameters, relied exclusively on the height of the column of liquid. It appeared, thus, that a more or less correct symbolic representation is by itself not sufficient to bring about an operatory compensation such as: narrow $\times$ higher = same quantity. However, the correct representation of levels will sooner or later become the indispensable auxiliary of reasoning once the child understands the phenomenon of conservation and when, instead of describing what he sees, he starts to explain it.

Displacement of a Stick in Relation to Another of the Same Length

This experiment was done as follows:

(a) The child had before him two straight sticks of equal length (say, 10 cm.). One was displaced so that it was almost completely masked by a screen. The child was asked to imagine how far the stick reached behind the screen, and, then, to draw the two sticks as if they were both entirely visible.

(b) With the same display, the child was asked to choose from among a mixed group of 18 sticks measuring 0.5–10 cm (actually 9 pairs), a stick that could exactly fill the space vacated by the displaced stick. Then he was asked to choose another stick equal to the hidden part of the displaced stick; for example, the child was told, "Now find another stick of the same length as the bit hidden by the tunnel."

(c) Without a screen, the child was asked whether the length of the stick remained the same after it was displaced parallel to the other stick (a displacement equal to about a third of the total length seemed to give the most interesting results).

The most instructive points for understanding the relation between anticipation and operation may briefly be summarized as follows:

1. The anticipatory image seemed to be quite separate from the preoperatory judgment since the imagined representation tended to diminish the length of the mobile stick (which to us seems to be a result of the frontier effect again), whereas the preoperatory judgment tended to overestimate the length of the displaced rod under the influence of the movement.

2. The anticipation of lengths seemed to precede judgments of

conservation of lengths. Of a group of children aged 5 to 9 (leaving aside fluctuations in estimations and judgments), 25% had neither a correct anticipation nor a sure notion of conservation; 28% succeeded in both anticipations and conservations; 4% had a notion of conservation without correct anticipation; and 29% anticipated correctly, but without reasoning, along lines of conservation.

3. When it came to comparing full and empty spaces, however, judgments of conservation quite clearly preceded correct anticipations. Here, in fact, 38% had neither conservation nor anticipation, 23% had both, 38% showed that they had acquired the notion of conservation but without being able to anticipate correctly, and none anticipated correctly without conservation.

It would thus appear that a correct representative image of the protruding part of the stick was not sufficient to secure the conservation of lengths, the full understanding of which calls for a complete symmetrical system of compensation between empty and full spaces. Nevertheless, it is of interest to note that when the child's attention was drawn to the lengths of the protruding parts, the idea of conservation seemed to be acquired more easily. Children who had done a certain number of exercises in anticipation generally acceded a little sooner to notions of operatory conservation than children who had not. It would seem that the image became adequate only when it was directed by operations that were being structured, but image formation, in turn, facilitated the operatory elaboration. The experiment thus provided a fine example of the distinction and also of the interaction between the formative processes of images and operations.

THE DEVELOPMENT OF IMAGERY

The Origin of Symbolic Imagery

It is certainly difficult to say exactly when the child's first images appear. Piaget's studies on the origins of sensorimotor intelligence and the development of object permanency would invalidate the hypothesis that imagery appears early, as certain psychoanalysts have contended. Piaget's observations of the development of spontaneous symbolic behavior in his own children, which have since been confirmed experimentally by our team, lend color to the hypothesis that imagery is linked to symbolic function, and symbolic imagery arises by genetic filiation from imitative mechanisms.

The earliest observed behavior implying evocative images is linked to deferred imitation. The child evokes physical as well as human models in their absence. His means of evocation are gestures, attitudes, and movements. Imitative movements seem to become interiorized subsequently in the form of incipient schemes that, in our experiments, are seen as movements and drawing gestures that enable the child to symbolize the models figuratively. This filiation from imitation is, moreover, part of the general process of the development of symbols. From the second year onward, we witness a great development of symbolic function that is marked by the progressive differentiation of signifiers and signified. On the one hand are the multiple signification and the elastic extension, which the child attributes to symbols in his imaginative play, verbal (prelogical) concepts, and evocative imagery; this signification and extension result from assimilative processes of nascent thought. On the other hand, however, the accommodating mechanisms of imitation play a striking role in the constitution of the forms and contents of signifiers.

The fact that the developmental pattern of elementary forms of imagery—far from constituting an isolated process—encompasses a series of linked filiations that lead from imitation to symbol formation, strongly supports the modern conception according to which images have the status of symbols.

The Relation between Elementary Forms of Symbolic Imagery and Preoperatory Thought

An essentially static quality was seen to dominate symbolic imagery that corresponds to the level of preoperatory thought. This quality generally determines the difficulties of the child in passing from a reproductive image, itself frequently deformed, to an anticipatory image. The static quality of the image is seen particularly in the child's efforts to conserve certain features of the figure while neglecting others and by his incapacity to symbolize the continuous transformations of shapes and movements. Retaining certain typical features of the figure leads the child toward what one might call pseudoconservations and to a certain reluctance to exceed or cross the frontiers.

A whole set of converging indices point to the importance that the child attaches to certain figure frontiers: the translation of a square in relation to another gives rise to a pseudoconservation of the terminal frontier at the expense of surface conservation. As a complement to the conservation of the outer frontier, the child refuses to draw the inner frontiers of a figure when transparent squares are partially superimposed and thus neglects the intersection of the figures. In the experiments on folding, the child similarly refuses to represent the envelopment of a small circle in a square or the intersection with the frontier of the latter as long as the square is a figure and not a background surface.

The most tenacious frontier effect—reinforced as it is by the notional system of preoperatory thought—is the refusal to anticipate the projection beyond the extreme frontiers of an arc: the straight line derived from the arc is given as its chord. Another example of the interaction between the figurative and notional aspects of preoperatory thought is the systematic way the children have of wrongly judging the total length of open figures by the coincidence of their terminal frontiers. On the one hand, the child centers on the frontiers of the figure and, on the other, estimates the equality or inequality of spatiotemporal displacements by arrival order. The ordinal pseudoconservations, which, in a general way, dominate preoperatory thought, are here linked to figural pseudoconservations. Because of its static quality, the imagery fails to symbolize the different stages of a transformation. The almost insurmountable difficulties of imagining the intermediate stages between the arc and the straight line will be recalled, as will the children's clumsy efforts at symbolizing the successive positions of a somersaulting tube.

The insufficiently coordinated centralizations and irreversibility of preoperatory thought go together with an essentially static imagery. Anticipatory imagery, imitating in fragmentary fashion certain aspects of what is perceived, at first leads to distortion, as does preoperatory thought itself. This conjunction seems to involve a form of interaction; figural schematization is in many ways influenced by conceptualization and vice versa, and preoperatory notions are, as Piaget would say, "molded in the frame of the image." If symbolic imagery in its figurative aspect always retains a certain static quality, since its role is to imitate and not to construct, operation by its very constructiveness rapidly increases in mobility, and, in turn, acts on symbolic imagery.

The Relation between the Higher Forms of Symbolic Imagery and Operatory Thought

With the progress of operatory thought, which conceives of changes in a state as the results of reversible transformations, imagery gradually acquires sufficient mobility to become anticipatory; it will succeed, first, in representing the results of figurative or kinetic transformations and, later, the successive steps of such transformations.

In each of the experimental situations, we noted, in fact, a qualitative and progressive modification of figurative symbolization and a remarkable increase in the number of adequate solutions, the two going together with the development and generalization of concrete operations. The hypothesis of a concurrent development of the operative and figurative aspects of thoughts is easily demonstrated, but it still remains to be seen whether their progress is achieved through mutual or unilateral influences. The data available would bear out the second alternative; they show that the formation of operations directs the progress of figurative symbolism, which serves as a support for operative thought.

By examining not only the figurative results but their elaboration as evidenced by the children's trials and errors and their commentaries, we realized that anticipatory images are not simply derived from a spontaneously arising suppleness of reproductive images; the suppleness is, rather, achieved under the influence of operations. The concordance of the results of each experiment sufficiently illustrates the role played in anticipatory images by ordinal operations, in their twin aspect of change of order and serial order. Finally, operatory reversibility disengages representative imagery from figural pseudoconservations and orients it toward the symbolization of conceptual conservations.

The study of clinical cases brings an interesting confirmation of the results of developmental investigations. Some children who suffer from deficiencies in figurative symbolization may obtain a quasi-normal operatory level; their shortcomings in the field of representative imagery can be assimilated to behavior belonging to a more elementary level; sometimes they even succeed in compensating for certain lacunae of their imagery, although only by costly deductive procedures. While operativity thus directs the progress of symbolic imagery, imagery that has not yet been made supple by the effects of operativity does not seem to be sufficient to prepare operativity. This is shown by the fact that even the children who, thanks to evoking their daily experiences, can correctly anticipate certain changes of state (e.g., the level of the liquid after pouring into a different vessel, or the distance a stick protrudes after displacement) do not understand any better than the others the conservation of quantities and the compensation of dimensions. If the image is not orientated by operativity, it just does not seem to lead to the understanding of transformations, even if they are figural.

The situation, however, becomes quite different once symbolic imagery is moulded by operations. Images symbolizing the successive steps of figural transformations facilitate the representation of the transformation. The act of symbolically translating successive events into simultaneous spatial images does not only fix the information from which the judgment is elaborated but also serves as a continuous support for the elaboration itself. Although it is true that symbolic imagery, because of its imitative quality, never attains the dynamics of operatory construction and does not constitute an element of thought on an equal footing with operativity, it nevertheless fulfills the role of a symbolic tool that is complementary to that of language and, like language, promotes the progress of thought.

In conclusion, we shall consider the relation between operative thought and its symbolic imagery from both the functional and the structural points of view. From the point of view of the functioning of cognitive activity, it would seem that there is, concurrently, a complementary relation and a certain interdependence between the operative and figurative aspects of thought. According to the distinction established by Piaget, operativity consists in transforming, by action or in thought, a piece of reality considered as an object of knowledge. Thanks to a series of reversible operations, the child discovers, for example, the invariability of the quantity, although the matter is transformed. The figurative aspects of thought, on the other hand, are limited to copying, or, more precisely, to imitating in a schematic way the piece of reality. At each moment of development, operativity directs the formation of symbolic imagery by providing it with meanings, and the figurative signifiers, once they have been built up, favor the acquisition and the fixation of information that is food for thought.

By considering the development of operatory structures and symbolic imagery, we are entitled to suppose that their modes of construction do not enjoy an equal degree of independence from outside influences. The successive structures of operative thought, as Piaget has shown, are engendered one from the other according to a constant and integrated order. They may be accelerated or inhibited by many external factors; their mode of construction, however, does not seem to be modified by such factors.

The development of symbolic imagery, we believe, depends to a large extent on external contributions. It is as if, in the initial phases, symbolic imagery bore the imprint of motor-imitation schemes from which it stems; as we have shown, the later development of figurative symbolism is modified through the progress of operativity.

11

The Sensorimotor Origins of Knowledge

BÄRBEL INHELDER

For some years now, we have been witnessing a prodigious growth of research into the beginnings of mental life, and scientific effort has tended to become increasingly centered on furthering our understanding of the developmental mechanisms themselves.

While the developmental psychologists had already progressed beyond the troublesome dichotomy of maturation versus learning, the advent of new theories of language, stemming from the linguistic work of Harris and, above all, Chomsky, have reopened the controversy between empiricism and nativism. Their studies have shown decisively that grammars, i.e., linguistic competence, have features which cannot be explained by recourse to the empiricist and associationist theories. Chomsky's work led him to make two hypotheses on the acquisition of language: first, that the basic linguistic structures are innate, and second, that when the child is in contact with the language spoken around him he makes a choice between the possible grammars (there are important restrictions on these grammars). His followers went further and stressed this rationalist aspect of linguistic theory; they saw in language the most important example of human cognition and from this evolved a neonativist argument going well beyond language itself.

Translated by Mrs. S. Wedgwood (aided by a Ford Foundation grant).

As regards linguistic competence, this led to the hypothesis of a language acquisition device with a strong inner structure—a concept with which we can hardly quarrel. However, we begin to disagree when this structure is considered genetically preprogrammed and when no attempt is made to link the appearance of the first comprehensible utterances to the sensorimotor forms of behavior which precede their appearance.

Considering the question from the Genevan developmental angle, we think it is possible to trace continuous links between the first sensorimotor coordinations and truly cognitive structures, and to hypothesize that language and, in a more general way, the semiotic function of which it is the most obvious expression are not suddenly constructed but prepared by the elementary development of knowledge at the sensorimotor level.

Such a developmental point of view fits in with an explanatory system according to which the hereditary (both genetic and epigenetic) connections and the learning processes are controlled by more fundamental and more general mechanisms (e.g., regulatory and self-regulatory).

In the first part of this chapter, we shall try to trace the development of the fundamental categories of knowledge (space, time, and causality) which, according to Piaget, are developed as early as during the preverbal period and form the basis of the fundamental operations and concepts of thought, culminating in the structures of scientific thought. We are trying to show that these first cognitive elaborations can be explained in biologic terms such as assimilation; the development of intelligence is to be understood as a particular case of biologic adaptation.

Second, we shall describe some current research which we hope will throw light on the passage from sensorimotor activity to the semiotic function such as it appears in the first forms of symbolic play and language.

We shall conclude with a few remarks on the heuristic value of a constructivist genetic concept which, of necessity, leads us to have recourse to self-regulatory models such as those found in modern biology and cybernetics.

THE DEVELOPMENT OF THE UNIVERSE: THE ORIGIN OF THE CATEGORIES OF KNOWLEDGE

Certain remarkable studies of animal psychology, some of which have been transposed to the human level, have long convinced us of the existence of a sensorimotor intelligence which phylogenetically and ontogenetically precedes language. Nowadays, according to the epistemological perspective, the Kantian problem of the origin of knowledge has been placed in a context of developmental psychology. From this point of view, it is very interesting to follow step by step the child's progressive construction of his practical knowledge of the universe, a construction which has been compared to a miniature Copernican revolution.

In fact, knowledge begins in a sort of dualism, as J. M. Baldwin pointed out long ago. It does not stem uniquely from a subject already conscious of himself nor from an object which the subject simply accepts without question. It results from interaction between the subject and the object, and the progress of knowledge depends on the construction of modes of interaction or mediation.

Baldwin also showed us that the neonate manifests no awareness of his own person, nor of a stable boundary beween the internal and external worlds until the construction of the ego becomes possible both in correspondence and in opposition with that of other people, at which time we now know, thanks to Piaget, that the child's primitive world begins to contain the first permanent objects. The first objects to be endowed with permanency are in fact the people closest to the child who, as objects, are particularly interesting.

At the outset, the neonate considers everything in relation to his own body as if he were the center of the world, but he remains totally unaware of this fact. During the first 18 months the revolution consists in decentering his self-centered actions, and culminates in the child's considering his body an object among others in space.

He gradually becomes able to link his actions and discover that he is the source or even master of his movements.

The progress which characterizes the constitution of the universe during the sensorimotor period is due to the progressive coordination of the subject's actions and their relationship with the displacements of objects in the immediate environment. The undifferentiation of the self and the outside world and the centration on his own body stem from the noncoordination of the actions: each action at the origin constitutes a small but isolatable whole and these actions directly link the body to the external objects (sucking, grasping) whence the undifferentiation between the subject and the objects. Later on, the coordination of his actions will dissolve this direct link and objects can acquire permanency; the subject then becomes capable of coordinating their movements into a coherent system.

Piaget's longitudinal observations on his three children, since confirmed by some excellent studies of large groups of children carried out by Gouin-Décarie, Escalona, Hunt, and Lézine, enable us to reconstitute the stages of this construction of the universe. We shall limit ourselves to describing the interdependency of the various aspects of this development.

During the period from about 6 to 8 months, in which the.

maturation of the central nervous system is sufficiently advanced to allow the indispensable coordinations of vision, prehension, hearing, and smell, we witness the constitution of the first systems of spatiotemporal and causal relationships. These reveal a certain understanding of the universe, which, as it results from the subject's actions, is still subjective.

The beginning of object permanency is clearly linked to the child's activity (Piaget, 1954b):

> Jacqueline at 0;8 takes possession of my watch which I offer her while holding the chain in my hand. She examines the watch with great interest, feels it, turns it over, says "apff," etc. I pull the chain; she feels a resistance and holds it back with force, but ends by letting it go. As she is lying down she does not try to look but holds out her arm, catches the watch again and brings it before her eyes. By contrast, if, in front of her I hide the watch without her having an opportunity to handle it, Jacqueline does not react and seems to forget it immediately.

> Laurent at 7 months loses a cigarette box which he has just seized and thrown away. He touches it involuntarily outside his field of vision. He then immediately brings back his hand to where he can see it and looks at it for a long time, with an expression of suprise and disappointment—something like a feeling of loss. But far from considering this loss irreparable, he starts to swing his hand, even though empty, after which he looks at it again . . . as if he hopes that the object has been brought back.

At this level, the child is capable of following the movement of objects and even of anticipating rapid trajectories, but everything happens as if for him objects were not provided with autonomous movements.

> Laurent at 7 months is sitting in his cot opposite my office door. I open the door, appear and make him laugh, then I move slowly to the back of the room; Laurent follows me with his eyes, but even before seeing me disappear from his field of vision he turns back toward the door, and does this several times in succession.

When the moving object really disappears, the child does not credit it with the power to continue its course.

It is just the same for the reconstitution of temporal sequences. The child already clearly perceives the "before and after" of events: for example, the mother's footsteps and her movements when she prepares herself for nursing are immediately interpreted as an indication of forthcoming satisfaction, but the child cannot, as yet, reconstitute the history of phenomena outside his own activity.

> Laurent at 8 months sees his mother come into the room and follows her with his eyes until she is seated behind him: he returns to

his play activities, but turns round several times to see her again, despite the fact that no sound evokes her presence. However, when his mother gets up and leaves the room, Laurent follows her with his eyes until she reaches the door, then, immediately after her disappearance, again looks for her behind him in the place where she was before.

The spatiotemporal organization centered on the activity of the subject himself naturally leads to a causality concept of the magico-phenomenist type, according to which action can be efficient from a distance without spatiotemporal contact.

Jacqueline at 8 months is in her cot when the canopy is shaken without the child being able to see the cause of the movement. At first she seems a little afraid, but then shows her joy by sitting up and then falling back into her cot. When the phenomenon is repeated she follows it with acute interest. When the movement of the canopy stops she sits up again, staring at the canopy as if waiting for it to move.

Similar manifestations are observed when her father meows, or puts out his tongue, which amuses her greatly.

To make interesting spectacles recur, she uses a number of ways and means, such as sitting up and shaking her hand; it is as if she believed in the efficiency of her gestures and movements.

Toward the end of the sensorimotor period, i.e., around the middle of the second year, the different action systems, instead of constituting little self-contained systems, become coordinated, and a connection between methods and goals which characterizes intelligent behavior is attained. The child thus discovers the possibility of using instruments to reach objects that are too far away. He becomes aware of himself as the source of actions and knowledge, since the coordination of the various actions supposes an initiative which goes beyond the immediate fusion between his own body and the external world. To coordinate actions to attain a specific goal or result supposes the progressive understanding of how to move objects and of how they can move autonomously. The child now behaves as if these movements comport systems, which are in a certain sense, as Piaget has shown, isomorphic with Poincaré's grouplike geometric transpositions. The child becomes capable of assigning a number of successive, determined positions to objects. The latter acquire a certain spatiotemporal permanency, which in turn "de-subjectifies" the causal relationships. In a way, this differentiation between subject and object on the level of activity results in the objects' acquiring a status of their own. This decentration places the child's own body, as an object among others, in a universe with a certain temporal and causal consistency.

In fact, Piaget's observation of his three children's behavior, at a slightly later age, reveals a practical understanding of the permanency of objects whatever their movements. The children manage to reconstitute the trajectories even when the objects themselves become and remain invisible, as shown by Jacqueline's search for an object:

> At 1;7, Jacqueline is seated in front of three objects A, B and C, underneath which something can be hidden; these objects, in this case a beret, a handkerchief and her jacket, are equidistant from each other. I hide a small pencil in my hand saying: "Cuckoo the pencil," I show her my closed hand which I put under A; I then show it to her again before putting it under B; I then show it to her a third time before putting it under C where I leave the pencil and afterwards show her my open hand, repeating "cuckoo the pencil." Jacqueline immediately looks for the pencil under C. She finds it and laughs. When I change the object, its hiding places and their order, e.g., CAB, etc., Jacqueline succeeds nine times in finding the object.

It is clear that the child does not only remember the last position; proof of this is given by the fact that he sometimes tends to go back to the place where he saw the object disappear for the first time and that he temporarily relapses into less developed behaviors when the task becomes complicated.

Another example will convince us that the child is now capable not only of reconstituting the movements but also of anticipating them.

> Jacqueline at 1;8 arrives at a closed door with a blade of grass in each hand. She stretches out her right hand towards the knob, but sees that she cannot turn it without letting go of the grass. She puts the grass on the floor, opens the door, picks up the grass again and enters. But when she wants to leave the room, things become complicated: She puts the grass on the floor and grasps the doorknob. But then she perceives that in pulling the door toward her, she will simultaneously push away the blade of grass which she placed on the floor. She therefore picks it up in order to put it outside the door's zone of movement.

As regards the reconstitution of small temporal series, we have several examples where the child reproduces a series of events and starts to evoke them by a beginning of symbolic representation.

> At 1;7, Jacqueline picks up a blade of grass which she puts in a bucket as if it were one of the grasshoppers which a small cousin had brought her a few days before. She then says "Totelle, totelle, hop-la, boy" ("totelle" meaning "sauterelle," the French word for "grasshopper"). The perception of an object which reminded her symbolically of a grasshopper enables her to evoke past events and to reconstitute their order.

Finally as regards causality, this period is rich in important discoveries.

> Laurent, at 1;4, tries to open a solid garden gate but does not
> manage to do so because the gate is held back by a piece of furniture.
> He cannot see why the gate will not open nor does any sound give him
> a clue, but having tried to force it, he suddenly seems to understand: he
> goes round the wall to the other side of the gate, moves the chair
> that was in the way and opens the gate with an exclamation of
> triumph.

We thus see that the coordination of the subject's actions is inseparable from the spatiotemporal and causal coordinations he attributes to reality; these two sorts of coordination together form the source of differentiation between the pole of the subject and that of the object. This decentration tending towards bipolarity paves the way, on the level of the action, for rational thought, and forms the basis of the knowledge categories of space, time, and causality.

How do we explain, in psychological terms, this progressive construction which we witness during the first two years of life?

Those who support learning theories based on behaviorist methodology tend to invoke connections of the associationist type, while Piaget explains these same phenomena biologically in terms of assimilation. In fact, the concept of association refers essentially to the external links between elements associated in time and/or space, while the concept of assimilation implies the integration of new data in an already existing structure or even in the construction of a new structure in the forms of schemes.

As regards the very elementary and uncoordinated actions, two interpretations are possible. In the first, the structure is already in existence, being hereditary: for example, the sucking reflexes. In this case, the assimilation consists only in the incorporation of new objects in the structure which belongs to the organic programming. In the second, the activity is not preprogrammed: for example, the baby tries in vain to grasp a suspended object, then he succeeds in just touching it and it swings, which he finds a most interesting and unexpected spectacle. When the spectacle stops, he tries to reproduce it by what Piaget calls a reproductive assimilation (to repeat the same gesture) which results in the formation of a scheme. In the presence of another suspended object he will assimilate it to this same scheme; this implies an assimilation by recognition and, when he repeats the action in this new situation, a generalizing assimilation.

The coordination of actions by reciprocal assimilation represents both a novelty in relation to what preceded it and an extension of the same mechanism.

In the progress towards the elaboration of new behaviors we can thus distinguish two successive stages. A first stage is above all an extension of what is already known: it consists in assimilating simultaneously one object to two schemes, which is a beginning of reciprocal assimilation. If, for example, a swinging object also makes a sound, it can become in turn (or simultaneously) something to look at or listen to; a reciprocal assimilation can then lead, for example, to shaking any toy to find out what noise it makes. At first, goal and means remain relatively undifferentiated, but at a more advanced stage, the baby assigns a goal to his act before carrying it out: he uses various assimilatory schemes in order to produce sounds; for example, he pulls the canopy cord.

Such assimilatory processes will progressively result in the construction of new combinations. These discoveries stem at the same time from knowledge of the objects themselves (a suspended object is something which can start swinging) and knowledge resulting from action schemes which the subject uses on them (coordinating the means and goals while respecting the order of succession of the movements to be carried out).

We thus witness as early as the sensorimotor level that the growing differentiation of the subject and the object is marked by the formation of action coordinations, but among the latter we can, from the beginning of mental life, distinguish two types; on the one hand, those which link the subject's actions, one to the other, and on the other hand, those which concern the effect of actions on the objects and vice versa.

The first, thus, consists in combining or separating certain action schemes, in embedding them one in another, or ordering or putting them in correspondence, etc. They constitute the first forms of these general coordinations which are at the root of the logicoarithmetic structures whose further development at the level of thought will be considerable. The second confer a spatiotemporal, kinematic organization to the objects and this organization is the point of departure of the causal sequences.

Even before the appearance of language, therefore, we see that the coordinations of the sensorimotor actions result in the structuring of knowledge with its bipolar (logicomathematic and physical) nature. The subject and the objects thus start to become differentiated when the modes of interaction between subject and object become more refined. But at this level the modes of interaction are still only concrete actions. carried out by the child, and it is only thanks to the semiotic function that these actions progressively become thought operations.

FROM SENSORIMOTOR ACTIVITIES TO THE SEMIOTIC FUNCTION

We still do not know enough about the links between sensorimotor and symbolic (or semiotic) behavior. Symbolic behavior is sometimes considered to have different origins from sensorimotor behavior—the two slowly converging; other psychologists consider that a continual process of interiorization takes place. While we favor this second working hypothesis, it is a rather weak one since it tells us no more than that processes similar to sensorimotor development take place without any external manifestations.

The common sense answer maintained that it was through the use of language as a system of socialized signifiers that the cognitive functions become free from the sensorimotor context and accede to the level of representation. However, since Pierce introduced to psychology the concept of the symbolic function and Head showed its importance in neuropathologic studies, we can no longer consider language an isolated phenomenon, but rather a particularly important aspect of a more general function. Piaget's work, although not specifically concerning the beginning of language, has revealed the existence of a developmental interdependence between the various forms of the semiotic function, i.e., deferred imitation leading to imagined representation, symbolic play, and the first verbal schemes. In addition, he was the first to give a psychologic interpretation of holophrases. All semiotic behaviors have in common the differentiation between the signifiers and the signs. While at the sensorimotor level signals cannot be separated from the actual objects or events, at the level of the semiotic function the signifiers are distinct from the context and the differentiation is introduced by the subject himself. A child who makes a shell slide along a box, saying "meow" knows very well that his shell is not a cat, but symbolizes one and that the box is not a wall, but represents one. Even if at first he regards the word "cat" as an intrinsic part of the animal, the word as such is for him a symbolizer (or signifier) and not the object itself. It is not surprising that the different aspects of the semiotic function first appear almost simultaneously in the same child.

Deferred Imitation

> Jacqueline 1;4 has a visit from a little boy of 1;6, whom she sees from time to time, and who in the course of the afternoon gets into a terrible temper. He screams as he tries to get out of his play-pen and pushes it backwards, stamping his feet. Jacqueline stands watching him in amazement, never having witnessed such a scene before. The

next day, she herself screams in her play-pen and tries to move it, stamping her foot several time in succession.

The imitation of the whole scene is striking. Had it been immediate, it would naturally not have involved representation, but coming as it did after an interval of more than twelve hours, it must have involved some representative and pre-representative element.

Motor Symbolizer

At 1;4, Lucienne tries to grasp a watch chain which she has seen being put into a match box which she does not know how to open. The opening is reduced to 3mm. As a result of her previous experiences she possesses only two schemes: turning the box over in order to empty it of its contents and sliding her finger into the slit to make the chain come out. She immediately tries these two processes which fail. A pause follows during which Lucienne manifests a very curious reaction, bearing witness not only to the fact that she tries to think out the situation and to represent to herself through mental combination the operations to be performed, but also to the role played by imitation in the development or representations: she mimics the widening of the slit. She looks very carefully at it, then several times in succession, she opens and shuts her mouth, at first slightly, then wider and wider. She wants to enlarge the slit. The attempt at representation which she thus furnishes is expressed plastically, that is to say, due to inability to think out the situation in words or clear visual images she uses a simple motor representation as signifier or symbol.

Immediately after this phase of plastic reflection, Lucienne unhesitatingly puts her finger in the slit, pulls so as to enlarge the opening and grasps the chain.

Play

At 1;3, Jacqueline sees a cloth whose fringed edges vaguely recall those of her pillow; she seizes it, holds a fold of it in her right hand, sucks the thumb of the same hand and lies down on her side, roaring with laughter. She keeps her eyes open, but blinks from time to time as if alluding to closed eyes. Finally, laughing more and more, she cries out "Nono" ("Nono" meaning sleep). The same cloth starts off the same play behavior on the following days. Later it is the tail of her donkey which evokes the fringes of the pillow and from the age of 1;5 onwards she makes her animals, a bear and a dog, also do "nono."

Language

At 1;5, Laurent says "aplu" ("n'a plus" meaning literally "no more" or "all gone") signifying first of all a departure, then the act of throwing an object onto the ground; he then applies it to an object which is knocked over but does not disappear. He thus says "aplu" to his blocks when he knocks them over. Later "aplu" simply indicates that something is moved away (outside his grasp), then the game of giving someone an object to throw back to him. At 1;6, he even says "aplu" when another person has an object in his hand which he wants. Finally at 1;7 "aplu" becomes the synonym of recommencing any interesting play or action.

The development of signifiers has been described by Piaget in functional terms. The development of the intelligence at each of its principal stages culminates in states of equilibrium between the two opposing and complementary tendencies of assimilation and accommodation. In the formation of the signifiers, sometimes one and then the other predominates. The accommodating aspects are clearly predominant in imitation and images, while those of assimilation play the major role in symbolic play. In language, the two tendencies are present in proportions varying with the stage reached in its development.

However, one problem remains completely open: How, in general, does the child acquire the capacity of substituting signifiers for objects or events? This is important since it is these substitutions which render possible the first symbolizations, which in turn are one of the conditions of the acquisition of language.

One of the best ways of studying the origins of symbolization would appear to be the systematic observation of a large group of children between 1 and 2 years old, some of them being followed longitudinally. Our Paris colleagues, Irène Lézine and Mira Stambak, specialists in the study of very young children, have been good enough to associate my psycholinguist colleague, Hermina Sinclair, and myself in such a study. A group of 66 children between 12 and 36 months is currently being observed in nurseries, with a longitudinal examination (regularly once or twice a month) being carried out on some of them.

The technique referred to in this chapter consists of an observation effected from behind a one-way screen and the material used is made up of objects and toys with which the child is familiar, such as a sponge, spoon, plate, mug, pot, broom, feather duster, miniature baby's bottle, cloth, paper, books, mirror, doll, baby, and teddy bear. The child is put in front of these objects on the floor and one of the experimenters draws his attention to each of them and encourages him to touch them and play with them.

During the period between 12 and 26 months, we witness a development in behavior in which we can distinguish three levels of growing complexity.

In our first, inevitably superficial, analysis of this corpus of minute observations, we chose three different aspects of behavior, which allow us to distinguish different types of activity at each level of complexity.

The first type of activity is oriented toward knowledge of the object—the child is discovering the properties of the objects he is handling.

In the second type of activity the child himself introduces an organization into reality, rather than discovering something about a particular object.

The third type includes all the "make-believe" activities. It is, however, only at the most advanced level that one can clearly distinguish these types; at the lower levels, they are still too closely intertwined. For this reason, we shall begin with a description of the most striking characteristics of the most advanced level.

At this level, we witness the appearance of a host of new activities which can be classified according to the three different types we have distinguished.

Activities of the first type. We observe that the children are beginning to handle the objects in the accepted, usual way, both as regards the choice of the object-agent and that of the object-patient.

For example, Peter, at 26 months, sweeps the floor with the broom, brushes his hair with the hairbrush, and dusts the book with a cloth.

Activities of the second type. The children begin to put objects together in groups which can be interpreted as based on a first "category" criterion.

At the same session, Peter carefully puts the broom and the feather duster beside one another.

Activities of the third type. Several subcategories may be distinguished in this group of symbolic patterns.

(*a*) The doll and the teddy bear are treated as partners in a game. Peter holds the mirror up to the doll's face, inclining it so that she can look at herself.

(*b*) The activity includes symbolic evocation of a missing object. Peter pours some water from the bottle (in reality empty) down his neck which he wipes with his other hand.

(*c*) The activity includes the symbolic substitution of one object by another. Having put the doll in the nursing position, Peter puts the broomhandle in its mouth as if he were giving it the bottle.

One of the general characteristics of this level is the organization by the child of long sequences of actions which are linked, although sometimes very loosely, by a common situation.

The same Peter takes the brush and, using his right hand, slowly brushes his fringe, then he starts brushing the doll's hair. Then he holds the mirror up to the doll's face so that she can look at herself, then again brushes first the doll's and then finally his own hair.

To discover which behaviors precede and pave the way for these more developed ones, we must examine the intermediary level, which in our population is found at between 15 and 19 months of age. The following are some of the activities (still classified according to the same three types) which were witnessed.

> 1. The children carry out a group of activities (this time with less obvious connections between them) in which one of the objects, the agent, already plays its normal role while the patient-object is still more or less devoid of specific significance: Peter, now aged 19 months, dusts the baby's face with the feather duster. He puts the spoon on the plate and then presses it into the sponge. He brushes the baby's bottle with the hairbrush. Thus the action is performed with its usual instruments, but applied to an unusual object.

> 2. The children put various objects together, but at this level it is more difficult to distinguish a "category" criterion; these groupings have spatial, "category," and functional characteristics which cannot be isolated: Peter puts the spoon in the mug and, using his left hand, presses it well in, takes the mirror with his right hand, knocks the spoon into the plate, puts the mirror into the mug then takes it out, puts the spoon back into the mug, then puts the spoon on the plate, puts the mirror into the mug, puts the spoon back into the mug, and finally puts the spoon back onto the plate.

Sometimes the spatiotemporal and causal aspects of the behaviors are more accentuated:

> Peter takes the spoon with his right hand and puts it on the floor, stands it up vertically, swivels it round flat on the floor, stands it up again with his right hand, makes it turn around in this position, puts it on his right leg, then under his leg and then taps the floor with it.

Activities of the third type. At this level we can distinguish the following subcategories:

(*a*) Symbolic activities using the child's own body:

> Peter, again at the age of 19 months, rocks himself and pretends to sleep holding his head with his hand, his eyes closed. He stays like this for 2 minutes, getting more and more in a hunched-up position. As soon as the observer approaches, he opens his eyes and starts laughing.
> At another time, he pretends to eat without food, using the spoon and the plate.

(*b*) Play activities making use of the doll or the teddy bear, but without these being treated as active partners:

> Peter hugs the bear and gently rubs the doll as if he were caressing it.

At this developmental level, the sequences are shorter and less well integrated into a coherent framework of organized activities.

At the most elementary level examined in this research, which, in our population is situated between 12 and 15 months of age, the activities are even more disjointed. It seems to be the objects themselves which trigger the motor schemes and almost any motor scheme can be applied to almost any object.

Activities of the first type. We observe an "instrumental" activity which prepares the way for the discovery of the properties of the object: Peter, at 12 and 13 months, carries out a number of activities using two objects, such as hitting the mug with the broomhandle and pushing the pot with the feather duster.

The activities using only one object are: shaking the mug, shaking the feather duster (without our being able to recognize a precise imitative activity), throwing, rubbing, pulling, and pushing one of the objects at hand.

Activities of the second type. The child puts one object on top of another (for example, the bottle on a plate, the mug on the mirror), into another (for example, the mirror into the pot), and beside another (for example, the spoon beside the broom).

Activities of the third type. No such activities can be observed at this first level. It is at this age that we see the most activities using the child's own body, but without being able to recognize a symbolic scheme in the true sense of the term: For example, Peter puts the bottle on his leg, bites the broom, scratches himself, pulls his hair, and explores the objects by putting them into his mouth; at this age, this last way of learning about things is still important.

In what way does this rather rapid examination of behaviors throw new light on the constitution of the symbolic function? Once the sensorimotor cognitive adaptation is complete, what necessary conditions have to be fulfilled before the symbolic function can develop?

As regards the "object-knowledge" pole, it seems that the object may be evoked in its absence or replaced by a signifier only after the child has endowed it with properties giving it significance.

As regards the subject's structuring activity, the detachment of the schemes from the material context can take place only after his activities have been organized into sequences within a coherent framework.

There is always, of course, close interaction between these two poles of activity, since the subject's structuring activity furthers object knowledge and since the differentiation of the former is a function of the characteristics of the objects and especially of their kinematic properties.

Our point of view, as regards the first verbal productions, is inspired by the Piagetian concept that the first utterances are the translation of schemes whose subject- and object-poles are indissociable. Piaget calls these schemes "action judgments." Using the terminology of George Miller and Gruber (who consider the distinction between theme and commentary and the possibility of a theme becoming a commentary and vice versa to be one of the fundamental characteristics of language) it seems to us that the first holophrases represent a fusion between theme and commentary. By contrast, the slightly more sophisticated utterances, which Piaget calls "observation judgments," already reveal a distinction between theme and commentary (which does not imply that the two are necessarily present). At this same period, the child begins to refer to familiar objects in more or less stable and conventional terms.

It is possibly this aspect of knowledge, which we have called "discovery of object-properties," that will result in the acquisition of an organized lexicon; syntax, on the other hand, has its roots in the type of knowledge gathered from the subject's own organized activity. Evidently, there is an interdependence between these two aspects and each is constituted as a function of the other.

The first results of this type of research seem to give some weight to the hypothesis of a developmental construction on an interactionist model. We should like to emphasize the fact that when the development of sensorimotor activities is seen in the light of regulatory, rather than associative, mechanisms, it is easier to show its continuity with subsequent symbolic activities. The two aspects of action, one tending towards the object-pole and the other towards the subject-pole, cannot be interpreted without reference to the hypothesis of regulatory mechanisms. The latter cannot be rendered explicit through naturalistic observation and experimental studies have yet to be carried out.

FINAL REMARKS

Developmental Model

A developmental theory which is neither empiricist nor neonativist (but, in a sense, intermediary between those two positions) in the interpretation of the progressive construction of the cognitive functions sooner or later leads to the invocation of feedback-organizing mechanisms. It is only these which provide a possible explanation for subject-object interaction and the progress resulting from this interaction.

Piaget's fundamentally biologic conceptions have led him from the start towards a model with regulatory and even self-regulatory characteristics: the young cybernetician Cellerier was moved to say that Piaget became a cybernetician even before the science was invented. The heuristic value of Piaget's hypothesis received confirmation when he compared psychodevelopmental factors with those of Waddington's embryogenetics (Piaget, 1967a) and, in a more general way, with those of some of the contemporary biologists, e.g., Dobzhansky and Wallace.

In fact, according to Piaget, the regulatory systems are found on all levels of the organism's functioning, right from the genome up to psychologic behaviors; thus they appear to be among the most general characteristics of the organism. Self-regulations seem to constitute at the same time one of the most universal characteristics of life and the most general mechanism to be found in both organic and cognitive behaviors. This is so regardless of whether we are concerned with what (at the level of the genome) Dobzhansky's school calls genetic homeostasis, with the dynamic equilibrations of the embryogenesis named homeorhesis by Waddington, with the multiple regulations of the nervous system including the reflex feedbacks or, finally, with the regulations and equilibrations observable at all levels of cognitive behavior.

Each self-regulatory system supposes the existence of several types of feedback, which are caused by interaction of subject and environment and by the changes in the environment itself.

In cybernetics one can consider that a self-regulatory system can be self-constructing. A system is modified through the influence of a feedback constituted by the results of its own action by which it treats the input coming from outside.

We hope we have shown in this discussion some of the reasons why we feel that the development of the cognitive functions during the first phases of development and, in particular, the continuity between sensorimotor and semiotic activities can best be explained through self-regulatory mechanisms.

12

The Development of Systems of Representation and Treatment in the Child

PIERRE MOUNOUD

AN INTRODUCTION TO DEVELOPMENTAL PSYCHOLOGY OR THE STUDY OF THE DEVELOPMENT OF BEHAVIOR IN THE CHILD

To appreciate the originality of developmental psychology and the specificity of its problem, it is of course essential that we refer to Piaget and in particular to his early training and interest as a biologist. More precisely, we must examine the problem and the theories of evolution which were reevaluated at the beginning of the century in the light of new discoveries in heredity. Since that time, interest in these problems has readily increased, as a result of contemporary concepts in population genetics and new contributions in cellular biology.*

Throughout his theory of genetic epistemology, combining both the method of developmental psychology with the historical-critical method, Piaget has attempted to elucidate the problem of evolution. The most recent and complete formulation of these ideas can be found in his book *Biologie et Connaissance* (Piaget, 1967a; Engl. trans. 1971a).

* The problem of communication as considered in linguistics or cybernetics is equally of interest in this case.

The Concepts of Evolution and Development

The problem of evolution is to determine the basis for variation whether at the level of the individual (ontogenetic) or at the level of the species (phylogenetic). It is necessary to define the roles of the organism and of the environment (i.e., the roles of the subject and the object respectively) when we consider such phenomena as selection and adaptation. Are the observed variations due to changes or resistances of the environment? Are they produced by internal variations? Could there be more subtle interactions between the organism and the environment?

The originality of Piaget has been first of all, his rediscovery of the continuity across the different adaptive variations found in living organisms, and secondly, in his considering our thought as the "organ" or instrument most specialized for adaptation to the external world. He has considered human intellectual operations as a perfect system of regulations, as Ashby uses the term, that enable total compensations to external changes in relation to a set of problem situations. Consequently, a system in evolution attains only relative equilibrium, and is always confronted with new changes or new problems. These new problems can result, either from new possibilities of the organism (e.g., because of maturation, which gives access to new situations, opens up new possibilities) or to changes in the external world. Thus the organism (or the species) is faced with changes for which it cannot entirely compensate (integrate) by means of the instruments it has available (even if they are perfect for another set of problems), and therefore must by necessity create new instruments.

Some examples of regulatory systems are: changes of climate or vegetation which posed survival problems to certain species which consequently had to modify their means of protection (e.g., skin) or their nutrition. For the baby, passing from a supine to a sitting position, and then to a vertical position, necessitates a series of organizations of movements of parts of the body in relation to other parts; in other words, the reorganization of the postural schema. The loss of an object as we shall see later, poses another series of problems for the baby. In a different domain, geographic changes, agriculture, and animal domestication have continuously raised problems for mankind which have resulted in the invention of innumerable instruments. On another level, the fall of an apple raised issues that led man to elaborate new theories in order to solve them. These theories, considered here as instruments, allow the assimilation of the problem situation (or the phenomenon).

As these examples have shown, there is no single solution or definitive comprehension of a given phenomenon, and consequently every theory or every instrument is relative to the issue raised or to the disturbance experienced. It is easy to see how the possibility of setting up a problem or of recording new variations depends strongly on past theories or instruments. We have shown (Mounoud, 1970) how the simple act of reaching for an object either can constitute a problem or not, depending on the level of development of the subject, and especially how one can transform the situation, introducing new limitations, so that it becomes a problem situation on other levels.

These analogies among phenomena which are obviously so different were not made for the purpose of pure speculation. On the contrary, they permit us to study behavior (actions and mental operations) in a new light. From such a point of view, we can define an action as a real or virtual transformation introduced into the environment, for the attainment of a goal, or for the satisfaction of a need. In a general sense, we can speak of the prehension of an object (assimilation) for the purpose of incorporating or understanding it (knowledge being a kind of incorporation or appropriation). But as we have already said, in a number of cases, the object or the environment does not allow itself to be incorporated, especially not completely incorporated. Such an incorporation would necessitate a reorganization of the existing behavior or the emergence of a new behavior. This reorganization would then allow the subject to make the correct transformation (which need only be a simple movement or a mental conjunction between different parts of the object).

An important remark is necessary here in order to clarify certain frequently noted confusions. Developmental psychology, unlike experimental psychology, does not specifically study the synchronistic aspect of behavior, it does not concern itself with the regulations made by structures already formed or with the conditions and limitations of the functioning of such structures. Developmental psychology is fundamentally concerned with the diachronic aspect of behavior, i.e., it is concerned with the regulations which appear when the ongoing operations of a given organization fail and the subject has to create new instruments or, when possible, a new organization. In order to solve this fundamental problem, it is first of all necessary to characterize the levels of organization that differ qualitatively. This essential task has been the preoccupation of developmental psychology until quite recently.

Keeping these remarks in mind, it is now possible to examine two complementary approaches to research in the field of developmental psychology.

Levels of Organization and Organizing Processes (or Regulation Processes)

There are at least two complementary methods to study the behavior of the subject throughout his development, according to whether one seeks to characterize different successive levels of organization or the processes by which the subject passes from one level of organization to another. Since the characterization of levels precedes the study of organizing processes, the initial research carried out in developmental psychology has been, for the most part, of the first kind. This type of study has defined the successive levels of organization in terms of the different aspects or categories of reality (space, time, etc.). Situations were devised in which different series of transformations were introduced (e.g., two trains made to vary their speed and points of departure; two wooden rods; two plasticine balls; two sets of counters or two model landscapes etc.; where one object of each pair underwent transformations). The clinical method is used to record the successive responses of the child, in order to show his possibilities for operating (or acting) on these sets of transformation situations.* In other cases the experimenter gives the subject a set of disarranged objects (or a set which is partially arranged) and then asks questions about certain relationships among the given objects, or asks the child to act upon the objects or elements of the object in order to arrange them in terms of the inherent relationships. The common characteristic in all of these situations is that the subject is not allowed to estimate the correctness of the organization or the operations by which he has integrated the objects. This important characteristic allows the estimation of the possible limits of the instruments then available to the child, and especially does not entail a questioning or a attitude of doubt. In consequence, this type of research is not useful for the study of the passage from one level to another, that is, the study of the filiation of structures. These kinds of situations lead us to think that the child always responds correctly to the questions he asks himself. This is confusing—for then one cannot understand why the child continually modifies his responses and their underlying organization in the course of his development. No one would purport that an organism evolves solely in terms of the influence of the environment (social or physical). It would therefore be preferable to say that the child (or adult for that matter, or any organism) asks only those questions for which he has a partial answer.

There is another category of situations, complementary to the preceding one, where one gives the subject a task with a given goal (as is found in all organisms in their natural behavior). This kind of situation has been seldom used in developmental psychology with the exception of Piaget's work on the sensorimotor period (Piaget, 1936, 1937). Our research on the construction and utilization of tools or instruments (Mounoud, 1968, 1970) belongs to this category of situations and requires some clarification.

---

* In order to understand, in particular, the invariants which exist at different levels of organization.

Recently, research in this area has been undertaken at the Center of Epistemology in Geneva. In the case where the subject does not attain the given goal, the situation causes him to question his response, i.e., the arrangement which he has made or the strategies which he has used. This is what we have previously referred to as a questioning or attitude of doubt. The regulations or corrections made by the child permit us to explain the development of a new organization or the development of the organizing processes themselves.

All the contributions of biology and psychology show that no organization or new structuring can be accomplished without being founded upon previous organization. We have sought in our previous work

1. to define the initial organization upon which the new organization is formed;
2. to determine the relationship between this initial organization and the organization being formed;
3. to show the respective roles of these organizations as regulating systems and their progressive combination.

We are presently in the process of attempting to do the same for the sensorimotor period. Our current considerations will help to clarify these points by separating the study of systems of treatment from that of systems of representation.

THE SENSORIMOTOR ORGANIZATION OF BEHAVIOR

The main objective of developmental psychology has been to make evident the internal structures of the subject, that is to say, the different *systems of treatment* (or systems of calculation) defining the successive stages of development. These systems of treatment are therefore the determinants of behavior; they characterize what can be called the levels of resolution of various "sets of problems." The sets of problems result from the confrontation of the subject with natural phenomena. This is what we will see in the first section. These systems of treatment [by which all organisms (individual or social) can be characterized], just like computers, cannot act directly on external objects. It is necessary that they incorporate what is called a language, a code, an index, or a system of signifiers. It is especially necessary that the organism make a translation of the objects into a given code, or from a first code to a second one (coding functions). We will consider problems of this type in a second section, that we have called "Systems of Representation."

We could say that for every system of treatment there corresponds at least one defined system of representation. From a synchronistic point of view one can avoid these distinctions, and speak, without too much risk, of stimuli and responses. On the other hand, from a diachronic point of view, it is preferable to dissociate these two aspects and to treat separately the elaboration of systems of treatment and systems of representation.

Even when there is a concrete assimilation-incorporation of objects as in nutrition, for example, this assimilation is really the transformation of a part of the constituents into one's own substances and the rejection of the part which is not able to be assimilated by the system of treatment (gastric juices). The substances which will become the food after the assimilation-transformation can be considered as internal representations. It is in this sense that the mathematician Thom has been able to define the bones of the arm, for example, as simulators of a metric group.

We shall begin the discussion of these systems at the first period of development of the child, called the sensorimotor period (the first 18 months). This is the best level to study these problems and it is essentially from the study of this period that Piaget (1936, 1937) has defined his psychology.

Systems of Treatment

LEVELS OF PROBLEM SOLVING

We will first consider the behavior developed by the infant in his search for an object which he has lost. The behavior, which can be observed vary greatly with age and constitute what we call *levels of resolution*. At about 4 to 5 months of age the object is searched for through the prolongation of whatever activity the infant is engaged in at the time. We can speak of a behavior (or an action-transformation) which does not allow the solving of the lost-object problem, except for one particular category of disappearance. At about 8 to 10 months, the infant looks for the object in particular places, using actions by which he has previously succeeded (as for example, in the experimenter's hand). At this level of resolution, the infant is less concerned by the movements of the object than by his own actions (movements of his arms). This is a new strategy or action-transformation that only permits the solution of a subclass of the set of possible disappearances of the object. It is not until about 18 months that the child acquires what Piaget has called "object permanency," that is to say, the capacity to credit the object with an existence after its disappearance, and to organize the set of successive movements given the object in order to find it. In other words, the child knows how to act so as to cancel out the transformation movements which the object has undergone, or yet again, he knows how to control and correct the external changes (for this defined set of problem situations).

We shall discuss two behavior patterns, typical of this sensori-motor period, one which appears at about 4 months and is called "behavior with the cord" and the other appearing at about 12 months and called "behavior with the blanket."

Behavior with the Cord (about 4 months)

The baby is in his crib. A number of toys are attached to his canopy and also a cord that the baby can take hold of. When the baby pulls the cord, the first time by chance (that is, in relation to an initial goal), he makes the toys move and rattle, causing an interesting sight and noise. The baby repeats the action and causes the satisfying effect (which defines the new goal). Piaget observed that the new means is then generalized in the sense that it tends to be utilized to make any interesting spectacle reappear, without taking into account the relationships among the objects.

Behavior with the Blanket

Some months later, when about 12 months old, the baby is capable of using an intermediary tool to retrieve an object which is out of reach, such as the cover on which the object lies or a string attached to the object. In this behavior the subject realizes certain connections among the objects.

These two behaviors are generally described separately in order to characterize two distinct levels of organization. But we think it is highly probable that by excessive generalizations of the first level (which have sometimes been described as errors or meaningless behaviors) the baby comes progressively to discover the connections and real relationships between the objects, or between his action and the external world. It is evident that these generalizations are instantly sanctioned by external facts and that the desired effect has little chance to reappear if it has no connection with the baby's action. This is an important source of feedback which facilitates the corrections necessary for the formation of a new organization.

THE PROCESSES OF RECONSTRUCTION AND RECOORDINATION*

At birth, the neonate has a certain number of hereditary assemblages called reflexes; for example, the sucking reflex, the grasping reflex, etc. These reflexes define and contain the organization of the first behaviors. From a neurologic point of view, there are circuits and nervous centers already formed and capable of functioning. One can say that these assemblages connect certain groups of effectors with certain groups of

* Piaget uses the term "vertical decalages" or "reflexive abstraction" (cf. Piaget, 1967a).

receptors. These assemblages or reflexes therefore define the structure of actions and it is in this sense that they correspond to what Piaget calls sensorimotor schemes.

From a psychologic point of view, these reflexes or hereditary schemes are the source of the ontogeny of behavior (psychogenesis), from the phylogenetic and embryologic points of view they constitute an end, a point of arrival. There are however several ways of considering this psychologic beginning: either as a series of isolated assemblages, or as an organization of a whole set of assemblages. At this point, we diverge from Piaget's interpretation. According to Piaget, the different reflexes or hereditary schemes each constitute segmentary behaviors (isolated or independent) which define heterogeneous spaces. These independent behaviors or heterogeneous spaces eventually undergo a process of coordination. The schemes, wrote Piaget (1967a), coordinate because of their tendency to mutually assimilate each other. This position is curious because Piaget also admits the current conceptions of the embryology of reflexes which are "considered as the product of differentiation on the part of the spontaneous activities of the whole."*

According to our point of view, the assemblages or hereditary schemes define a first level of whole organization, that is to say, of coordination. It is necessary to take into consideration not only the sucking reflex, the grasping reflex, the head–eye reflexes etc., but also the postural reflexes. It is then possible to define a whole structure of movements and positions of the body and of its parts which can be called the postural schema. This organization or structure defines all the stimulations the baby receives, that is to say, it interprets them and gives them meaning. This whole structure also defines what can be considered as a homogeneous space. Certain manifestations of this whole structure are frequently interpreted in a negative way as "tonic participation," "discharge interference," "associated contractions," etc. We think however, that without such a total structure, it is absolutely impossible to consider the eventual coordination of the different hereditary schemes and we consider the initial process of coordination to be the organizer of the new system.

The process that appears after birth is a dissociation of the initial structure into substructures, and it is these substructures which are momentarily heterogenous and which define isolated spaces. A recoordination follows this dissociation. This reinterpretation of initial behavior results in important theoretical modifications.

Our interpretation has two fundamental origins: the first is the relationship between two fields which, at least from our point of view, have been kept separate, the fields of developmental psychology and

---

* Many authors agree with this point of view; many make reference to Piaget's work.

neurophysiology; the second is exemplified in our previous research. This research has enabled the analysis of how the prehension scheme, when completely evolved at about 16–18 months (in the sense of a whole structure of movements of the arm and hand in relation to the objects which are handled), constitutes the organizing program of reelaborations that the subject accomplishes later on in relation to the representation of objects (3–8 years). Piaget has given the name of reflective abstraction to the reelaborations or reconstructions of this level. But, although for Piaget the schemes are coordinated only because of their tendency to assimilate each other, in our opinion, they are coordinated because of their previous state of coordination which directs and partially determines the new construction.

The Processes of Differentiation and Dissociation

We shall now attempt to define more precisely, by means of an example, the way in which a hereditary reflex characterizes an organization of the actions of the subject, in other words, a scheme, and to examine the way it evolves. The sucking reflex is a suitable example. What we usually call the sucking reflex does not only concern the rhythmic movements of the jaws and lips for swallowing,* but mainly the movements of the head relative to cutaneous stimulation of the area surrounding the mouth [this is called rooting reflex (Prechtl, 1958; Ingram, 1962)]. These coordinated movements have as their goal the incorporation of the source of stimulation. The fact that this assemblage initially belonged to a total structure, to a global state of coordination, is demonstrated by a series of relationships between the sucking activities and activities of other segments or parts of the body; the hand, in particular, is associated with rhythmic suction through synchronistic contractions. Conversely, the stimulation of the hand can bring about sucking (this technique is well known by wet nurses). The respective positions of the different parts of the body are equally interdependent with predominance of the proximal over the distal, and the head over the trunk. In consequence, the position of the head during sucking determines the position of the arms, trunk, etc.

Initially the sucking reflex only functions in an approximate way, and it is only by trial and error that the goal is achieved (capture of the source of stimulation). Does this approximation cause one to doubt the idea of structure or of organization? Certainly not. We can imagine that the structure initially defines the movements of the head as concerns their direction and orientation and not their amplitude or speed. Having thus demonstrated the existence and nature of an organization or initial scheme, we must now consider its development. After functioning for several days,

---

* This aspect of the assemblage is also very important and more complicated than might be imagined, because it exerts a subtle control to avoid in particular suffocation, and this necessitates variation in rhythm and intensity.

this behavior is refined and becomes more precise. The source of stimulation is directly incorporated without gradual correction [Piaget (1967a) speaks of a gradual consolidation of reflexes]. This means, in terms of our schematic and somewhat arbitrary analysis, that the amplitude or the speed of movements is also shaped. We think this transformation of the scheme allows the definition of one of the general processes which underlies any developing organization: the *process of differentiation*, which means that the initial organization has assimilated new sources of information and has thus increased its capacity of treatment and of discrimination (cf. following paragraph). This explains in particular the gradual growth of the field of behavior during its development, which is wrongly considered by many authors as the cause of development. As an illustration it can be said, that in our example, the initial scheme was only concerned with cutaneous stimulations and that through differentiation it became possible to deal with proprioceptive stimulations. This process of differentiation is correlated with the *process of dissociation* by which the different reflex assemblages separate themselves from the initial whole structure (cf. above).

It is thus that the functioning of the sucking reflex or scheme is no longer associated with other activities (like manual contractions) and becomes autonomous in a certain way (it is often called the inhibition of associated reactions). We can add that the different assemblages become heterogenous (one from the other) before they recoordinate in a new level as we have examined above. A good example of this recoordination is the "systematic thumbsucking," as Piaget refers to this activity (so as not to use a term implying intention, "will," or "conscience"), at about the age of 2 months. This behavior demonstrates a coordination between hand and mouth or, more exactly, between the arm–hand assemblage and the head–mouth assemblage, that is to say, between the sucking and grasping reflexes. These two organizations unite reciprocally and organize themselves. It is this that Piaget calls the reciprocal assimilation of two schemes. We are now studying the progressive elaboration of this coordination (in collaboration with A. Bullinger).

Development, the fundamental mechanisms of which we have just discussed in reference to particular behaviors, is made possible because of the appearance of new instruments (Piaget, 1967a); at the sensorimotor level it results from the maturation of certain nervous pathways or centers.

Systems of Representation

PERCEPTION AND CONFIGURATION OF INDICES

Another form of knowledge develops, parallel to the one we have considered previously, and in a way not dissociated from the elaboration of the movement-displacement of the object or of the body: the knowledge of the representation of the object and of its properties (spatiotemporal and physical). In Piagetian terminology, one can say that the knowledge of the states and properties of the object corresponds to the knowledge of the transformation of the objects (singular or collective), these two aspects being complementary and very closely tied to each other.

This knowledge of the object (its states, its internal relations, its physical properties) is supplied at the sensorimotor level, by perceptions, which translate the object in the form of a configuration of indices. These configurations of indices are more or less rich and complete, depending on the systems of treatment with which they are connected, on which they depend, or from which they were constructed. This is why we first of all considered the development of systems of treatment, which provide the foundation of the developmental pattern, because "all modes of knowledge . . . suppose a structuration as a previous and necessary condition . . . (Piaget, 1967a)."

This aspect of knowledge and of behavior has been extensively studied in psychology, in particular at the sensorimotor level in relation to shape and size constancy, and in a more general way, to the discriminatory abilities of the neonate. Numerous studies have been carried out in the laboratory. However we shall characterize this development by means of two typical spontaneous reactions which Spitz (1952) has very aptly demonstrated the symptom value of, in relation to different levels of organization. These reactions, by themselves, do not permit the formulation of hypotheses. It is because of laboratory experiments that the nature of these organizations has been partly analyzed (Fantz, 1961, 1963; Bower, 1966; Ahrens, 1954, etc.).

LEVELS OF PERCEPTIVE SCHEMATIZATION

These two typical reactions are the smile in the third month and the anxiety response in the eighth month. Concerning the smiling reaction, Spitz has shown the discriminatory possibilities that correspond to it. The results show that a certain configuration—eyes, nose, forehead—presented to the child, provokes the smiling response. This means that for the 3-month-old baby, all faces presented in front of him, even masks or reproductions of configuration, are identical (constitute a class equivalence) and consequently the mother is not differentiated. This conclusion is certainly rather precipitous and it is necessary at least to say that she is not differentiated *visually*. It is probably true that the baby is capable of finer and more subtle discriminations in other categories of indices or groups of indices (in particular somaesthetic, auditory, olfactory, etc.). These indices allow him to identify his mother or at least, reduce the number of substitutions and consequently, define a class of equivalence more restricted in extension than the visual class. A mother is not altogether mistaken in thinking that her child recognizes her at this age.

As for the anxiety observed in the eighth month, it betrays a very different level of organization, because the crying reaction is caused by every strange face; this means that the mother (or her substitute, or another familiar person) has been very precisely identified by a considerable perceptual capacity (visual). The mother constitutes a unique class. From this level, the baby must still build a structure of classifications which will allow him to group these unique classes and include them in a hierarchical system of classes. It is not until 8 to 10 months later that this is attained (at a sensorimotor level).

DISSOCIATION OF FORM AND CONTENT AND CATEGORIES OF SIGNIFIERS

At the level of hereditary assemblages, the scheme can be defined as a closed set of perceptions and movements (Piaget, 1936) thus grouping both aspects of knowledge, the knowledge of transformations (movements), and the knowledge of states (perceptions). The development of behavior shows a trend toward their dissociation, which begins at the sensorimotor level. This has allowed us to treat separately these two aspects: the organization of action-transformation on one hand, and the organization of perceptions on the other (this separation of behavior remains nevertheless, arbitrary). All the subsequent development of cognitive functions is characterized by a slow and laborious liberation of forms (or structures) from content (Piaget, 1961a). Piaget has frequently defined the scheme as "what is repeatable, transposable, or generalizable in an action." In other words, the scheme is the structure or form of the action in opposition to the objects which serve as variable contents to it. Sometimes however he states that forms are not elaborated independently of content (Piaget, 1968b). In *Biology and Knowledge* (1971a) one finds a slightly different way of defining the relations between form and content. There, the structure is said to "consist of the elements and the relations which unite them, but without this it would be possible to characterize or define these elements independent of these relations . . . [although] . . . a structure can be considered independent of the elements which compose it . . . as the 'form' or the system of relations, that is essential to our comparisons, for it is the principle of all isomorphism." But we would add that although this principle (the foundation of the structuralist method) has been of great utility, it also entails a danger to the behavioral sciences. It is in particular this notion which caused Piaget to declare once that he had only studied psychologic development from the subject's point of view (that is, structure or operations) and not from the object's point of view (that is, representations or translations of the object as content). This remark was the point of departure of recent studies carried out by Piaget on causality. Having collaborated on these studies we think that the developmental study of the child's behavior cannot be carried out while dissociating form and content. We have demonstrated this point in our analysis of the relations between simple abstraction and reflective abstraction (Mounoud, 1970). A system of relations must necessarily take into account the nature and the role of the elements on which it is based.

Following this line of discussion, we will now try to demonstrate the nature of this dissociation of form and content after the sensorimotor period. This is above all made possible by the semiotic or symbolic function which appears at approximately two years of age. This function allows the emergence of new categories of signifiers, in particular the systems of images and the systems of signs (verbal, graphic, or mathematical, etc.). The signifiers are distinguished from perceptive indices by the fact that they are dissociated from the signified (operations or schemes or actions).* Systems of signifiers (which comprises perception) define what Piaget calls figurative instruments, which furnish the knowledge of states; while the systems of relations (schemes of action and operations) define the operative instruments which deal with the transformations. If this distinction is not important at the sensorimotor level, due to the relative undifferentiation of form and content, it is necessary to introduce it for the study of the operative organization of behavior.

THE OPERATIVE ORGANIZATION OF BEHAVIOR

We will now examine the period called "concrete operations" that extends from 2 to 9 or 10 years of age (which follows the sensorimotor period), in relation to the development of spatial representation. We will consider, in the first place, the development of children's drawings (the drawing defining what can be called "graphic space").

Children's drawings have been analyzed by numerous authors, from different points of view. The main perspectives are to consider pictures as tests: test of either intelligence or of emotional development. Another dichotomy is to consider children's drawings or pictures either in relation to their structure or degree of organization, or in relation to their content and to the meaning they represent.

An original study of the development of children's drawing from a structural point of view, is that of Luquet (1927) and his classification is still well accepted. Luquet distinguishes three periods of development in the child's drawing: the first, a period of "synthetic incapacity" extends from 3 to 5 years; the second period of "intellectual realism" is found from 6 to 8 years; and the third period of "visual realism" that begins at 8 years, is

---

* We think it is preferable to say "dissociable" in the sense that the signifiers can be projected in reality to constitute artificial objects (which are the systems of signs and of images in the manner of tools-instruments, cf. Mounoud, 1970).

achieved between 9–10 years. These drawings correspond to those of an adult.

Mental Images as a System of Signifiers

It is not possible to explain the development of these drawings in terms of motor development. To understand it we must consider the development of what is generally called representation (which appears along with the symbolic function) and constitutes in fact one of the systems of representation. In this way, drawing supposes an internal pattern, a representation or a mental image, which is different from simple perception, as Luquet has said, although the "simple perception" becomes at once a schematizing construction as we have previously seen. (Piaget's hypothesis in this field is to consider simple perception as the result of sedimentary perceptual activities.) Through drawing, we can trace the spontaneous development of this new system of signifiers: the image signifier or the mental image [the drawings constitute pretty good approximations (Piaget and Inhelder, 1948)]. It is evident that the study of spontaneous drawings does not in itself allow us to characterize the exact nature of different successive organizations; it only provides a number of indications for the interpretation of which, a series of experimental situations were created (Piaget and Inhelder, 1948), in order to be able to define the nature and limitations of successive structurations to which the subjects arrive. The approach is the same as for the baby's spontaneous reactions (which we have already mentioned) which we can interpret in relation to laboratory experiments.

The system of image signifiers is built in coordination with the system of relations (or operations) with which they define another series of organizations. In the previous section we have seen the different translations or schematizations of the human face that the baby makes during the first two years, without indicating every time, the system of relations they correspond to. These schematizations were made as part of a first system of signifiers that constitute perception (with indices and signals); we can also speak of a first system of *"indexation"* or a first system of *signalization,* to join Pavlov and other Soviet authors whom we will mention later. The system of relations that corresponds to the first system of signalization is defined (as we have seen), by the coordination of actions which we usually call movements (from the point of view of the structure that coordinates them). Movements and perceptions are in part inseparable at this first level, and for this reason, Piaget defines the perceptive indices as signifiers undifferentiated from the signified (movements). On the contrary, at the age of two, the symbolic (or semiotic) function renders possible the elaboration of new systems of signifiers (in particular the images) now differentiated from the signified, which are the mental operations or pre-operations of the subject. In this way, a single operation (as a system of relations) can be applied to different signifiers. [We are not very favorable to this dichotomy "differentiated–undifferentiated." If movements (the structures that determine them) as signifiers are more highly connected with perceptive indices than operations with images, this is only a question of degree. On the other hand, the differentiated signifiers stay connected to the relational system.]

Different Levels of the Schematization of Drawings

Following the interpretation of Piaget and Inhelder (1948), we shall examine briefly the three general groups of drawings, from the point of view of the operations or systems of relations that sustain them.

The child's first drawings (period of synthetic incapacity) respect in their general lines, certain topologic relationships, whereas in detail, these relationships are often incorrect. The topologic relationships are relationships of nearness, separation, order, inclusion, etc. The first drawings of the human body, with arms and legs attached to the head, are good examples of this first level.

The graphic productions of the second period (of intellectual realism), reveal that the child now respects topologic relationships and evidences the first steps toward the elaboration of projective or Euclidian relationships. More precisely, the frequent *fold downs* that characterize this level are only pseudo *fold downs*. (The term "fold down" refers to a specific type of distorted drawing. A four-legged table, drawn in the manner of a "fold down," is shown in Fig. 12.1.) They indicate much more an in-

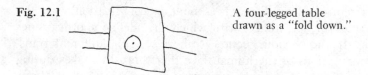

Fig. 12.1   A four-legged table drawn as a "fold down."

capacity to coordinate different points of view that are placed side by side, than they do real *fold downs* that have been found in older children through appropriate tests. The design of a spool of thread for example, can be made from three different points of view at a time.

The productions of the third period, called visual realism, correspond to adult drawings and indicate the presence of a metric and projective organization of space. The child has acquired the system of coordinates.

Findings of spontaneous drawing have been enriched by the study of the copy of geometric figures (Piaget and Inhelder, 1948). This evolution permits a comparison with what we have seen at the sensorimotor level. We can recall that at three months the visual translations of the human face into perceptive indices are global enough to render equivalent a great number of subject-objects. In the same way, the translations that a child of three to five years makes by means of the developing system of images and sufficiently general to render equivalent the objects assimilated. These objects are therefore indentifiable by the previous sensorimotor organization. For example, at the age of four, the child can already differentiate the square from the round by means of the instruments of the sensorimotor period (he can differentiate perceptively), but is not capable of furnishing clear translations in his drawings, that is to say, by means of imagined signifiers and their corresponding operations. Human faces are therefore equivalent in relation to this second system. (We think that the discordance between these two translations is one of the main origins of the evolution of the whole system.)

The Process of Image Formation

We have characterized, up to now, only certain levels of the elaboration of image signifiers, mainly to indicate to which type of structuration they correspond. Now the main problem is the formation of these systems of signifiers (or of signalization), in other words, the construction of images.

For many years the origin of representation has been investigated in exploratory activities. The tracing of ocular movements has been extensively carried out, but mainly in order to study perceptual mechanisms and their relation to operations.

Tactile explorations have been used in preference to explain the formation of images and representations (often not dissociated from thought). Soviet psychologists have done a great number of studies on the subject, which we learned of only recently (O'Connor, 1961; Pick, 1964; Cole and Maltzman, 1969). It is also through the study of tactile explorations that Piaget and Inhelder (1948) conducted a study of image formation, using a haptic perception test. As for North American authors (J. J. Gibson, 1966; E. J. Gibson, 1969), they chiefly use this means of exploration to study intersensory relations or cross-modal transfer.

It would be very long to describe here the different conceptions and techniques used in these studies. A simplified view of the development of explorations, common to these different studies is, that from being very poor or nonexistent, these explorations become more and more complete until finally they are systematic and exact, in the sense of a complete examination of the object, i.e., they are of an imitative type. Aside from all the methodologic questions raised by these different studies, the interpretation of explorations poses delicate problems. From our point of view, we find it difficult to consider explorations (visual or tactile), either as faithful models of the subject's operations, or as the direct origin of a mode of knowledge (or a reflective type or a probabilistic-inference type). There has always been in psychology a certain realism in the concepts of action or activity and in their interpretation.

According to our interpretation, the absence of actual exploration can indicate a level of organization already established, whereas a very minute exploration can be the sign of an organization in elaboration. In this perspective, we have reconsidered the study of haptic perception (in collaboration with L. Hay). A detailed analysis of tactile explorations of free geometric figures (not fixed to a support) has allowed us to state how children at different levels arrive at exhaustive explorations of the object (between 7, 10, 14 years of age). The explorations consist of following the contour of the object in a servile way and so form an imitation of its shape. We could say that in this case it is the use of strategies of an *imitative type*. To these strategies correspond the possibility of correctly reproducing the object through drawing. (The recognition of the object does not require the same type of elaboration.) They characterize stages in which the systems of treatment or of organization are established.

It would be possible to conclude, from this type of strategy, that the explorations are entirely directed by the object and by consequence the knowledge is obtained from the object. But on the other hand we know that neither Soviet authors nor Piaget believe in the idea of "copy knowledge." In order to explain that the imitation is schematizing even though it gives a faithful picture of reality (from a spatial point of view in any case), the Soviet authors resort to the notion of the orientation reflex, i.e., to previous schematization (Vekker, 1961; Sokolov, 1966; Lomov, 1966), and Piaget resorts to the fact that imitation or accommodation are always related to an assimilation scheme.

We have considered this imitative-type strategy in relation to strategies that precede it developmentally and in a positive sense in order to demonstrate the former's nature and role. These explorations, (which are more discontinous, which proceed by establishing relations, and which are in appearance more systematic), indicate the elaboration of systems of treatment and of representation. We shall call these exploration strategies of a *constructive type*. Once elaborated, these systems can integrate successive information and introduce relationships in a less elaborate way by means of an imitative-type of strategy. Thus we understand why these imitative strategies are not simple copies of the object, nor are they the origin of simple reflection, but overall *their function is much more to obtain or "capture" information than to elaborate it*. Consequently, the gesture of the hand that follows the contour of the object obtains information regarding certain properties or elements for which the subject has "normative" representations (and by consequence, has corresponding motor patterns). These properties or elements are integrated by the systems of treatment already constituted. In this sense, the imitative strategy is a schematization.

In conclusion, the constructive strategies which introduce relationships by actions are necessary for the elaboration of new systems of treatment and representation, and later, the imitative strategies are only meaningful in that they are collectors of information. Only in this sense we can mention Claparède's (1898) expression "touching is spelling shape." This statement is only correct if the subject posseses a lexicon, a code, or a grammar, and hence posseses constituted signifiers and significates (system of relations). In a synchronistic perspective, this point of view is sufficient. What makes this evidence and analysis difficult is that during the child's development we find only rarely pure strategies, because the developmental process is continous and there are, at all stages, completed forms of organization and others in formation.

Figurative Instruments

Mental images, as percepts, furnish what Piaget calls the knowledge of states as opposed to the knowledge of transformations. These different systems (mental images and perception) constitute what he calls "figurative instruments," because they translate or represent external objects in opposition to systems of relations that define the transformations and constitute the "operative instruments."

We should specify that there are not only mental images for spatial objects (properties and operations), but also for physical and logicomathematical features. Piaget attributes a special character to the images of spatial objects, since the image is spatial by definition. Consequently, the development of an image of spatial objects consists of translating into spatial forms the transformations that take place in space and this therefore presents a figurative aspect and not exclusively an operative aspect, such that transformations are for themselves, figures in space. On the other hand, the elaboration of an image of logicomathematical operations consists of a translation into spatial forms (necessarily) of nonspatial transformations. These images are more or less arbitrary. We find, for example, many varied representations of the numerical series. In many cases the figuration of logicomathematical operations is based on the existing isomorphism among logical operations, applied to discontinuous elements or collections of objects, and operations that Piaget calls "sublogical" (or spatiotemporal), which are applied to continuous elements, that is to say, on the parts of the object (an example of the figuration of logicomathematical operations is the Euler circles). It is evident that the figurations or signifiers most appropriate to logicomathematical objects are the systems of signs and it is those which are most frequently used.

Correspondences

We have tried to analyze in this chapter different levels of translation or representation of objects. This is what we suggest be called the internal representation systems of the external universe. We have described different schematizations, either at the level of perceptive indices, or at the level of mental images. We have also tried to demonstrate how these instruments of representation or of figuration, called systems of signifiers, are elaborated and the existing dependence between the systems of signifiers and the systems of relations or of treatment (the significates).

In conclusion, we would like to outline some correspondences between the levels of representation seen in children and other levels of representation.

Studies on instinct, among the best known being those of Tinbergen and Lorenz, indicate that elaborated translations of external reality (as in the case of reflexes) already exist; that is to say, for a given receptor (e.g., a visual receptor) in certain conditions, a specific configuration of indices is directly meaningful. These configurations release sequences of behavior, which are arranged genetically in a hierarchial way. For example, during nest-building, the red abdomen of the male stickleback releases a parade activity in the female and a fight reaction in the male. [Instinctive behavior poses, in fact, more delicate problems because it activates behavior adjusted reciprocally among individuals, and consequently it is only characteristic on a "trans-individual level" as Piaget says, that is to say, at the level of the population (Piaget, 1967a).]

At the molecular level, it is possible to observe how certain substances directly produce a given reaction in relation with what is called the "stereospecific" properties of molecules (Monod, 1970), which implies a certain internal representation of external substances. We point to a correspondence among configurations of indices which produce instinctive reactions, among releasing stimuli that produce reflex responses, among configurations perceived by the 3-month-old baby that provoke the smile, or among the graphic schematizations accomplished by a 4-year-old child, etc. The comparison with an artist should not surprise us, because his productions provoke in him an interpretation or a given emotion.

From a synchronistic point of view, the correspondences do not pose great problems and we can say that all organisms, at a given point in history, possess internal representations of external reality that are directly meaningful, and can release a specific behavior. By means of certain instruments (e.g., the symbolic function) and from a certain level on it is possible to project these representations into reality and to construct artificial objects (tools, theories, pictures, designs, etc.).

From a diachronic point of view, the correspondences are more difficult. The transformations or variations of (systems of) representations are a general phenomenon, whether they take place at the level of the organism, of the population, or of the species. This is one of the problems of development in general and especially of child development, for which we have suggested some steps toward a solution. In this perspective I would suggest, for example, that we consider Picasso's successive translations of the human face through his paintings, designs, and sculptures, as a reflection of the development of his internal representations. This development must be produced by mechanisms comparable to those we have already analyzed (the role of his history, of his initial representations, the role of the models which inspired him, of the materials etc. (cf. Mandelbrodt and Mounoud, 1971)).

What should be avoided are too direct comparisons, based on manifest contents in psychoanalytic terms, or superficial structures in linguistic terms. The comparisons we are trying to establish are those relative to the mechanisms by means of which we pass from one organization to another. It does not matter whether the second organization is superior or inferior to the first. What we are hoping to be able to characterize are two stages of evolution that are qualitatively different, and the transformation processes that relate these two stages. In other words, we want to know how the subject, during his development, decodes reality and makes successive reinterpretations of it.

Finally, we wish to point out a fact not mentioned until now—that there is a constant tendency for every established or constructed organization (schemes, operations, or structures) to generalize itself abusively and force the subject to lose momentarily certain discrimination possibilities. In an experiment dealing with relationships between perimeters and surfaces, using spaghetti of the same length, it is surprising to see how a child of 5–6 years is capable of correctly seriating differently constructed surfaces, while a child of 7–8 years is no longer capable because he generalizes the conservation of the perimeter to the surface, and thus cannot perceive the differences (Vinh-Bang, 1965). We can therefore state "that submitting to facts is only a way of submitting to nature in order to adjust to it, and later to impose a law on it. The shock of the subject in contact with external world actualizes the possibilities of the organism" (Lévi-Valensi, 1970).

THREE

Developmental Approach to Language

13

Developmental Psycholinguistics

HERMINE SINCLAIR

One of the questions a Genevan psycholinguist who works with Jean Piaget hears often is: how does language figure in Piaget's theory? Does his theory of cognitive development provide a framework for the acquisition of language? Does he have an epistemology of language? It is difficult to answer these questions in a straightforward manner; the more so, since the few articles Piaget himself has written on language are almost uniquely concerned with the problem of language as a factor in development, and may seem to be written almost reluctantly (one of them starts off ". . . il aurait fallu me poser cette question à une epoque ou. . . ." 1963); his very early work, *Le Langage et la pensée chez l'enfant* (1923) concerns far more "la pensée" than "le langage." On the other hand, it is quite wrong to assert, as many authors do, that Piaget leaves language completely outside his considerations, and that, in fact, his experiments may lose some of their meaning because of this refusal to consider language as a separate, important variable.

To live with, or rather in, Piaget's theories for a number of years may have curious effects on a psycholinguist: from an initial irritation at the rather off-hand manner in which language is dealt with in many of Piaget's works and in much of his experimentation, one reaches the conviction that, spread over a number of works, Piaget has in fact provided the bases for a general theory of both language acquisition and of the role of language as a factor of development. However this may be, the following is an attempt to explain and elaborate Piaget's views on language. These views will be presented in two contexts: language viewed as a factor in cognitive development, and as a possible theory of language acquisition.

PIAGET'S CONCEPTION OF THE ROLE OF LANGUAGE IN COGNITIVE DEVELOPMENT

In several articles Piaget has been most explicit on this relationship between language and intellectual operations. The two main points that recur in his writings on the subject are the following:

1. The sources of intellectual operations are not to be found in language, but in the preverbal, sensorimotor period where a system of schemes is elaborated that prefigures certain aspects of the structures of classes and relations, and elementary forms of conservation and operatory reversibility. In fact, the acquisition of the permanency of objects (elaborated between 6 and 18 months) constitutes a first "invariant." The search for an object which has disappeared is conducted in function of its successive localizations: these localizations depend on the constitution of an elementary *groupe de déplacements*, in which detours (associativity) and returns (reversibility) are coordinated.

2. The formation of representational thought is contemporaneous with the acquisition of language; both belong to a more general process, that of the constitution of the symbolic function in general. This symbolic function has several aspects; different kinds of behaviors, all appearing at about the same time in development, indicate its beginnings. The first verbal utterances are intimately linked to, and contemporaneous with, symbolic play, deferred imitation, and mental images as interiorized imitations.

The first point is elaborated in many works by Piaget and his co-workers (Bärbel Inhelder in particular). Intellectual operations are actions that have become interiorized and reversible, but they are still actions. The coordination and decentrations of sensorimotor activity are not limited to this first period of life, but are found, in a different form, at work in the constitution of operational intelligence as well. And, as Piaget frequently remarks (1963), they are also found in linguistic acts. This may account for a partial isomorphism between language and logic. It is important to bear in mind that already in the sensorimotor period object permanency is a general acquisition. It would be a contradiction in terms to speak of one specific operation, since an operation is always part of a structured whole, of a system of operations; but in the same way, object permanency is not to be understood as the permanency of one or of some objects (a toy, the baby's bottle) but of objects in general. Similarly, the *groupe de déplacements* does not mean that the baby can make one specific detour, or return to his starting point in one particular case: these first prefigurations of associativity and reversibility are, again, general. Thought has its roots in action; at the end of the sensorimotor period, and before the appearance of language or of the symbolic function in general, the baby has overcome his initial perceptive and motor egocentrism by a series of decentrations and coordinations. The construction of operations demands a new series of decentrations; not only from the momentary, present perceptive centration, but also from the totality of the actions of the subject.

As regards the second point, Piaget has devoted a whole work to *La Formation du Symbole chez l'Enfant* (1945, Engl. title *Play, Dreams, and Imitation in Childhood*, 1961b). This important work cannot be summarized in a few pages, but the main concepts bearing on the role of language in the development of thought may be expressed as follows.

At the end of the sensorimotor period the first decentrations appear in the child's dealings with his *hic-et-nunc* environment; action schemes appear that permit the child to attain his practical aims, which are limited to the immediate present and to the manipulation of concrete objects within his reach. These spatiotemporal restrictions will slowly disappear with the development of thought. Moreover, the activity of the baby is directed toward success in his manipulations (from the cognitive point of view) and toward personal satisfaction (from the affective point of view). Later on, his activity takes on another dimension: cognitively, immediate success will no longer be the sole aim, but he will search for explanations and will reflect on his own actions; affectively, he will seek not only satisfaction, but also communication; he will want to tell other people about his discoveries, that now become *knowledge of* objects and events rather than *reactions to* objects and events.

One might be tempted to regard language, in the sense of learning to speak one's mother tongue through contact with the persons in one's environment, as the sole or main instrument that causes this transformation. Piaget, however, shows clearly that language is only a symptom and not the source of this change. Retracing the development step by step through careful observation of his own children, he demonstrates that language, despite the fact that later on it becomes most pervasive and takes on the guise of an autonomous capacity, is only part of the symbolic function. The symbolic function can be defined essentially as the capacity to represent reality through the intermediary of signifiers that are distinct from what they signify. The important term in this definition is the word *distinct*. In fact, around six months of age the baby already is capable of treating a partial perceptive datum as an indication of the presence of the whole; even if only a bit of the object is visible, it indicates the presence of the object. But such signals are directly linked to the objects, or are part of the object, whereas distinct signifiers imply a differentiation between signifier and signified, *introduced by the subject himself*. Signals (like the tracks an animal leaves in the snow, or the smell of food, or visible bits of partially hidden objects) are temporally and spatially restricted; the most distinct signifiers (words, algebraic symbols, and such) are free from such restrictions. Using a slightly different terminology, the linguist Bally said that the signal is a signifier only for whoever interprets it; and that a sign (distinct signifier) is a "voluntary act," and also meaningful for whoever uses it.

The child who pushes a small shell along the edge of a box saying "meow" knows fully well that the shell is not a cat and the edge of the box is not a fence. And even if for the child the words "meow" or "cat" are at first somehow inherent in the animal, they are signifiers, and certainly not the animal itself. Piaget introduces a dichotomy in the distinct signifiers themselves: (1) symbols, which like the shell have a link of resemblance with the object or event, and (2) signs (words), which are arbitrary. Symbols, moreover, are usually personal; every child invents them in his play, whereas signs are social. Finally, we may add, symbols are mostly isolated, though within the context of symbolic play they may be loosely associated; signs on the other hand form systems.

According to Piaget, this capacity to represent reality by distinct signifiers has its roots in imitation, which starts very early in the sensorimotor period (around six months of age) and which already constitutes some sort of representation by action. At the end of the sensorimotor period imitation becomes possible in the absence of the model, and evolves from a direct sensorimotor model to gesticulative evocation. First one sees action schemes appear out of their proper context as representations (for instance, pretending to be asleep), then these representations become detached from the activity of the subject (for instance, putting a doll to sleep). Slowly these deferred imitations become interiorized, and constitute sketchy images, which the child can already use to anticipate future acts. Piaget gives several examples of these action imitations that announce interiorization: when L. tries to open a box of matches (which is not quite shut), she first manipulates it, but without result; then she stops acting, seems to reflect on the problem and opens and shuts her mouth, several times in succession: she uses a motor-signifier to represent the problem and to find a way of solving it. After this short period of "reflection" she pushes her finger into the small opening and pulls to open the box completely.

A wealth of such observations throws light on the development of the symbolizing capacity, which has many different aspects that are at first inextricably linked in observable behavior. Small children pass extremely swiftly from what looks like pure imitation to symbolic play and to acts of practical intelligence accompanied by words (or onomatopoaeia), but at first these different aspects cannot even be distinguished. Language as seen by Piaget is thus part of a much larger complex of processes that go on during the second year of life; it has the same roots, and in the beginning the same function as symbolic play, deferred imitation, and mental images; it does not appear *ex nihilo* (nor simply from early, prelinguistic vocalizations) but partakes of the entire cognitive development in this crucial period. It is, of course, just as closely linked to affective development; but this aspect of the question has been frequently dealt with by other authors, and the aim of this chapter is restricted to the relationship between language and intellectual operations.

In summary, Piaget considers language not to be a sufficient condition for the constitution of intellectual operations, and he has said so, explicitly, in several articles (1954a, 1961b, 1962, 1963, 1965a, Piaget and Inhelder, 1966b). As to the question of whether language (in the sense of the normal acquisition of natural language by the young child) is, if not a sufficient, all the same a necessary condition for the constitution of operations, Piaget leaves the question open as regards the operations of formal logic. He notes (1963) however, that these operations go beyond language, in the sense that neither the lattice of possible combinations nor the group of four transformations is as such present in language; they cannot even be expressed in ordinary, natural language. As regards concrete operations, Piaget considers language (again, in the limited sense) not even a necessary condition for their constitution, though he has not explicitly said so. However, he does state:

> . . . the sensorimotor schemes seem to be of a fundamental importance from their very first beginnings; these schemes continue to develop and structure thought, even verbal thought, as action progresses, up till the constitution of logicomathematical operations, which are the authentic end-product of coordinated action-logic, when the latter can be interiorized and combined into group structures (1965).

Moreover, as regards concrete operations, Piaget quotes experiments with deaf-mute children, which clearly seem to point to the fact that the symbolic function is an obvious necessity for the constitution of these operations, but that the normal acquisition of a natural language is not. A brief summary of experimental data pertaining to the relationship between language and thought can be given and two different kinds of experiments can be distinguished.

(1) The comparison of the reactions of normal children to Piaget-type tests with those of deaf-mute children on the one hand, and blind children on the other. The deaf-mutes have intact sensorimotor schemes, but have not acquired spoken language (or are only at the beginning of an "oral" education), whereas the blind are in the inverse situation.

Studies of deaf children have been made by Oléron (1957) and Furth (1966) among others. Their results concur fundamentally, and indicate that deaf children acquire the elementary logical operations with only a slight retardation as compared to normal children. The same stages of development are found as the ones established by Piaget on a normal population. Both Oléron and Furth point out some differences in the reactions of their deaf subjects (particularly in the conservation of liquids). In the case of the conservation of liquids, however, certain difficulties in the presentation of the tests may account for these differences (e.g., in the pouring of liquids, the distinction between the quantity of liquid and the volume of the container is difficult to convey).

Furth notes an interesting difference in the comparative performance of deaf and hearing on "logical symbol discovery" versus "symbol use" tasks. While the deaf are inferior to the hearing on the former, they show equal ability on the use of logical symbols in a structured task. Furth points to several factors that could explain the results: among others, a different approach on the part of the deaf towards problems that call for invention, which may be due to a general lack of social contact. Oléron finds that seriation tests are only very slightly retarded, that spatial operations are normal, and that classifications possess the same general structures and appear at the same age as with normals, but seem slightly less mobile or flexible (when classificatory criteria have to be changed). Here again, the cause may be more due to a general lack of social exchange and stimulation than to operational retardation.

These results with deaf children are all the more striking when it is considered that the same tests are only solved by blind children, on the average, four years later than by normal. The sensorial deficit of the blind has retarded the constitution of sensorimotor schemes and inhibited their coordination. The verbal acquisitions cannot compensate for this retardation, and action learning is necessary before blind children reach an operational level comparable to that of the normal and the deaf (Hatwell, 1960).

(2) A second group of experiments, directly bearing on the relationship between language and intellectual operations has been carried out in Geneva by Inhelder in collaboration with the author. These experiments have been described in detail elsewhere (Sinclair de Zwart, 1967a), and in this chapter we shall do no more than briefly indicate their technique and summarize the results. Our aims were twofold: (a) to see whether the profound modification that occurs in the child's thinking with the constitution of the first concrete operations is paralleled by a linguistic development; (b) if the answer to (a) were in the affirmative, to determine whether a child who still lacks a certain concept or operation would show operatory progress after having undergone verbal training aiming to make him acquire expressions used by children who already possess the concept in question.

Consequently, we first chose some Piagetian tasks (conservation of liquids and seriation) that call for understanding and using certain expressions (quantitative and dimensional terms and comparatives). We explored the child's verbal capacities in this domain by first asking him to describe simple situations (which do not touch upon conservation or seriation problems: e.g., we present the child with two dolls, to one of whom we give four big marbles and to the other two small marbles, and we ask: "Is this fair? Are both dolls happy? Why not?" Or we ask him to tell us the difference between two pencils, e.g., a short thick one and a long thin one). After this exploration of the child's use of certain expressions, we study his comprehension, by asking him to execute orders couched in "adult" but simple terms (e.g., "give more plasticine to the boy than to the girl"; "find a pencil that is shorter but thicker than this one").

After dividing our subjects into three groups according to their results on the Piagetian conservation task (total absence of conservation, intermediary stage, and conservation acquired), we compared their answers in the verbal task. The results can be summarized as follows:

(a) No difference was found among the three groups in the comprehension tasks; in fact, almost all subjects executed all orders correctly; only a very few young children (four years old) had some difficulties in questions of the type: "Find a pencil that is longer but thinner."

(b) Striking differences were found between the two extreme groups (no conservation at all and conservation acquired) as regards the description tasks.

Of the children with conservation, 70% used comparatives (without adjectives) for the description of different quantities of plasticine, and 100% did so for the description of different numbers of marbles: *le garçon a plus que la fille* (the boy has more than the girl).

Of children without conservation, 90% used absolute terms (in contrast to comparatives): *le garçon a beaucoup, la fille a peu* (the boy has a lot, the girl has a little).

An interesting point was that 20% already used comparatives for discrete units (marbles) whereas they did not do so for continuous quantities (plasticine); and the conservation of discrete units is acquired before that of continuous quantities.

Of the children with conservation, 100% used different terms for different dimensions, using two couples of opposites (e.g., *grand/petit, gros/mince,* big/little, fat/thin).

Of children without conservation, 75% used undifferentiated terms for the two dimensions, i.e., they would use at least one word to indicate two dimensions: e.g., *gros* (fat) for long and for thick, or *petit* (small) for short and for thin.

Of children with conservation, 80% described two objects differing in two dimensions in two sentences, coordinating the two dimensions:

ce crayon est (plus) long mais (plus) mince, l'autre est court mais gros [this pencil is long(er) but thin(ner), the other is short but thick].

Of children without conservation, 90% either described only the one dimension, or used four separate sentences, dealing first with length, and then with thickness: *ce crayon est long, l'autre est court, ce crayon* (the first one again) *est mince, l'autre est gros.* (Percentages are approximate; slight variations occurred in different groups of items and with different materials not described here.)

In a second series of experiments we tried to teach children without conservation the expressions used by children with conservation: comparative terms, differentiated terms and coordinated description of a difference in two dimensions. After this verbal training we again tested their operational level in the conservation task. The results of these experiments were as follows:

It was easy (in the sense that only a small number of repetitions were necessary) to teach the children without conservation the use of differentiated terms; it was more difficult (and about a quarter of the subjects did not succeed) to teach them to use the comparatives *plus* (more) and *moins* (less) in our situations; it was still more difficult to teach them the coordinated structure *long et (mais) mince, court et (mais) gros.*

Even for children who succeeded in learning to use these expressions, operational progress was rare (10% of our subjects acquired conservation).

On the other hand, more than half the children who made no clear operational progress, changed their answers in the posttest. Instead of simply using the level of the liquid to decide that there was more to drink in one of the glasses, they now noticed and described the covarying dimensions (higher level, narrower glass); they sometimes explained that the liquid goes up higher in a narrower glass, but this did not lead them to the compensation argument and conservation.

From this first series of experiments we drew the following conclusions:

(a) A distinction must be made between lexical acquisition and the acquisition of syntactic structures, the latter being more closely linked to operational level than the former. The operatorlike words (e.g., more, less, as much as, none) form a class apart whose correct use is also very closely linked to operational progress. The other lexical items (e.g., long, short, thin, thick, high, low) are far less closely linked to operativity.

(b) Operational structuring and linguistic structuring or rather linguistic restructuring thus parallel each other. The lexical items are already being used or at least easily learned at a preoperational level; the coordinated structures and operatorlike words are correctly "understood" in simple situations; but the latter are only precisely and regularly used with the advent of the first operational structures. Moreover, the difficulties encountered by the child in the use of these expressions seem to be the same as those he encounters in the development of the operations themselves: lack of decentration and incapacity to coordinate.

(c) Verbal training leads subjects without conservation to direct their attention to pertinent aspects of the problem (covariance of the dimensions), but it does not ipso facto bring about the acquisition of operations.

An additional experiment may be briefly mentioned: in interrogating a group of severely retarded children (age 8 to 15, IQ 50 or below) we found that when we used the description patterns of children with conservation for simple orders (*donne plus à la poupee-fille, moins au garçon*), the retarded children were incapable of reacting consistently; but if we used the descriptive terms of our normal nonconservation group (e.g., *donne beaucoup à la fille, et peu au garçon*) their reactions were both correct and consistent. This result illustrated the psychologic "reality" of the different descriptive patterns used by normal children.

A second group of experiments dealt with seriation and its verbal aspects, and yielded comparable results.

These Genevan results, together with the results of the research on deaf and blind children mentioned earlier, confirm Piaget's view on the role of language in the constitution of intellectual operations: language is not the source of logic, but is on the contrary structured by logic.

A POSSIBLE THEORY OF LANGUAGE ACQUISITION WITHIN THE GENERAL FRAMEWORK OF PIAGET'S DEVELOPMENTAL THEORY

No theory of language acquisition has been explicitly proposed by Piaget. We can, however, speculate on the general form that such a theory might take. The problem is complex for several reasons.

In the first place, language, in Piaget's terms (1966) is "a ready-made system that is elaborated by society and that contains, for persons that learn it before they contribute to its enrichment, a wealth of cognitive instruments (relations, classifications, and so on) at the service of thought." The knowing person expresses his "knowledge" in this code. As such, language takes the place of symbolization in the relationship knower–symbolization–known. But this code is itself an object of knowing; as such it takes the place of the "known" in the knower–known relationship. Piaget stresses mainly the first aspect; most psycholinguists pay attention only to the second.

A second difficulty lies in the fact that language, though it is a system of signs (in terms of the distinction between signals on the one hand and symbols and signs on the other) that can be used for rational discourse and communication, it need not only be used as such. In fact, linguistic forms can be used as signals "to be reacted to" rather than "to be understood": trivial examples are animal training and verbal conditioning; they can be used as symbols, as in rituals and certain kinds of literature.

Consequently, a theory of the acquisition of language would have to be based on a theory of the developmental changes in the knower–symbolization–known relationship: in other words, on genetic epistemology. On the other hand, it would also have to be based on a theory of the formal properties of language, in other words, on linguistic theory. To understand *how* something is acquired, we first have to know *what* is acquired.

Modern linguistics (since de Saussure) has been concerned with the establishment of systems of elements and procedures for making inventories of elements (segmentation, substitution, association, classification, and so on), For this reason, Chomsky (1964) calls this type of theory taxonomic linguistics.

Taxonomic linguistics was combined with associationist learning theory to produce theories of language acquisition that left honest observers of young children mystified and that failed completely to account for the fundamental fact of language: the ability to produce and to understand an indefinite number of sentences that have not been previously heard. The comparative ease and rapidity with which young children learn their mother tongue remained completely mysterious as long as both the learning organism and the verbal behavior to be learned were thought to be as amorphous in structure as associationist theory supposed them to be. Thanks to Chomsky's nontaxonomic theory of language, which aims at a system of rules rather than at a system of elements, our insight into the structural properties of natural languages has so far deepened that it becomes possible to begin to envisage a theory of language acquisition which would be in accordance with the linguistic facts, with the known facts about children's verbal behavior, and with the theory of cognitive development in general. Chomsky's theories are most often referred to as "transformational linguistics" or "generative grammar," highlighting two important aspects of his conception of language.

While no attempt is made to summarize Chomsky's far-reaching theory, it seems necessary to underline certain points that have often led to confusion.

A generative grammar is an explicit description of the internalized rules of a language as they must have been mastered by an idealized speaker-hearer. It is adequate insofar as it corresponds to the intuition of the native speaker. However, it is *not* a model of performance; first, the speaker-hearer may not be aware of (or even capable of becoming aware of) the grammatical rules; and second, and more profoundly, the grammar assigns a structural description to a sentence, but the derivation of this sentence as made explicit by the grammar does not tell us how a speaker actually (and psychologically) proceeds to produce the utterance.

A generative grammar is said to be descriptively adequate if it meets the criterion of corresponding to the competence of the native speaker. It is said to attain explanatory adequacy if it is linked to a theory of language that deals with the form of human language as such (and not only of the particular language). In this case it contains an account of linguistic universals. It is the universal grammar that deals with the creative aspect of language. General linguistic theory would ultimately provide a theory of the fundamental form of possible human languages and of the strategies necessary for selecting a particular grammar. In this sense, general linguistics belongs to epistemology; in this sense, also, it would give an explanatory model of language acquisition.

A generative grammar contains a system of rules that have three components—syntactic, phonologic and semantic. The syntactic rules account for the creative aspect of language. The phonologic and semantic components are purely interpretive. The syntactic component consists of a base, which generates deep structures according to certain rules. The basic strings of elements form a highly restricted set; within this set there is a subset of "kernel" sentences. These kernel sentences (exemplified by simple affirmative-active sentences) have played an important role in psycholinguistic experimentation, though often in a confused way. The rules of the base are a very special class of those that are studied in recursive function theory, and may be mostly universal, and thus not part of particular grammars. In addition to the base, the syntactic component contains a transformational subcomponent. These transformational rules are concerned with generating a sentence—with its surface structure—from the base. Elementary transformational rules are drawn from a base set of substitutions, deletions, and adjunctions.

This necessarily superficial account of transformational linguistics, points to its deep concern with the creative aspect and epistemology of language. Because of this epistemological position, a psycholinguist who accepts Chomsky's theories of generative grammars for particular languages, cannot at the same time simply reject his, be it tentative, model of language acquisition. His model is still in the nature of a hypothesis; and though many of his fundamental discoveries about language seem to stem from the fact that he considers the problem from the viewpoint of a language acquisition device, not all assumed properties of the device would appear to be necessary to the theory as a whole. The following is a brief discussion of Chomsky's (and his followers') hypotheses about the device and of the points on which a Piagetian psychologist would raise objections.

Katz (1966; following Chomsky, 1957, 1965) who uses the model of a language acquisition device that has as its output the internalized linguistic rules and as its input speech (and, he adds, other relevant data from senses), shows conclusively that such an input is far too impoverished to produce the rules if the device were to be constructed according to empiricist, associationist hypotheses. Up to this point, a Piagetian psychologist cannot but agree. Subsequently, however, Katz develops the rationalist hypothesis that "the language acquisition device contains as innate structure each of the principles stated within the theory of language." Once again, we encounter the epistemological dilemma of structuralism without development or geneticism without structure. But is the choice really restricted to these two extremes? And is it necessary, in order to enrich the internal structure of the learning organism, to postulate innate linguistic structures?

Chomsky's own treatment of the rationalist hypothesis seems at the same time more cautious, more supple, and more far-reaching than that given by Katz. Chomsky poses the problem as follows:

> A theory of linguistic structure that aims for explanatory adequacy incorporates an account of linguistic universals, and it attributes tacit knowledge of these universals to the child. It proposes, then, that the child approaches the data with the presumption that they are drawn from a language of a certain well-defined type, his problem being to determine which of the (humanly) possible languages is that of the community in which he is placed. Language learning would be impossible unless this were the case. The important question is: What are the initial assumptions concerning the nature of the language that the child brings to language learning, and how detailed and specific is the innate schema (the general definition of "grammar") that gradually becomes more explicit and differentiated as the child learns the language? For the present we cannot come at all close to making a hypothesis about innate schemata that is rich, detailed and specific enough to account for the fact of language acquisition (1965).

And

> A consideration of the character of the grammar that is acquired, the degenerate quality and narrowly limited extent of the available data, the striking uniformity of the resulting grammars, and their independence of intelligence, motivation and emotional state, over wide ranges of variation, leave little hope that much of the structure of language can be learned by an organism initially uninformed as to its general character. . . . The real problem is that of developing a hypothesis about initial structure that is sufficiently rich to account for acquisition of language, yet not so rich as to be inconsistent with the known diversity of language (1965).

From the point of view of developmental psychology, three criticisms can be made:

1. This view of language acquisition fails to take into account the knower–symbolization–known relationship indicated above; it only considers language as the object of knowledge in the knower–known relationship.

2. It assumes tacitly that from the moment the child starts to understand language and to talk, he somehow considers language as a system of signs (as opposed to signals and symbols).

3. No account at all is taken of the structural richness of the learning organism as demonstrated by the acquisitions during the preverbal sensorimotor period.

In other words, there would be agreement on the nature of the output, i.e., the internalized grammar, and also on the need for postulating a structural richness within the acquisition device. But there would be disagreement on the degree of innateness of the·structure of the device and on the nature of the input, which would be much richer and more structured than merely speech samples of a limited and degenerate quality plus (unspecified) "other data from senses."

Much of the need for postulating specific, innate linguistic structures seems to vanish if one considers language acquisition within the total cognitive development and, in particular, within the frame of the symbolic function. This manner of considering language acquisition would moreover be compatible with two facts that seem to be difficult to explain within the theory of innate structures: (1) the time lag between the first manifestations of practical intelligence during the sensorimotor period and the first verbal productions; (2) the particular character of these first verbal productions.

Concomitant with the development of the symbolic function, the child changes from an organism that reacts to objects and events as signals to a being that "knows" objects and events and expresses this "knowledge" by means of signifiers. His knowing, however, is always "acting upon," and the first use of signifiers is only possible in function of the internal richness of coordinated action schemes. His first verbal productions recognizable as "words" are far from being signs in the sense of belonging to a fully structured system. They resemble far more symbols, which can be loosely associated but are essentially isolated representations of schemes. They share the characteristic of symbols in that they are inextricably entwined in the complex of objects, actions the subject can perform on objects, and symbolic representation of the objects. In Piaget's terms (1945), the first words "retain the imitative character of the symbol, either as onomatopoaeia (imitation of the object) or as imitation of words used in adult language, but extracted from this language and imitated in isolation. Especially, they retain the disconcerting mobility of symbols, in contrast to the fixity of signs." And (1945) "The first language consists almost solely in orders and expression of desire. Denomination is not the simple attribution of a name, but the expression of a possible action." Examples abound in all recordings of child language; to quote two of Piaget's examples:

> J. around 1;6 knows better and better how to take advantage of adults to get what she wants; her grandfather is especially docile in this respect. The term *panana* ("grandpère") is used not only to indicate her grandfather, but also to express, even in his absence, her desires; she points to what she wishes to have and adds *panana*. She even says *panana* to express a wish to be amused when she is bored.
>
> L. at 1;5 uses the term *a plus* ("il n'y en a plus," or something similar, but, of course, *a plus* should not be taken to represent two separate words) to indicate a departure, then to indicate the throwing of an object onto the floor, then it is applied to an object that falls over (without disappearing) for instance when he is playing with building blocks. A little later *a plus* means "remoteness" (anything out of reach), and the game of handing over an object for somebody to throw it back to him. Finally, at 1;7 *a plus* takes on the meaning of "to start over again."

The transition from what Piaget calls *jugements d'action* to *jugements de constatation* takes place soon after: "words" then no longer simply translate sensorimotor action, but describe past actions and events (though usually in the immediate past). At this point begins the slow transition from symbols to real signs, which furnish a re-representation; and at this point the first concatenations of words begin to appear.

Both these facts, the relatively late start of the first verbal productions, and their particular character, seem difficult to reconcile with the theory of innate linguistic structures. The time lag might conceivably be explained by an allusion to imprinting and critical periods: Katz (1966), speaking about the fact that the effortless way in which children appear to acquire a language terminates at about puberty, says, "thus this ability of the child's is much like the abilities of various animals described as imprinting with respect to the existence of a 'critical' period." The peculiar character of the first productions, coupled with the fact that these do not yet show real concatenations of words, might lead a staunch adherent of the theory of innate structures to refuse these verbal schemes the status of linguistic productions. This seems, however, completely unjustified psychologically; whatever their nature, they most certainly prepare the way for further verbal acquisition, and moreover they already have some of the traits of signs: they show a certain detachment from the subject's own actions and a desire to communicate by way of sound-complexes which the other person also uses.

It seems more in accordance with the facts, though less simple, to suppose that the coordination of sensorimotor schemes, which are actively built up during the first 18 months of life, starting from hereditary reflexes, is a necessary condition for language acquisition to become possible, which, like all manifestations of the symbolic function, takes place within a context of imitation. It is true that Chomsky remarks (1965), "It would not be at all surprising to find that normal language learning requires use of language in real-life situations, in some way." However, according to him, this would not affect the *manner* in which the acquisition of syntax proceeds. In our view, however, the way in which sensorimotor schemes, coordinated into practical groups, become transformed into operations would determine the manner in which the linguistic structures are acquired. Though it is not possible to make hypotheses about this mechanism detailed enough to account for language acquisition, this approach to the problem seems nearer to the psychologic truth. The Genevan research on the parallelism of language acquisition and operational development of which a few examples have been given, indicates that this hypothesis is at least not in contradiction with the admittedly very few and limited results obtained so far.

Two other experiments (1970, 1971) also give results that seem to run counter to the inate structure hypothesis. Briefly, the technique is as follows. We give the child a collection of toys, dolls, cars, animals, sponges, sticks, cups, and so on, and we ask him "to act out" with these objects a sentence we pronounce, after an introductory period during which the child gives names to the dolls, tells us something about the toys, and such. The sentences used are simple active and passive affirmative ones. We use different kinds of verbs, and "reversible" as well as "irreversible" sentences (reversible: "Peter washes John" or "the red marble pushes the blue marble"; irreversible: "Peter washs his car"). Inversely, we perform an act with some of the toys and we ask the children to tell us what happened. We also try to elicit passive sentences by asking the child to start his sentence with the noun indicating the object of the action performed. (We let Peter wash his car and we ask "Now tell us what happened; but I would like you to start this way: the car. . . .") Finally we perform the action and at the same time we pronounce the passive sentence; then we ask whether what we said was correct, and we ask the child to repeat it.

To mention only one of the types of behavior that appear in this experiment, and which we are still far from being able to interpret conclusively, at about four and a half years old several subjects decode a passive sentence into a reciprocal act: "Peter is washed by Mary" is acted so that Peter and Mary both take a sponge and wash each other; "the red marble is pushed by the blue marble" is acted by taking a marble in each hand and making them hit each other, whereas the corresponding active sentence is acted by taking the blue marble in one hand, leaving the red marble on the table and hitting the latter with the blue one. In the items where we try to elicit passive sentences, the children also produce sentences in this way: "*Pierre et Marie se lavent*," "*La bille rouge et la bille bleu roulent ensemble*." We also find passive sentences decoded according to active word order: "Peter is washed by Mary" is acted as "Peter washes Mary." In these items some children also say that what we ask them is impossible: "you can't start with Peter, it's Mary who washes." It is the reciprocities that intrigue us most; and it seems that they cannot be accounted for by a triggering of innate structures.

Epistemologically, the difference between Piaget and Chomsky seems important, but the two are certainly much nearer to each other than either is to a defender of the empiricist point of view. Moreover, their difference may be less marked than it appears. For instance, Chomsky (1965) warns us that what he is describing as the process of acquisition is an idealization in which only the moment of the acquisition of correct grammar is considered. He adds: ". . . it might very well be true that a series of successively more detailed and highly structured schemata (corresponding to maturational stages, but perhaps in part themselves determined in form by earlier steps of language acquisition) are applied to the data at successive stages of language acquisition." This seems to indicate that his position is much less extreme than is often thought. However, without knowing more precisely what is means by "schemata" and "maturational stages" it is difficult to interpret remarks such as these.

It is clear that we are in great need of experimental results. As far as experiments go, approaches starting from either Piaget's or Chomsky's theories would have several points in common. They would share the emphasis put on the creative aspect of language. They would share also the wish to make a clear distinction between performance and competence. Where Chomsky (1964) only seems to stress the fact that performance is bound to appear far poorer than an investigation (if this were possible) of real competence would show the latter to be, the Piagetian psycholinguist would add that there is also the opposite danger, namely, that performance can easily induce an overrating of competence. We would assume that the verbal productions of the child may contain prestructures and pseudostructures, just as there are preconcepts and pseudoconservations; the prestructures would be isolated instances of certain syntactic structures, strongly content-bound and context-bound; pseudostructures would be strongly imitation-bound. The prestructures are both important and understandable within a developmental interactionist theory; they would be hard to explain within the rationalist theory. The main difference between the two approaches corresponds to the fundamental epistemological difference that has been stressed all along in this chapter the Piagetian psycholinguist would always try to study language as part of the symbolic function, within the frame of the total cognitive activity of the child rather than as an autonomous "object of knowing."

14

Epistemology and the Study of Language

HERMINE SINCLAIR

It seems that everyone with an epistemological axe to grind has used language as a grindstone. Only fairly recently, though, has the question of language itself as a type of knowledge rather than as an instrument for expressing knowledge been brought to the fore. It is now more and more widely accepted that linguistics is the study of knowledge of a certain type, and a rather special type at that, and that therefore it belongs either to psychology or to epistemology or to both.

In Piaget's view, the task of epistemology is to understand the nature of human knowledge in the different fields; one of his postulates is that this can only be achieved through the study of how knowledge has been constructed. More specifically, what Piaget calls "genetic epistemology" is the study of how knowledge has progressed from early, simple forms to more complex and powerful constructs. This genetic epistemology uses several sources of data:

1. The study of the cognitive development of the child, i.e., the study of the gradual construction and elaboration of basic concepts, rather than that of the acquisition of particular skills and the learning of specific information.

2. The study of the history of science, from the point of view of how a level of knowledge that surpasses a previous level has been reached, what it was in one theory that paved the way for the creation of new scientific knowledge.

3. Formal models of the state of some scientific knowledge at one particular point in time. Such formal models presuppose the existence of experimentally determined laws or regularities and the choice of an abstract deductive framework. This framework renders precise otherwise imprecise deductions and permits the discovery of new relations between regularities and laws. These formal models do not exclude or prejudge the existence of a "real substrate," such as society, or physiologic and neurologic maturation.

These three sources complement each other in many ways. The study of the cognitive development of the child allows us to go back to the roots of knowledge—in logic, in physics, in mathematics, etc. Reciprocally, the history of science can provide fruitful insight into what problems to study, what questions to ask, and generally what to look for in cognitive development. Obviously, no question of ontogeny and history is intended. It could be hoped that formal models would give us more precise indications as to acquisition processes than just suggestions about what problems to study; however, this does not seem to be the case at the moment, and the use of formal linguistic models for the study of language acquisition has been particularly contested (for discussion of this problem, cf. Mehler, 1969; Bever, 1970; Watt, 1970). Of course, formal models, even if they are "generative" in the mathematical sense, are mainly output, or structural models; and what genetic epistemology and developmental psychology look for are process models. Developmental psychology, by contrasts, has been fruitful for epistemological studies beyond the limits of a simple provision of working hypotheses; however, this is due to the establishment of cognitive universals—or basic concepts—and of developmental stages in cognition rather than to attempts at formalization.

Before going into the question of the study of language and its importance for our understanding of the nature of human knowledge in general, it may be useful to clarify certain terms of developmental psychology, such as *basic concepts* and *cognitive stages*.

BASIC CONCEPTS

There are different kinds of basic concepts, but roughly they may be divided into logicomathematical concepts on the one hand, and concepts belonging to physics on the other. Though not acquired in exactly the same way, both kinds of knowledge depend on the subject's interaction with the environment, the accent being on *action*. The experiences resulting from this interaction are constructed by the child according to his competence—i.e., his level of cognitive structuring. It is to be stressed that the terms *interaction* and *environment* should not be taken in a narrow sense. Interaction and action are not restricted to manipulating, and environment is not restricted to concrete objects. Making mud pies, planting flowers, and constructing mechano-models may be important activities for children, but so are being fed or dressed, looking at objects from different angles, cuddling toy bears, and communicating with other people, at whatever level of competence.

Logicomathematical knowledge derives from the actions of the subject, from their coordination and integration, and does not depend on particular properties of objects. To take one of Piaget's favorite examples, whether a collection of pebbles is divided into a group of three on one side and of four on the other, or a group of two on one side and five on the other, makes no difference to the total sum of the pebbles. Finding this out does not depend on the characteristics of pebbles, but on the organization of the action patterns and their results. Whether these actions are performed on biscuits, blocks, or pebbles makes no difference to the logical result, as long as the objects are solid; drops of water or milk would not be suitable. From many experiments it seems clear that children arrive at the concept of natural numbers (with all that this concept entails: additivity, commutativity, ordinality, cardinality, etc.) via an understanding of one-to-one correspondences. This is one of the many examples where a· scientific discipline rediscovers, or at least explicity states, a concept that existed many centuries earlier: barter, or the exchange of one object for another, preceeded arithmetic, but it was only Cantor who formulated the principle and used it to construct transfinite numbers.

Physical concepts are also action-dependent, but by contrast with logicomathematical notions they imply knowledge of object properties. Finding out that certain objects float and that others sink does depend on the particular properties of the objects involved, and not only on the organization of the subject's actions. Knowledge of object properties and the capacity to design and profit from experiments depends also, at least partly, on the presence of logical structures. The distinction between the two types of knowledge should not be seen as a dichotomy, but rather as a polarization, with logic at one pole and physics at the other. Evidently, since logicomathematical knowledge is acquired through action, and since it can only experimentally be observed through action (at least in children and in adult nonmathematicians), experiments always include real objects; the knowledge gained, however, does not depend on their specific properties. The same problem exists in language experiments: since very few subjects can be asked to deal with uninterpreted structures, research on syntax always has a lexical aspect as well.

The polarization of the two different types of knowledge becomes more marked as the child grows older. During the preverbal stage of practical intelligence, the distinction only indicates that actions present two aspects: each particular activity provides the occasion for the apprehension of object-properties and as such it prepares the future notions of physics, but at the same time each particular action is repeatable and generalizable to different objects, and it can be coordinated with other actions; as such it constitutes the source of later logicomathematical structures. Despite this close connection between the two aspects, it is supposed that until the appearance of the first concrete operations there is a predominance of the physical-causal aspect over the logical aspect (Piaget and Garcia, 1971). The young child is mainly interested in obtaining a certain result, and less likely to reflect on the organization of actions necessary to obtain this result. However, the application of action patterns to new objects often presents a problem, and the child's desire to solve this problem can provide the occasion for new constructs on the logical, deductive plane.

In much the same way, the child begins by uttering lexical, information-bearing elements; the syntactic structure is hidden in what is generalizable in the combination patterns. Just as in the case of the discovery of object-properties, the acquisition of new lexical items raises syntactic problems. Consider, for instance, the syntactic problems inherent in the first apprehension and use of the word *see*, as in the following conversation with a two year old. Mother: "See Daddy? He's cleaning the car." Child: "Daddy car." Mother: "He can see that we're ready and waiting." Child: "Daddy see."

In Piaget's view, cognitive development proceeds through the active construction of a gradually widening and at the same time more solid framework of logical thinking and of a progressively more ordered world of physical objects. Much, if not most, of this development takes place so to say subterraneously, without any direct change in behavior being observable. Piaget's well-known tasks tap this basic knowledge and allow us to observe the transition from one type of solution or manipulation to another. The acquisition of these basic concepts does not depend on external reinforcements, and they are never lost, except in pathologic cases. Their elaboration does depend, of course, on a stimulating environment in general and on discussion and contact with other people, just as it depends on physiologic and neurologic maturation. What is acquired is neither an externally imposed link between events, to which the subject passively submits (as extreme empiricists would maintain), nor an emergence of latent, inborn concepts released by experience which only acts as a catalyst (as extreme rationalists would maintain).

STAGES IN COGNITIVE DEVELOPMENT

Piaget's formalization of the successive stages in cognitive development consists of structural models of the output of the knowing subject. At the same time, Piaget is concerned with the process itself; and although on this point he has not gone as far in the construction of a formal model, it is clear from many of his works that his process model is of a biologic type, based on regulatory mechanisms. Just as lower organisms compensate for disturbances (brought about by the environment) through a recombination of already existing elements, which results in a new adaptative complex, new patterns of thought grow out of the combination of already existing patterns—with the possible difference that it is precisely the growing thought patterns themselves that create the disturbance. By assimilating more and more varied contents a certain pattern of thought or action will encounter an obstacle to which it cannot be accommodated; the subject will then search for a different, but allied pattern, which is already established, and will find a new combination to deal with the situation, thereby creating a new pattern. In this way, each acquisition opens up possibilities for conflicts, whose resolution leads to new constructs. Cognitive functioning, as observed in actual behavior, always presents two aspects: an assimilatory, i.e., generalizable and in a sense abstract aspect, and an accommodatory aspect, i.e., the adjustment to a unique situation. The cognitive stages themselves are species-specific, but the regulatory mechanisms by which transition from one stage or substage to another takes place are rooted in the biology of all living organisms. Since these mechanisms are linked to the underlying structures, they acquire a special significance in the human context.

Both structures and mechanisms are universal. Cognitive development is obviously dependent upon environment and external stimulation, but apparently very little on specific situations. Many experiments have shown that environment can accelerate, retard, or stop development, but that the successive stages are maintained (Bovet, 1968; Dasen, 1970). However, physics concepts may be more content-bound than logical concepts, and this is certainly true of any but the simplest physical notions.

This constructivist view of cognitive development in children as being governed by processes that are rooted in biology is also the main tenet of Piaget's theory about human knowledge in general. Epistemology is seen as the study of the gradual construction of more and more powerful insights and theories, and its task is mainly to understand this succession of new constructs. The human mind neither passively undergoes outside reality, arriving at more and more exact copies of this reality, nor is it equipped with *a priori* concepts that only need activating by the environment. It actively constructs more and more powerful logicomathematical frameworks and it acts upon and transforms reality. Reduction theories have no place in this conception of human knowledge: one cannot maintain that every more complex structure or theory should be reduced to the more simple, earlier one; e.g., it is impossible to translate electromagnetism into classical mechanics. Vital biologic processes cannot be reduced to physicochemical reactions. Logic, by constructing operations on operations, is far more than a simple notation of judgments derived from experience. In psychology, stimulus–response theories cannot account for cognitive development. A different, but equally reductionist, trend is represented by vitalist or finalist theories which equate the more simple theory with the complex one, considering the complex theory as already contained in the simple one. In Piaget's view, the history of science and the development of the child show that more powerful constructs are genuine novelties, derived by transformations from earlier ones. The cognitive development of the child demonstrates that the first forms of knowledge are far more different from later forms than could have been expected, and that the latter's construction is far less predictable than was thought.

LANGUAGE ACQUISITION

What is the role of language in cognitive development and what is the course of its acquisition?

In Piaget's view, language is one of the manifestations of the symbolic or representative function. This capacity of representing absent objects and events, by mental images, by gestures, by play, or by language, is essential to thought; without it, we would not progress beyond the practical intelligence of apes and infants. However, this does not mean that knowledge of one or more of the natural languages is necessary for the development of thought, but only that some kind of symbolization is required. Though fortunately it becomes more difficult to find deaf-born children who at the age of primary schooling are found to possess virtually no language at all (neither a natural language in its written form nor any type of conventional sign language), several researchers have conclusively shown that such children solve cognitive problems in the same way as normal children when these are presented in a nonverbal way (Furth, 1966, 1970). This confirms Piaget's theory that knowledge has its roots in sensorimotor activity, and that its logical organization is not derived from language. How deaf-born children arrive at sufficiently precise and mobile representation without the use of language is a fascinating problem, but there is no doubt that they do so without the help of what to hearing subjects is the most handy and usual system of representation and communication.

Language is different from other means of representation. In the first place, language is conventional. In other representational activities the subject can invent his own symbols and make his own rules, but to communicate verbally he has to adopt the language of his community. In the second place, language is a highly structured system with intricate rules; other representational activities may imply techniques (drawing) and creative behavior inside a common framework (dramatic play), but no knowledge comparable to that of grammar (though a special position is occupied by games such as chess—de Saussure's favorite analogy with language).

Comparisons between animal communication patterns and human language are hazardous; no animal species appears to have anything approaching grammar. Still, studies of animal communication are valuable for the study of human language (quite apart from their intrinsic interest and fascination)—if only because they stress some essential differences.

Certain birds do not seem to be able to change the vocalizations of their species no matter what experiences they are subjected to. Others, mostly song birds, can adopt the pattern of foster parents, or they can even be brought to imitate human beings. Thorpe (1969) has shown that if chaffinches are reared in a soundproof room or deafened at birth, they develop "what you might call the most elementary schema of what is normally regarded as the song of the species." With deaf-born infants, no such schema emerges. Vocalizations indicating distress, discontent, pleasure, surprise, etc., appear during the first months but tend to disappear soon afterwards. We cannot rear infants in soundproofed rooms, and no demonstration exists that human infants, if left alone together, would not elaborate something resembling a natural language. Some such process must have taken place in prehistoric times. However, several cases are known of hearing children born to deaf parents; until they come into contact with talking people these children do not develop any kind of verbal pattern. In contrast to cognitive development, language acquisition depends on exposure to a specific model. Since this is clearly the case, many psychologists have supposed that language learning is simply a result of associative, imitative learning, and that cognitive development only intervenes in the use the subject makes of what he has learned. Since Chomsky's critique of this view, no serious psycholinguist can continue to defend it. Moreover, any parent or teacher knows only too well that children actively construct their language: *he goed, I taked it, my foots*, are not mere imitations of expressions heard, but examples of rule-governed behavior.

How does the very young child acquire such rules as plural and past-tense formation to the point that he applies them in cases where adults do not? How does it happen that young children, the world over, whatever language they hear spoken around them, seem to go about their language acquisition task in the same manner? They all start their careers as communicators by conventional language with holophrastic utterances such as *aplu, alle alle, allgone, 'nito* (all indicating absence or disappearance); they then progress to two- and three-word utterances, *sock dirty, Papa parti*, and at least in the early period one gets the impression (confirmed by many observations in many different languages [cf. Slobin, 1968]) that they go about their language acquisition task in exactly the same way: paying attention to and producing certain, but not all, features of the speech they hear around them, creating rules that have something to do with adult sentence patterns, but whose results are far from a parrotlike imitation.

Language acquisition reminds us forcibly of the fact that all natural languages are the creation of the human mind and that they must have characteristics in common. Traditional grammarians were interested in language universals, but in more recent times this interest was frowned upon until Chomsky revived the question. Language learning and the form it takes would be impossible unless the child approached the learning of his mother tongue with some idea of what the structure of human language is like—some way of treating the quite heterogeneous samples of speech he hears around him. As Chomsky puts it: "What are the initial assumptions concerning the nature of language the child brings to language learning, and how detailed and specific is the innate schema . . . that gradually becomes more explicit and differentiated as the child learns the language? (1965)." But for the word "innate," Genevan psycholinguists agree that this is the important question. In our view, however, it is precisely the fact that this initial schema is not innate in the obvious sense (though it may be so in the sense of a predisposition) that can provide hypotheses about the child's assumptions. Children do not start to talk (in the sense of communicating about reality by conventional words) before they are in their second year. By that time they have reached a certain level of practical intelligence that shows structural properties which Piaget has brought to light. This intelligence-in-action is the basis for all later cognitive constructs which elaborate on different levels the initial grouplike structure. We would like to suggest that this group of action patterns also serves as the heuristic model for language learning; that it is precisely what the child (every child) has learned during his first 18 months or so which provides him with the necessary assumptions to start language learning. That these assumptions are adequate for doing so is due to the fact that there exist language universals. In a certain sense, something like a basic schema of human language *does* exist, and so does a set of basic assumptions permitting an oriented approach to the input. Both derive from fundamental properties of the human mind and therefore, in a sense, from neurologic coordinations.

As already mentioned, it can be supposed that the two poles of human knowledge are also reflected in language behavior; a parallel can be drawn between the acquisition of lexical items and knowledge of properties of physical reality, on the one hand, and between syntactic structure and logical organization of action and thought patterns on the other.

Natural languages, however, have moved far away from any hypothetical "basic schema." After a first period of language acquisition the differences in the learning of mother tongues become more marked than the similarities—although quite striking correspondences in experiments and observations have been noted. Something very like the progressive integration and differentiation of action and thought patterns as described by Piaget also seems to take place in language learning. Ervin (1964), for example, has noticed that such irregular plurals as *feet* appear at first as isolated items, apparently without connection with the rest of the plural system which is being elaborated. Subsequently, these forms are absorbed into the system, and appear as *foots, feets,* and even *feetses.* A little later they reappear in their correct form, but this time, one supposes, they are exceptions to a system rather than isolated items. Similar phenomena have been observed in Klima and Bellugi's (1966) account of negation formation; *can't* and *won't* appear as unanalyzed entities before the appearance of *can* and *will.* The auxiliary system takes a long time in getting installed.

These well-known phenomena suggest an active construction process on the part of the subject in interaction with his environment. Experimental work on the comprehension of sentences by young children also shows, in our opinion, such active construction or elaboration of underlying syntactic substructures in close connection with cognitive development in general. Other psycholinguists have proposed different explanations: e.g., Bever (1970) and Mehler and Bever (1968) who argue that rather than new structures being elaborated, more adequate perceptual strategies account for changes in performance.

It may well be that our knowledge of the course of language acquisition is still so poor that as yet it hardly clarifies the epistemological problem of the nature of human language. Nevertheless, the study of acquisition is certainly one of the main sources, if not the most important one, for any theory of language that aims at explanatory adequacy.

DIACHRONIC AND COMPARATIVE LINGUISTICS

How about the second source of epistemological information, history?

Historical linguistics has always been concerned with reconstruction, but until recently mainly with the establishment of hypothetical original forms. Nevertheless, as expressed by Watkins,

> we are in a position now to study the dynamic aspects of the process
> of linguistic development and frame hypotheses about them. . . . A
> problem in historical linguistics today presents two aspects: on the one
> hand the establishment, by the techniques of the comparative method,
> of an arbitrary initial stage of the phenomenon, and on the other
> hand a reconstruction of the historical processes whereby the
> original system was more or less eliminated, transformed, or restructured
> in the form in which it may appear in the different systems of the
> historical languages (1969).

However, this constructivist, or reconstructivist approach to language has as yet few facts to offer for the study of the nature of human language. Our knowledge of the history of human languages is extremely fragmentary and does not extend beyond certain narrow spatiotemporal limits. Nevertheless, an example of work done in this spirit is that of Benveniste (1958). In his paper on the functionally primordial position of the third-person singular (characteristically published in a psychologic journal), Benveniste explains this position within the verbal paradigm by psychologic arguments. The fundamental role of the third person singular is that of pure predication, divorced from the implications of "personalness" (first and second person) and "subjectivity" (first person). The first- and second-person singular are often marked by special desinences, whereas the third person is typically the bare stem without ending. Moreover, the tendency to derive the other persons from the third-person singular which either has a zero ending, or is *felt* to be the bare stem, is present in many languages and at many points in time: it therefore constitutes a kind of dynamic constant.

An example of the possibility of combining formal models with a reconstructive approach is given in the work of Postal (1968) on diachronic sound change, who, like Halle (1962) appeals to child language to arrive at an explanatory hypothesis. Postal's examples and technical discussion are convincing, but his explanatory hypothesis (1968) may seem far-fetched. His conclusion is worth quoting:

> . . . following Halle, we agree that sound change is of at least two
> different types. First there is the addition of rules to the grammar.
> This, he points out, is the only way the grammar of adults may change.
> However, since the addition of a rule R to a Grammar G1 may
> define a language of which the optimal grammar is not G1 + R, it
> follows that children in the next generation will in such cases learn not
> this, but the optimal grammar, in effect yielding a different type
> of sound change.

Until we know much more about language acquisition, this hypothesis will remain untested; but clearly the study of the acquisition of language also has its part to play in phonologic studies.

Despite this new constructivist approach, historical linguistics has hardly ever been used to construct hypotheses for the study of acquisition processes, as Piaget has done with cognitive development and the history of logic and physics. An example is a study by Bronckart on the acquisition of the verbal system (Bronckart and Sinclair, 1973).

Since Ferreiro (1971) completed her study of temporal relations in child language, Bronckart undertook an investigation of aspectual relations in children's use of verbal forms. Ferreiro's work contains some indications of the fact that young children seem to use what to adults are forms expressing relations of anteriority, posteriority, and simultaneity as aspectual distinctions, i.e., to express a temporal or modal contour of the action described. Bronckart also uses the technique of asking children to describe simple events acted out by the experimenter. For instance, a sheep jumps over a fence, or takes a series of short hops over several barriers, to arrive at the barn; a doll is made to cry either six or seven times in rapid succession, giving separate small wails, or in one long drawn-out cry. In some more complex items two events are presented, either successively or simultaneously, and taking up different or equal amounts of time. The results show that, at least for the youngest subjects, verbal forms are not felt to express temporal relationships; these forms are indeed used to express aspectual and modal differences. We would like to suggest that such findings can be in some way connected with historical analyses (from which the working hypothesis was derived in this experiment), as for example elaborated by Kurylowitz (1956), Watkins (1969), and Ivanov and Toporov (mentioned by Watkins). *Grosso modo*, the latter authors suggest that the injunctive (cf. injunctive forms in Vedic, which constitute one of the oldest layers in the Indo-European verbal system) represents the predecessor of the entire indicative system. Watkins remarks: "They are surely right in maintaining the original absence of temporal oppositions in the verb; but the existence of the perfect implies at least one aspectual correlative in the system . . . (1969)." Many facts, indeed, point to the very early existence of an opposition between perfective and imperfective. The latter opposition is easily modified into a temporal opposition: past-present. The place of the future is left unfilled, but this function is often taken over by an older desiderative. In the different historically attested languages such functional rebuilding of the verbal system did not necessarily take place in the same manner; but to all of them can be applied Slobin's dictum (1973) about language acquisition: "New forms first serve old functions, new functions are first expressed by old forms." Bronckart's results suggest that something like the proposed evolution of the verbal system from proto-European to historically attested languages takes place in the elaboration by the child of the adult verb system (which retains, in French, a certain mixture of temporal, modal, and aspectual relations).

We cannot but be intrigued by the parallel between certain hypotheses of Watkins (1969) and McNeill's (1970) proposal of nouns as strong linguistic universals. Discussing the -s morpheme with reference to the sigmatic aorist, Watkins affirms that the origin of the -s is to be sought in the configuration of root with final enlargment -s-. The original radial form in final -s becomes reinterpreted as a third-person singular with zero ending; on this basis the rest of the paradigm is supplied. Finally, through analogy with other third person singular forms showing a phonetic body, the third-person singular with zero ending is itself transformed. It is Watkins' hypothesis about the original function of enlarged root forms that interests us:

> ... when we consider the neutral, intransitive value still present in such forms in the historical period, as well as the formal identity of -s with the mark of the nominative singular, then it is hard to avoid the supposition that the formation was originally nominal. We may tentatively suggest that such nominal forms could be used simply predicatively [in historical linguistics, asterisks indicate hypothetical, reconstructed forms]:
>
> > * Hnecks 'unnatural death (occurred)'
> > * preks 'asking (occurred).'
>
> The syntatic point of contact between the nominal and verbal expression could have been furnished by the nominal phrase where no verb at all is present" (1969).

Let us emphasize once again that we have no intention of equating such historical evolution with language-acquisition processes. We would rather insist on their heuristic value. In fact, holophrastic and two-word utterances show many parallels with Watkins' historical hypothesis. We would, however, hesitate to assume that the verbal formation was originally nominal, preferring, at least for language acquisition, the hypothesis that originally verbal and nominal predicate forms are fused, and that only later differentiation takes place.

FORMAL MODELS

The third source of our understanding of human knowledge, formal models, is certainly the main contribution of modern linguistics to the study of the nature of human language. Since Chomsky proposed his first formalizations of grammar, we have gained a far deeper insight into the fundamental features of language in general. These formalizations are structural models rather than process models, though they have been applied to the study of production, understanding, and acquisition of language as well. Many other papers deal with this aspect of the problem, and we will not insist on it. Though direct applications of formal structural models are being questioned nowadays, a theory of acquisition will certainly have to incorporate some model of the structure of the native speaker's linguistic competence.

So far, it has been argued that linguistic theory as a theory about the fundamental nature of human language is still in its beginnings and will have to combine the study of acquisition, of historical change, of comparisons between different languages, and of structural models of grammar to reach an explanatory level.

The other side of the question of epistemology and language is the following: will an as yet to be established theory of language contribute to our understanding of human knowledge in general?

On the one hand, it can be argued that language is no more than a special kind of symbolic representation and communication, and that its nature is such that it has to be distinguished from those aspects of knowing which are able to produce novelties. As expressed by Furth (1970), the understanding of a symbol cannot exceed the available level of operative understanding—"operative" meaning understanding acquired by actions, either concrete or formal. From this point of view language plays the role assigned by positivists to logic: it is no more than a formal translation of physical experience, which does not in itself create new structures. If in the case of logic the assignment of such a subordinate role appears unjustified, in the case of natural languages it would appear plausible. It is difficult to imagine that language creates new structures that announce or make possible new scientific discoveries—language would then be richer and more powerful than what it describes. If language is indeed essentially a system of representations (and a rather inadequate one at that), it lacks the capacity of creating new knowledge and as such it would take a subordinate place in epistemology.

On the other hand, it might be argued that modern linguistics, with Chomsky's distinction between deep and surface structure, has come closer to other disciplines, such as biology and mathematics. Biology has shown that the classic idea of organisms passively reacting to their environment has to be replaced by a concept of constant interaction. Man, as a knowing subject, can hardly be an exception and simply faithfully record outside events. Mathematics, by its very nature, goes beyond observable phenomena. Physics and chemistry transform reality and create new objects, which, in Piaget's (1970a) words, not only enrich our knowledge of reality, but also enrich reality itself. In these sciences the tendency to look for unobservable structures before attempting experiments has become very strong in the last decades. Similarly, modern linguistics searches for underlying, unobservable structures, and, as in other sciences, it seeks to construct models and formalizations. Moreover, if from the point of view of language in general and its historical development, it is difficult to maintain the existence of the creation of knowledge, for the child the situation is different: he does create new linguistic knowledge, even if this creation is a re-creation. What the child hears are actual utterances, which are only particular instances of underlying structures, and what he has to acquire is the unobservable system. Starting from what has to be a simple heuristic model, he becomes a fluent speaker who has no trouble understanding and producing an infinite number of sentences he has never heard in exactly the same form before—that is to say, a person who some-how implicity knows the system. This is no doubt a constructive and creative cognitive activity. Moreover, it is an activity which all humans indulge in very often indeed, and which, *pace* Washoe, is species-specific. Since language is a creation of the human mind, its study should help us to understand the nature of human knowledge. From this point of view we reach the opposite conclusion: the study of language is indeed an important part of epistemology.

FOUR

Psychopathology

15

Some Pathologic Phenomena Analyzed in the Perspective of Developmental Psychology

BÄRBEL INHELDER

In this section, I would like to discuss certain pathologic phenomena that have been analyzed in the perspective of developmental psychology during some of our studies at the University of Geneva. The following fields are involved: reasoning of the mentally retarded child, reasoning of the senile dement, reasoning of the so-called "pre-psychotic" child, and operativity and impairment of symbolic imagery in the dysphasic, dyslexic, or dyspraxic child. The discussion will follow that same order.

THE REASONING OF THE MENTALLY RETARDED CHILD

Our investigations on mentally retarded children (Inhelder, 1963) have shown that their reasoning is characterized by fixations or blocking of the operational activity at different stages of development. Their reasoning is also marked by the difficulty of integration from one level to the next, which in normal children assures the functional continuity of development. With mentally retarded children the operational construction remains unachieved. The imbecile remains fixed at a preoperational level and is ignorant of the principles of conservation. In contrast to these extreme cases, the retarded child attains in the course of his development the possibility of forming an integrated set of concrete operations without, however, acquiring even the slightest notion of formal operations. The developmental sequence of stages is, nonetheless, the same as that of normal children; the developmental speed differs. Whereas the normal child passes relatively rapidly through the various stages, the mentally retarded child follows the same development at a slower pace. Furthermore, when the retardate attains his upper limit, his reasoning often shows traces of previous levels. With the normal child the passage from one level to the next is accomplished more and more rapidly, which goes with the growing mobility of operational thought. But with mentally retarded children we observe a gradual slowing up of development, leading to stagnation. Whereas the thought of a normal child evolves with a progressive equilibration of operations, the reasoning of the mentally retarded child seems to end up in a type of false equilibrium, characterized by a certain viscosity of thought.

During recent years, we have been particularly interested in inferior and superior borderline cases in mental retardation. We have today an array of operational assessment methods at our disposal to demonstrate the various levels of concrete and formal thought, and we have been wondering whether all mentally retarded children reason in the same way.

Our first results indicate that in severely retarded, almost imbecile children there exists a striking homogeneity between the different forms of reasoning. This enables us to determine with precision the underlying structure of their operativity. The homogeneity is more evident in severely retarded children than in young children whose mental development is unimpaired.

It is for this reason that certain retardates between the ages of 12 and 13 years who have been assessed by about 20 measures of the operational type are situated, according to the hierarchic scale established by Vinh-Bang (in preparation), at a level characteristic of a normal 6 year old. It goes without saying, however, that the way in which they tackle the problems, their interest, and the way they make use of information are quite different from those of the normal younger child with his intellectually dynamic approach. It is, nevertheless, striking to see how the different arguments and justifications of the mentally retarded child are more or less isomorphic with those that we know in young children when they effect the passage from preoperational thinking to the first signs of operational thinking.

Some interesting observations have also been made on children 12 to 13 years old who are at the upper borderline of retardation. We have already characterized this borderline by a fixation at the level of the attainment of concrete thought. With these subjects, we find a very similar level of achievement in concrete operations—not only as regards conservation, but also in all the other operations such as classification, probability, geometric constructions, etc. However, we do not find even the beginnings of formal operations in any of these subjects. In fact, as soon as we present these backward children with problems whose solution requires a formal level of organization—for example, a combinatorial system—they do not behave like normal preadolescents of 10 or 11, but like young children of 6 or 7 who would be performing the most elementary concrete operations. Thus, it seems that as soon as the problem becomes too complex, the mentally retarded child gives up the idea of trying to organize the situation and simply repeats the same actions over and over again, in the hope that an accumulation of repetitions will, sooner or later, in some way have the desired effect.

Operational theory thus has a contribution to make to the understanding of pathologic phenomena, which in turn enrich operational theory.

The studies on mentally retarded children permit us not only to analyze the levels of operational construction, but also furnish us with hypotheses on the laws governing normal and pathologic states—for example, completion of structural levels in normal children and closure of structural levels in mentally retarded children.

With the mentally retarded child who has reached his ceiling, we seem to be in the presence of a systematic closure that is quite different from the completed system observed in the normal child. With the latter, a system is said to be completed when it has attained such a level of structuration that each of the elements has become consolidated with the others. A system completed in this way becomes capable of being integrated into larger systems. The completed system thus constitutes at the same time an opening; it has within it the germ of further development. In the mentally retarded child, however, access to certain structures seems to be an end in itself, without hope of subsequent evolution. Ceiling and closure are terms that suggest themselves, rather than completion or fulfillment. And this closure cannot really be said to lead to a state of equilibrium, since only a passive stability is attained. It does not seem exaggerated to us, therefore, to speak of a false equilibrium when we are talking about states that reach an apparent stability but which are subject to a certain viscosity.

THE REASONING OF THE SENILE DEMENT

It is true that we tend today to accord primarily a heuristic value to Hughlings Jackson's hypothesis on the hierarchic dissolution in the aged, and that today nobody really expects to find at the core of the degenerative process an inversion of the mechanisms of genesis. Nevertheless, it is interesting to compare the degeneration of certain modes of thought in the aged, in particular their mental operations, to those of normal children and mentally retarded children.

This comparison is possible nowadays, thanks to the research work carried out by J. de Ajuriaguerra, L. Tissot, and their collaborators Monique Rey-Bellet-Muller, H. Sinclair, and Marianne Boehme. In their comprehensive neuropsychiatric studies on senile degeneration they have used a number of our operational assessment methods. The results obtained clearly show that persons afflicted with senile dementia reason in a similar way to children at different levels of development. (See de Ajuriaguerra *et al.*, 1964; Sinclair *et al.*, 1966.)

Generally speaking, the more advanced the disintegration, the more we see the progressive breaking-up of operational structures. Some old people, who are only slightly impaired, are still able to handle problems that call for superior concrete operations, yet show themselves incapable of dealing with operations that require a formal level of reasoning On the other hand, other old people who, according to many neurologic symptoms, show a far more serious deterioration but whose case histories do not suggest any presenile impairment demonstrate reasoning processes that are clearly preoperational. Finally, in several cases of older people who have been observed over long periods of time, we note the gradual and progressive breaking-down of operativity.

The disintegration, it is true, does not affect operativity in a uniform manner. What seems to happen is that the operations concerning spatial relations and physical transformations deteriorate more rapidly than those of the logical and mathematical type. Yet we also find, in a more pronounced manner than with mentally retarded children, forms of reasoning that now operate on one level, now on another. And, in addition, we also sometimes find certain residues of the superior reasoning processes within inferior processes.

A preliminary study of the verbal patterns used by the senile dement, as compared to those of the child of the same operational level, reveals some interesting facts (Inhelder, 1965; Sinclair *et al.*, 1966). The senile person seems first of all to lose the possibility of understanding and carrying out verbal orders, while descriptive verbal patterns of a higher level are retained for a longer time. These verbal patterns seem to have become automatized and are often attached only to the static aspects of the situation. For instance, the relationships involved in the terms *more* and *less* may no longer be understood, but expressions such as "this pencil is longer" will still be used correctly. Or, the simultaneity or succession expressed by different tenses in a sentence may have no meaning for the subject, but he will be able to use the future tense correctly in a sentence containing the word "tomorrow." On the whole, however, there remains a certain parallelism between the deterioration of the instruments of communication and the processes of operational construction.

These few indications show that the disintegration of operativity, far more than that of social instruments of communication, seems to obey a law approximately corresponding to the inversion of developmental progression. We have here, indirectly, proof that the operational constructions are not entirely a cultural product. These constructions, whose inversion is seen in cases of senile dementia, seem to reflect more or less faithfully the laws regulating their developmental integration.

THE REASONING OF THE "PRE-PSYCHOTIC" CHILD

It is interesting, with the help of our operational assessment methods, to examine children and adolescents whose reality-testing behavior is so disturbed that one is inclined to call them "pre-psychotic."

These children, who suffer above all from difficulties in making contact with other people, show a type of reasoning whose main feature is what we call a deforming assimilation of reality. That is to say, their representation of the external world is often distorted and even their reasoning is disturbed. Discordances within the operational activity are especially striking (Inhelder, 1965). Within a reasoning process of a higher level, we often see arguments that decidedly belong to an inferior level. It is interesting to note that the reasoning processes most affected seem to be those concerned with problems of conservation. With respect to these problems the "pre-psychotic" child manifests primitive levels of reasoning. These infantile forms of thought differ, however, from those observed in the mentally retarded child—not only by their great incoherence, but also by the type of argument and explanation given. The justifications of these "pre-psychotic" children often reveal a lack of differentiation between the "self" and the external world and comprise a host of magical representations. This aspect has been investigated first by de Ajuriaguerra *et al.* (1959), then by Inhelder (1965) and Schmid-Kitsikis (1969).

The thought disturbances of the "pre-psychotic" child differ very clearly, however, from those which can sometimes be observed in the neurotic child. In the course of a neurotic child's reasoning processes—which in other aspects are normal—we often find exaggerated oscillations between two successive levels of thought. These oscillations, we feel, can to a certain extent be considered as symptoms of anxiety, indecision, fear to commit oneself, etc. With such children, however, we rarely find an abnormal distortion of their reasoning processes as such. "Pre-psychotic" children, on the contrary, seem to remain in a sort of intellectual and emotional adualism. They develop numerous avoidance and withdrawal mechanisms in order to escape from encounters with other people and with the facts of "physical reality." They have a tendency to assimilate in an egocentric manner the information received, and to alter it according to the needs and fears which dominate them.

These few observations would indicate that the elaboration and development of operativity depend not only on internal regulations but also require a motivational force that is directed toward adapting the person to reality. The disturbing effects which contact with other people has on the operativity of the child indicate that the formation of intellectual structures is closely tied to the adaptive functions of thought. Here again, psycho-pathologic studies show the interaction between emotional and cognitive aspects of development.

OPERATIVITY AND IMPAIRMENT OF SYMBOLIC IMAGERY IN THE DYSPHASIC, DYSLEXIC, OR DYSPRAXIC CHILD

Whenever a child with an impairment of language (de Ajuriaguerra *et al.*, 1963; Inhelder, 1965; Inhelder and Siotis 1963), or of reading or writing, can be shown to have a normal development potential—that is, when he has attained a certain operational level and displays a certain functional mobility of thought——it is important to know the extent to which his impairment is associated with a deficiency in symbolic be-havior and, in particular, with the evocation and anticipation of symbolic imagery.

As already indicated, we have been able to demonstrate a synchro-nism in the evolution of operations and that of symbolic imagery. In children with one of the impairments just mentioned, we frequently observe a gap between operative and figurative aspects of thought. And though their operational development is within the normal range, their symbolic imagery is at a less advanced level. For example, such a child may well be able to solve a conservation problem, but nevertheless exhibits typical phenomena of the static aspects of imagery and has difficulties in anticipa-tion. Both this gap and the difficulties in image formation lead us to sup-pose a specific deficiency of symbolic behavior. Similar discrepancies have been noted in the case of so-called dyslexic or dyspraxic children by our colleagues in France (Stambak *et al.*, 1964).

This discordance is even more striking in the case of young adult aphasics. As Tissot and his co-workers have observed, these aphasics may be able to construct certain combinatory systems characteristic of a formal level of thought but, at the same time, have extremely infantile forms of symbolic imagery and great difficulty in anticipating displacements and transformations of figures (Tissot *et al.*, 1964).

Our research work in all of the fields I have discussed here is, of course, continuing at the University at Geneva.

FINAL REMARKS

To summarize, I have tried to bring out in this paper the usefulness of applying to pathologic phenomena what we know about the cognitive development of the normal child. On the one hand, pathologic phenomena of thought are more comprehensible when analyzed in developmental perspective; on the other, the analysis of pathologic aspects of thought enriches the operational theory. In conclusion, the following points merit reiteration.

1. Discordance between the figurative and the cognitive aspects of an evolution lends weight to the developmental hypothesis that the operational construction is relatively independent of its symbolic support. In fact, it would seem that the operativity directs the progress of symbolism: when the development of symbolic behavior is obstructed, the child can go beyond and compensate for the difficulty. The transformation from static imagery to anticipatory imagery is mainly due to operativity. However, the image, in return, favors the functioning of operations, although it does not modify their structure in any way. Thus, it would seem that there is no complete reciprocity between the operative and figurative aspects of thought.

2. The fact that cognitive operations disintegrate, roughly speaking, in an order that is inverse to their evolution seems to us to confirm the notion that the development of operativity is an integrational process.

3. The studies of the mentally retarded child not only allow us to analyze the modes of transition from one operational level to another; they also furnish us with hypotheses on the laws governing normal and pathologic equilibria which reveal themselves, *inter alia*, in the completion of structural levels in normal children and in the closure or "ceiling" in mentally retarded children.

4. The disturbing effects that the distortion of interpersonal relations has on the operativity of the "pre-psychotic" child show us how intimately the formation of cognitive structures is linked to the adaptive function of thought. Here again, the mutually sustaining and complementary roles of psychopathology, psychoanalysis, and the study of cognitive development become increasingly clear. The emotional and the intellectual aspects of development cannot be dissociated, and a study of the dynamics of cognitive function finds its necessary counterpart in a study of the dynamics of emotional development. It is fortunate indeed that, when seen from this point of view, results obtained by research in either of these fields illuminate and confirm results obtained by research in the other.

16

Operatory
Thought Processes
in Psychotic Children

BÄRBEL INHELDER

Many psychopathologists are interested in Piagetian theory, mostly from a psychoanalytical point of view. We think that this theory of cognitive development also plays an important part in highlighting abnormal aspects of cognition. Mental retardation has long been studied from this angle. Until recently, however, child psychosis did not seem to lend itself to this approach. It might well seem that abnormal phenomena of the thought processes in child psychosis cannot be systematized as they may be in retardates. Recently, however, this approach has proved fruitful in the study of senile dementia and sensory deficit (blind or deaf children). Since then, I have been using this approach in a study of psychotic children. At first sight, it seems as if the pervading character of the very individual meanings these children attach to their physical environment and to the human beings who surround them makes it impossible to diagnose the cognitive levels and operatory thought processes. However, we have been able to distinguish some general characteristics from among the welter of individual particularities.

We* selected three types of experiments to be carried out with

* This study forms part of a research project undertaken in collaboration with Professor Ajuriaguerra and his colleagues from the Geneva University Psychiatric Clinic.

our first group of boys, aged between 10.4 and 15 years. All these subjects were able to communicate verbally, though often in a very limited manner due to their illness. They had all been under psychiatric care for about 10 years and the majority had experienced hallucinations.

The first type of experiment required logical class operations and took the form of inclusion and class-intersection problems. We used pictures in these experiments. The second required the physical or spatio-temporal operations underlying the concepts of conservation of matter. These experiments involved the transformation of a ball of plasticine or the dissolution of a lump of sugar in water. The third required the combinatory operations underlying the concept of probability. The child's probabilistic knowledge was tested by means of one experiment using counters with a circle on one side and a cross on the other (a sort of "heads or tails" experiment); another involved drawing lots and a third used what was essentially a roulette wheel.

Our *method of investigation* is as follows: while we carry out the experiments we keep up a continual clinical dialogue with the child. Although we follow the wandering thought of the young patient, we nevertheless try to center the child's attention on cognitive problems. Since the child sometimes becomes disturbed through our insistence on his giving reasons for his answers, he does not always give as good an answer as he might otherwise have done, but by this method we can discover the child's particular difficulties. These bear on his relationship with other people and his deformation and subjective assimilation of reality.

For this brief discussion, I should like to limit myself to describing some striking phenomena in subjects ranging from children at the level of elementary concrete operations to those who have reached the transition to formal operations. Between these two categories, we know, there is a wide range of concrete thought operations. We already know which of these operations are developed synchronously and where décalages occur in normal children. On one hand, we have the logicoarithmetic operations which are acquired when a child, for whom material objects only exist to be acted upon (classifying, ordering, counting), becomes able to coordinate his own actions; on the other, we have the physical operations which are also known as spatiotemporal or infralogical operations. The latter are also developed from the subject's actions, but this time the actions transform reality and in return are themselves modified by reality.

Probabilistic reasoning, which aims at organizing "chance events," cannot be worked out deductively. It requires the development of concrete and formal operations, even though these cannot be applied directly to chance events. By analyzing the thought of young patients in this developmental framework, we think it is possible to determine some abnormal constants. I shall describe some of the most striking. The most salient characteristics are the great "ups and downs" observed even during the space of one relatively short interview.

We believe that we can distinguish two groups of children from among our sample population: those whose thought structure is perfectly integrated (and either corresponds to their age level or is even more advanced) and those whose integration is only partial and consequently extremely fragile. The first abnormal constant is that these children cannot understand and assimilate chance phenomena and refuse to reason in probabilistic terms.

Even the children in the first category who have acquired the first formal operations and who show by their reasoning that their concrete operations are completely integrated (in fact only one case out of ten) are particularly reticent when it comes to chance phenomena. They act as if they consider everything in the world to be deducible. Therefore, as soon as they can no longer assimilate reality to simple causal sequences or predictable frequency of occurrence, they refuse to guess or to give a probabilistic judgment. Clearly, they do not lack the ability to work out the logicomathematical operations underlying the chance concepts (combinatory and proportion operations). Their difficulty stems simply from the fact that they find themselves face to face with uncertainty. The children who are at a less advanced operatory stage often imagine that there is some magical force at work or that the experimenter is tricking them. The boundary between the physical and the human world seems at times to be extremely woolly, the psychotic child sometimes falling back into primitive adualism of thought.

The second abnormal characteristic is the relative inferiority of physical operations in relation to logicoarithmetical operations. With children whose concrete operations are only partially developed, we notice, to varying degrees, a discordance illustrating an abnormal décalage between the capability of carrying out logical inclusion operations and those of conservation of matter at the corresponding level. With the mentally deficient child, we have noticed that the décalage is rather the other way round, since this child does less well in experiments concerning logic than those concerning physical matter. Hatwell (1966) also found this greater difficulty in coordinating actions concerned with transformations and compositions in the physical world in children who were either born blind or became blind very early in life. Stambak (Stambak *et al.*, 1964) also found this (but to a lesser degree) in the dyspraxic children she studied. In young psychotic children, as in those with sensorimotor or praxic deficiency, exchanges with the physical world are more or less deeply disturbed and their thought operations seem to be affected by this.

The third abnormal constant concerned the difficulty these children find in handling logical relations and more particularly the concept of conservation of continuous quantity. The physical concepts of conservation, or rather the structures underlying them, are extremely stable in normal thought. By contrast, in a psychotic child these concepts seem very fragile. It often happens that when the child has at long last acquired them, he suddenly reverts back to a much earlier stage of thought. And even in the rare cases where these concepts seem firmly established, we find that the operatory processes which underlie their formation are hardly ever the same as those of normal children. With the latter, the arguments which reveal these formative processes bear both on the compensations of the transformations (reciprocal operations) and on reversibility (canceling) and identity. In psychotic children whose reasoning is not completely integrated, we note almost exclusively arguments of identity, only exceptionally arguments of reversibility, and no valid arguments of compensation in the transformation of the dimensions of the type "longer but thinner," etc. It looks as if these children tend to mentally break up contents into fragments, or even countable units, but find themselves incapable when it comes to mastering the concept of conservation of continuous quantity.

Their difficulty is shown clearly, for instance, in the abnormally wide décalage between their solution of the conservation problem in the experiment concerning the changing shape of the ball of plasticine and that concerning the dissolution of sugar. The psychotic child, due in fact to his need to deal with fragments, easily brings a certain atomistic intuition to bear on the question and can picture the sugar in the form of little grains to count, but cannot represent the continuous process of transformation linking the initial to the final state and vice versa. This system of operations in the normal child precedes an attempt at an atomistic explanation. For the psychotic child, the sugar is first of all there and then suddenly it is "dead" as some of them say.

It is possible—but this remains to be proved through more adequate experiments—that beyond the particular difficulty of mentally compensating for the transformations carried out and grasped by the reciprocal mental operations, the psychotic child has more difficulty in handling logical relations than logical classes. His language is in fact poor in comparative terms and is more like that of the children at a preoperatory level studied by Sinclair (1967a).

The last abnormal constant I shall mention concerns the fixed aspect of the symbolic function and the particular difficulties these children find in reasoning from assumptions.

To understand the operatory tests, the child must accept the make-believe put forward by the experimenter: we shall play with the plasticine as if it were a cake; we shall pretend that the Indians have chased all the birds. To abstract a common characteristic (for instance color) we show pictures of green (or some other color) leaves, cats, etc. It is strange to find that children between 10 and 15 years old, who seem to be living in an imaginary world full of phantoms, have such great difficulty in indulging in the make-believe so popular with normal young children. But it is one thing to be enclosed in one's own imaginary world and quite another to share other people's imaginary worlds, and especially that of one's questioner. First, the psychotic child has great difficulty in getting away from himself and his subjective world. In addition, for the child to have a full range of possible actions from which he can freely choose within his grasp, his semiotic function must be operating normally. He must also be able to substitute symbols and signs for reality, have an elementary knowledge about the difference between the signifier and the significate, and realize that symbols are not part of reality itself but indicate it. In fact, everything leads us to believe that it is the symbolic function which is disturbed or has become static in these young patients. Their thoughts often lack consistency and they cannot conform to the behavior standards of their group. In addition, they also lack creativity, despite the fact that their thought is often full of imagery.

The dominant characteristics concerning the functioning of thought which we have briefly described stem from three types of troubles: (1) disturbance of the relationship with others (revealed in an inability to decentrate), (2) disturbance in the mastering of the physical world (revealed by the instability of the adualism), and (3) disturbances of symbolic activity (characterized by the various ways the child is unable to differentiate between symbols and signs on the one hand and reality on the other).

These studies are, however, only in the early stages, and it is far too early to draw clear conclusions. Nevertheless, I should like to emphasize two points: first, as is so often the case, results from psychopathologic studies can contribute to the explanatory aspect of developmental psychology through the dissociation of factors which often takes place in pathology; second, our procedures and assessment methods make it possible, at least to a certain degree, to avoid the widespread tendency to explore cognitive and emotional phenomena by means of totally different tests and methods. It is true that nobody would deny the link between cognition and personality structure, but the relationship between the two and even their partial similarity can be demonstrated in a particularly clear fashion by using the developmental frame of reference. On the one hand, the disturbing and sometimes spectacular cases of child psychosis can, through this kind of analysis, throw light on the normal mechanisms, and on the other, our comprehension of normal development gives us a better understanding of the dissociations and abnormal functioning found in pathology.

SUMMARY

Although the various examples I have given may seem rather disparate, they are nevertheless linked both by the experimental approach and by the underlying theoretical concepts. In fact, the convergence of fundamental research and its application for diagnostic purposes is illustrated in each of the three fields I have briefly described.

17

The Cognitive Mechanisms Underlying Problem-Solving in Psychotic and Mentally Retarded Children

ELSA SCHMID-KITSIKIS

INTRODUCTION

Few things are known about how the psychotic child acquires the basic logical thought structures. Most experimental work has sought to analyze the intellectual activity of these subjects in terms of the efficiency aspect. But not everyone is in total agreement concerning this: is the psychotic more productive in verbal or nonverbal fields? Are his conceptualization abilities inferior, superior, or equal to his other intellectual performances? On the other hand, much work along the same line has concerned the mentally retarded, and the problem of the homogeneity or heterogeneity of the levels of intellectual performance has been much debated. Finally, comparisons between these two groups of subjects have stressed the importance and meaning of the respective deficiencies.

The IQ analysis and the performance on different activity tests of these subjects have often brought to light contradictory results. The outline we shall draw here can only be skeletal. We may note the work of Goldfarb (1961) and Heuyer *et al.* (1956) who find in psychotics better verbal than nonverbal performances, Gillies (1965), Viitamaki (1964), and Wassing (1965) who find the contrary, Moor (1968) and Perrimond

---

Translated by Harold Chipman. Dr. Schmid-Kitsikis has also published under the name of Elsa Siotis.

(1965) who find no difference between these two types of production. Furthermore, we know how the concept of heterochronology attributed by Zazzo to the mentally retarded has given rise to controversy. But the performance analysis of both groups has shown new ways of approach. Direct observation has enabled Norman (1948) to account for how the psychotic gathers knowledge about object properties. Through the study of language in the psychotic and the mentally retarded, Kanner and Eisenberg (1955), Goldfarb *et al.* (1956, 1959), Garonne *et al.* (1969), and Luria (1961) have attempted to define the importance of the acquisition of verbal signification for direct verbal exchange and its positive role in the subject's subsequent development.

Certain investigations, mostly based on a longitudinal approach, have aimed at defining among other factors the rhythm of intellectual development (Lestang-Gaultier and Duché, 1967; Lockyer and Rutter, 1970). Finally, most researchers use the observation of behavior as the framework for interpretation of the particular intellectual productions. One has thus been able to establish a sort of catalog of the clinical characteristics of these subjects. Such inventories, while being strongly contested, are still frequently reproduced—for the mentally retarded: the lack of flexibility and adaptation, the persistence of animistic thinking, the flight into basic simple activities, attention span problems, etc.; for the psychotic: withdrawal with regard to human beings, the piecemeal character of habitual activity, the rich content of delirious manifestations, a seemingly "intelligent" and "expressive" expression, the greater facility of contact with objects, etc. (Kanner, 1943, 1968; Lecuyer, 1967; Aubin *et al.*, 1956). Concerning intellectually regressive psychoses, the work of Misès and Perron-Borelli (1972) and Lang (1969) stresses the difficulties encountered when attempting to dissociate so-called psychotic symptoms from retardation symptoms.

The experimental analysis of the dynamic aspect of reasoning beyond a volunteer learning situation has hardly been studied despite the importance of the problem: Inhelder (1963), Ajuriaguerra *et al.* (1969), Schmid-Kitsikis (1969). Furthermore, experimental attempts at comparing the dynamic thought processes of the two groups have not been systematic. Despite the fact that, in certain psychiatric milieus, the opinion persists that it is erroneous to distinguish psychosis from retardation as separate nosologic entities, our quick overview of the different research trends has shown that the problem is far from being solved, even in the case of intellectually regressive psychoses.

With the aim of understanding better the mental functioning of these subjects, we have undertaken a large-scale experimental and comparative study of which we shall present the first and exploratory phase. Our analysis and interpretation of the first results will permit us, we hope, to outline new dimensions for research.

THEORETICAL BACKGROUND TO OUR
EXPERIMENTS

We have undertaken our work within the Piagetian cognitive-developmental framework. In the course of the experimental task, we shall seek to note the information the subject gathers about objects and events (and this supposes the use of his assimilatory capacities); the information the subject derives from his own activity; and the type of inferences he formulates. If, as Piaget has written, the experimental subject may be defined as a "centre of functioning" since "facts imply the attribution of structures to the subject," our analysis of pathologic thought processes will seek to evidence, in the subject's constructions, forms of groping, corrections or precorrections of errors with intervening anticipatory mechanisms. These different types of construction will enable us to evaluate the stability of a given response in a given experimental situation, the manner in which the subject develops new coordinations to cope with a novel situation, how the subject modifies a situation which in turn requires, depending on the type of modification, the elaboration or not of new coordinations.

Our study will focus particularly on the coherence of thought processes in the course of their equilibration, with an aim to define the nature and role of contradictions that operate in the form of groping and self-correction, which in turn depend on a fundamental aspect of structural constructions: assimilation. Thus, as structures are formed (essentially but not solely) through assimilation, the analysis of the subjects' different modes of groping and self-correction, based upon the knowledge they derive from objects, events, or their own problem-solving activity, will tell us something about both the level reached by the different schemes and the possibility of developing new ones.

Our investigation concerns psychotic and mentally retarded children. With regard to the commonly admitted clinical characteristics of psychotic subjects, we find a perturbed relationship with the outside world and insufficient cognitive investments. With regard to the retarded subject, we find a poor relationship with the outside world and an insufficient level of cognitive realizations. Furthermore, it is generally admitted (which does not imply that we shall adopt this point of view) that it is the conflicting nature of the psychotic subject's interaction with the outside world that is responsible for the poor cognitive investments whereas in the case of the mentally retarded, inversely, the poverty of his interaction with the outside world is due to his insufficient intellectual capacities.

While voluntarily remaining descriptive in order to avoid an over-simplified explanatory outline, we can admit that, in both cases, the poverty of the cognitive sphere is an essential characteristic. What differs is the subject's relationship to the outside world. In the case of the psychotic there is either absence of this relationship owing to total withdrawal from reality, or a distortion of this relationship owing to the constant impinging of phantasmatic life in real life; in the case of the retarded, it is the extent and variety of the exchanges that are restricted.

Piagetian theory stresses the various interaction processes that intervene in cognitive development and that enable the elaboration and maintenance of a certain level of equilibration. This enables us to define the objectives of our study as follows and without commenting further at this point on the controversy that the distinction between retardation and psychosis may have caused.

1. Concerning the modes of cognitive organization in each group, we shall seek to analyze:

The degree of stability of an experimental response in a given situation.

The subject's capacity to develop new coordinations in a modified situation.

The subject's capacity to modify a situation in terms of a previously defined goal.

The experimental problem-solving procedures used in the course of the equilibration process.

The type of relationship between intellectual activity and outside interferences, and the subject's capacity to overcome these.

The coherence of the thought processes involved.

2. Concerning the comparison of the two groups:

Is it possible for the subjects of both groups to develop a stable cognitive construction process independently of their level of achievement and using an equilibrated action coordination system?

If this is not the case, does the state of disequilibrium entail special types of problem-solving procedures: discordances, deviations, fluctuations? If these special types exist, are they the same for both groups?

PRELIMINARY EXPERIMENTAL DATA

Population

Within a group of psychotic subjects presenting an intellectual deficit, we selected 15 subjects presenting an early psychotic syndrome. Furthermore, we chose 15 mentally retarded subjects presenting no evidence of organic damage. The age range for both groups was 9 to 12 years of age. All the children came from specialized institutions. The diagnosis of psychosis or mental retardation was formally explicated in a dossier for each child which contained all the usual information derived from school and family and the results of different medical examinations. The IQ range for each group, established by a competent consultative service or ourselves, varied between 60 and 75. All these subjects attended special education classes which were often mixed. The teachers frequently pointed out to us that the school performance of the psychotic children was inferior to that of the mentally retarded.

Type of Experimentation

Each child was interviewed separately by an experimenter. On the average, there were seven to eight sessions per child. The entire interview was recorded, and the manipulations, gestures, and emotional reactions were immediately transcribed. The subjects were encouraged to be as active as possible. Our approach was "clinical" and we tried, while maintaining a basic guideline in interrogations and presentation of items, to follow the subject, adapting our questions to his reactions.

Experimental Tasks

Four types of notion were investigated: one-to-one numerical correspondence (Piaget and Szeminska, 1941), invariance of physical quantities (Piaget and Inhelder, 1962), classification (Piaget and Inhelder, 1959), and spatial arrangements—a synthesis of the operations of combination and permutation (Piaget and Inhelder, 1951). This choice was not random in that it corresponds to two major preoccupations.

1. As the analysis of the experimental procedure will show, these tasks entail a variety of problem-solving activities.

a. The subject must assess the result of transformations modifying the appearance of an object.

b. The subject must, after verbal instruction, produce an organized totality from randomly placed objects through anticipation and direct action on the task materials.

c. The subject must, after verbal instruction, discover through successive constructions, real or anticipated (the experimenter gradually provides the necessary elements) the law which governs these constructions, a law which he must formulate and justify. He must integrate intermediate solutions into the following ones by a mechanism of retrocation and anticipation. Only short-term goals are imposed.

In analyzing the different types of interaction, we wanted to see whether the subject uses the same problem-solving procedures in the case where he simply has to assess the result of a transformation bearing on the appearance of an object and in the case where he has to effect a transformation on an object in terms of a more or less distant goal and then comment on the result of his own activity.

2. The tasks and the type of problem-solving procedures they elicit in the normal child are well documented and lend themselves quite easily to experimentation in pathology thanks to the variety of controls they permit. We thus felt it would be possible to show how pathologic

subjects attain logicomathematical structures, and what means they have to solve tasks dependent upon them.

EXPERIMENTAL PROCEDURE

Physical and Numerical Invariants

We selected five experimental tasks of increasing complexity which were proposed successively to the subjects according to the degree of operatory reasoning they exhibited. These tasks involve two notions: numerical equivalence in a one-to-one correspondence; and conservation of total quantities (liquids, matter), weight, and volume.

All tasks require the same procedure. The subject is at first confronted with two collections of objects numerically equivalent, or with two objects of equal quantity, and this equivalence or quantity is to be noted by the subject. Second, one of these objects or collections is transformed so that the physical appearance is modified. Third, the subject is asked to emit a judgment as to the quantity involved.

At the end of each task, we used a series of suggestions and control questions which enabled us to judge whether the preoperatory subjects had been able to develop new forms of thinking thanks to this kind of help. The control conditions were as follows: if a subject progressed with a first task, he was not subjected to the others, and so on.

1. The subject is asked to add or subtract a certain number of elements: liquid, matter, so as to reestablish the initial equality while maintaining the modification of appearance. The reestablishing of the initial shape or configuration may enable the subject to become aware of his errors and perhaps to rectify them.

2. The subject is asked to carry out the transformation himself, but slowly and following the contours of the object with his hands. For instance, he is asked to flatten the plasticine sausage he has to assess while checking with the free hand the varying dimensions of the object. After each slight transformation, the subject is asked to describe the object and refer to the original model and to determine the quantity of the transformed object. The sausage is thus totally flattened and elongated. The inverse procedure is then initiated, and the subject is asked to foresee what will happen. If there is progress in his reasoning, the subject is tested by means of a different standard task in order to assess the nature of the progress. This helping procedure is kept in the task concerning weight and volume, but the checks are rendered easier by the visual or empirical nature of the child's verifications (weighing, looking at water levels).

3. The subject is confronted with three equal plasticine balls A, B, C instead of only two. A remains as such, but the same transformation is carried out on B and C with, however, a certain time lag. More precisely,

the subject flattens B a little, C is flattened a little more and so on. The successive assessments bear on A and B, A and C, B and C. With this control situation, the child's notion of transitivity may be assessed. The effect of these facilitating procedures is always checked by means of different tasks.

Classification Notions

The subject first is asked to explore a rectangular plank on which 36 objects of geometric shape are glued. Their characteristics are: difference of shape (3), difference of color (3), difference of size (2). The subject is asked to classify these exhaustively and to specify each time the criterion he selects, as well as the number of envelopes to be used for the elements to be placed therein. After each attempt at classification, the subject is asked to return to the starting point and imagine another type of classification.

Second, the objects are no longer glued to a board but lie in disorder in front of the child who is then asked to classify these by this time acting upon the objects. Different pieces of paper instead of envelopes are used for the different "heaps." Before each classification, the child is asked to announce his choice of criterion. The difference between these two task variants lies in the spatial aspect of the latter procedure. This may help or perturb the subject. On the other hand, the action of classifying may enable a tighter control of the different choices of criteria since each of the subject's actions leaves fewer objects to be classified. The procedures may be summarized as follows:

1. The subject must announce his choice of criterion in order to prevent eventual digressions from the initial activity.
2. The subject hands the objects to be classified to the experimenter who puts them in the envelopes. He must therefore bear in mind what objects are in the hidden collection and this enables the experimenter to assess whether the choosing of the objects by the child himself has some reinforcement value.
3. The experimenter may suggest novel classifications by initiating new forms of classification himself.
4. The number of objects used may be diminished in the face of exceptional difficulties encountered by the child.

Arrangement Notions

In front of a series of numbers written on small pieces of cardboard, the subject is asked to construct the possible series of two digit numbers. Numbers with 1 and 2 are used, then 3 and so on. The law governing these arrangements is a synthesis of the operations of permutation and combination. The subject who discovers the law is asked to explain it.

The following variants were introduced if the subjects had evident difficulty:

1. The subject is presented with all the necessary numbers plus one or two more. For example, in order to arrange the 1's and 2's, there are five number 1 figures and five number 2 figures. The child is asked to combine these in all possible ways avoiding repetition of the same number. Later on, the same task is required for the numbers 1 and 3, 2 and 3, and then the subject is asked to state which numbers are missing. The task is to constitute the entire series using the best disposition of the objects.

2. If the number of elements is too great for the subject, only the numbers used for the construction of a series starting with the same numbers are given, for instance, all the numbers starting with 1. The subject is asked to continue the series by asking for the figures he requires. The experimenter seeks to assess whether the child conceives any limit to the number of arrangements and whether the child realizes the necessity of adding numbers so as to avoid repetition. The subjects who progressed during this task were submitted to a control two weeks later using the same task.

EXPERIMENTAL RESULTS

Physical and Numerical Invariants

In order to facilitate descriptions, the tasks will be referred to as follows: numerical equivalence (1), quantity of liquids (2), quantity of matter (3), weight (4), and volume (5).

Mentally Retarded Subjects

Spontaneous Reasoning

Three subjects out of the 15 are at a preoperatory level as evidenced in our tasks. In the numerical equivalence task, they deny the equivalence when the visual one-to-one correspondence is destroyed. However, the return to the initial one-to-one correspondence provokes a renewed assertion of equivalence. Preoperatory reasoning is also evidenced on tasks 2 and 3.

Three subjects attain numerical equivalence through counting activity during the experiment. A repetition of the same task two weeks later evidences the maintenance of the equivalence notion. Preoperatory behavior is exhibited in tasks 2 and 3, with however, correct anticipation of the increase in water level in the thin glass of task 2. The arguments given center on one of the dimensions only.

Five of the subjects attain the conservation of liquids level in task 2 but remain preoperatory on tasks 3 and 4. Only one subject attains conservation of matter without help during the experiment and derives this notion from the possibility of regrouping the bits of plasticine into the original ball. However, the conservation reasoning disappears in the face of extensive physical modifications (total flattening of the sausage). The spontaneous argumentation of these subjects is somewhat rigid, persistently referring to the initial state of equality.

Three subjects exhibit conservation behavior on task 3, but remain preoperatory on 4 and 5. Two subjects are immediately "conserving" in their reasoning, and one develops conservation behavior in the course of the experiment. The latter is consistently operatory in the face of any type of physical transformation and even concludes that "one can make any shape, it's always the same." The conservation notions are evidenced in similar tasks carried out two weeks later. These three subjects are noteworthy in that their conservation reasoning seems totally sure and unhesitant despite all physical transformations carried out in front of them. They always refer to the original situation in their justifications, and, as staunchly as they admit conservation in task 3, as staunchly do they deny it in task 4 despite spontaneous weighing behavior carried out symbolically in reference to their own bodies.

Finally, only one subject asserts conservation in task 4 despite some initial hesitation. However, the conservation behavior is only generalizable under certain conditions: for instance, conservation is denied if the object extends beyond the rim of the plate on the scales. The weight of the bits of plasticine that jut out "pull down." Thus, the possibility of completely overcoming physical conflicts through true logicomathematical thinking is, in this case, absent.

Task 5 was tried on all 15 subjects, at least in anticipatory form ("will the water level rise after immersion of an object?"). Three subjects anticipate a change owing to the weight of the object. One anticipates a decrease in water level owing to the flattening effect of the water on the object. Out the other 11, eight think there will be only a disturbance due to the introduction of an object, and three think that nothing will happen.

REACTIONS TO INTERROGATION

We were struck by our subjects' ease in this type of interrogation. No particular type of avoidance behavior was noted. But there was no spontaneous search for verification or proof as evidenced in normals. Only one subject spontaneously verified the return to the initial situation in tasks 1 and 3. Fluctuations in reasoning were absent, and the subjects seemed hardly to be influenced in their decisions. Contrary to certain descriptions, the mentally handicapped subject seems in no way hesitant or incapable of a personal point of view, even though we do not believe that this implies any real intellectual autonomy or equilibrated thought processess. However, we shall analyze this phenomenon as distinct from perseveration later on.

REACTIONS TO CONTROL SITUATIONS

We shall summarize our three controls as follows:

1. Modifications designed to test the subject's notion of invariance.
2. Slowing down of the procedure with emphasis on the physical dimensions of the objects.
3. Reinforcement through graduation of the different stages of the transformations effected.

This was done in the cases where the subject showed preoperatory reasoning only.

Control 1. All subjects underwent this type of control at some point during experimentation. Of the three subjects denying numerical equivalence in task 1, only one attained equivalence using this method. The procedure of adding or subtracting elements brings the subject to an awareness of equivalence and induces counting which brings about the correct solution. This same subject senses an analogy between tasks 1 and 2, but cannot overcome the conflict engendered by the differing water levels. Noteworthy however is the adaptative character of the progressive adjustments of the water levels which leads to inconclusive compromise solutions.

With the five subjects using conservation reasoning in task 2, the control bore on task 3. Out of the five subjects, one progresses significantly, while another attains an intermediate level. After successive additions and withdrawals of quantities of plasticine, the former subject concludes that "it's always the same because before it was the same ball." The latter hesitates, but in the face of lots of little bits admits that it's the same "because you just have to put all the bits together and that will make the ball." Two weeks later, the former subject is still at this level of reasoning whereas the latter had regressed to his initial level.

The control task was carried out with regard to weight (4) only with the subject who had progressed. The results show a great difficulty in integrating what was previously acquired into a new situation. After reasoning only of conservation of matter, the child was asked to focus on the weighing aspect of the situation. This provoked massive regression with denial of the identity of the original quantities of matter. It was shown that this regression was due to the proximity of tasks 3 and 4, since a further control established the solidity of the acquisition of conservation of matter. Concerning the subjects who did not progress with this type of control, it is interesting to note the astonishment provoked by the subjects' various adjustments: they spontaneously noted that they had made a mistake ("I shouldn't have added, I put too much . . .") but this did not lead to the notion of invariance.

Control 2. Only those subjects who progressed with control 1 were subjected to this procedure. It concerns only tasks 3, 4, and 5 in view of the tactile explorations of the object it requires. Consequently, the four subjects who did not attain conservation of matter were involved here. While this procedure did not provoke any operatory reasoning, four points of interest may be noted.

1. Two subjects admitted conservation of matter only in the case of small transformations. In the case of inverse transformations, conservation is admitted only when the original ball is reformed. A second attempt shows the same results. Invariance is apparently admitted only as long as the new shape is reminiscent of the original shape.
2. This type of task enabled the subjects to become aware of the possible regulation of the transformation, i.e., of the links between the different stages of the transformation without actually attaining operatory reasoning.
3. The direct manipulation of the object did not enable all the subjects to abstract therefrom the physical dimensions. Three subjects simply describe the terminal state ("it's flat, it's flatter") while only one talks about length or thinness to indicate a smaller quantity.

Control 3. These same four subjects underwent control 3. They all discover an analogy between the two situations which they thus express: "We do the same as before, we go slowly, but there are more balls." "It's the same, but there are three things and one goes faster with this one" (which means that one ball was transformed to a greater extent than the others).

In this task we see once more the children's ability to express the regulatory aspect of the transformation with, furthermore, the possibility of attaining a visual seriation of the different states.

Our attempt to analyze transitive reasoning by means of this task in subjects who had already acquired conservation of matter has evidenced the subjects' great difficulty in this domain. Whereas the subjects exhibit conservation when the reference ball is unchanged (comparison between ball A and sausage B; comparison between A and a longer sausage), they remain incapable of inferring that the sausages B and C are of the same quantity of matter. Their reasoning becomes preoperatory. Sausage C has "more clay because it's longer."

What remarks may we make concerning this series of results? Without wishing to minimize the subjects' difficulty in constructing an operatory reasoning process, we must underline certain positive aspects:

1. Certain subjects were able to go beyond and remain at a higher level of intellectual reasoning.
2. A better appreciation of the different transformation processes

that betray a growing awareness of the regulatory aspect of the transformation.

3. The discovery by the subjects of errors and contradictions, even if most of these are not corrected.

4. The discovery of relationships at the external level (analogies, seriation of states, etc.) despite the absence of an accomplished system of inferences.

In view of these results, may we suppose that such intellectually "adequate" behavior hides a perseveration factor which is so often invoked in the case of mentally retarded subjects? Without excluding this possibility in view of the slow growth of their thinking, it strikes us as most important to underline the positive aspect of their interactions with experience. While we abstain from evaluating the differences in cognitive acquisitions between normals and mentally retarded, we must recognize that the latter exhibited a certain capacity to adapt to the experimental conditions which, though limited, was totally adequate.

The Group of Infantile Psychoses

SPONTANEOUS REASONING PROCESSES

Of the 15 subjects in this group, two 12 year olds explicitly are at the level of invariance reasoning with regard to volume and one 9 year old attributes to a certain numerical collection a stable notion of equivalence. The other subjects exhibit in all the tasks used such fluctuating arguments that it is impossible to assess their structural level. Consequently, our analysis will bear mainly on this majority group.

Types of Fluctuation in Reasoning Processes. With all subjects we use the four experimental situations concerning numerical and physical invariance notions. Only the six 11–12-year-old subjects were tested for the invariance notions concerning volume. However, we wished to know whether all the subjects were capable of imagining the displacement of the water level after immersion of an object, and this aspect was tested in all subjects. Out of our 15, only two failed to anticipate the change in water level.

The investigation of these elementary notions was rendered necessary by the fact that we wished to ascertain whether the subjects attained a stable cognitive level and whether these fluctuations were characteristic of an intermediate level of acquisition

On the descriptive level, we noted the following: at all levels, we noted fluctuating types of arguments. These fluctuating types of arguments are clearly distinct from those heralding the future acquisition of a notion.

I. Fluctuations within preoperatory behavior. The subject's arguments bear on either one of the objects and he attributes to both the same quantitative value. Thus, when confronted with the ball and the sausage, he says, "Here there is more and there there is more," and in front of the standard and thin glasses, "Here there is a little less and there there is a little less."

II. Always within preoperatory behavior. The same object has two different quantitative values. In front of the thin glass, the subject says, "There are three kilos of sirup, there is one kilo of sirup"; in front of the cake, "There is more clay, there is less clay."

III. Fluctuation between arguments of different levels. The subject both asserts and denies conservation: "There is the same clay, there is less, there is the same," "There is the same sirup because nothing was taken away, there is more because the glass is big." These three types of fluctuation may be found in the same subject.

Before commenting on these results, we must note that these contradictory responses were emitted simultaneously and not at different moments during the interrogation. Furthermore, only very rarely did a subject cancel a previously emitted argument in favor of another. The experimenter's attempt to bring about in the subject an awareness of the contradictory nature of his responses was a failure. It seems as if the subject does not establish a fixed reference point be it an object or part thereof. This being the case, the subjects' responses were adequate only in that they follow the changing points of reference.

In Table 17.1, we may immediately note the considerable number of type III fluctuation responses. This type of response therefore excludes the hypothesis of a global cognitive deficit in these psychotic subjects since, despite their fluctuating nature, certain operatory arguments are evidenced. The analysis of these responses shows a predominance of identity reasoning (nothing was added or taken away) coupled with arguments implying centration on one dimension only (there is less because the sausage is narrow). This poses the problem we shall discuss later in our conclusions of the type of structuring process of these subjects and their ability to function on a grouping and integrated correction mode.

Table 17.1. *Table of Fluctuation Types*

			FR				
TASK	N	NFR	TYPE I	TYPE II	(I + II)	TYPE III	TOTAL
1	15	12	16	10	26	27	65
2	15	18	33	7	40	63	135
3	15	5	18	27	45	68	118
4	15	12	25	22	47	71	130
5	6	10	10	6	16	27	53

Code: N = number of subjects.
NFR = Nonfluctuating responses.
FR = fluctuating responses.

The Nature and Pattern of Argumentation. The analysis of the responses from the point of view of their adequacy as to the task problem shows two particularities: one evidences a fairly important difficulty in maintaining a certain continuity in the response argumentation partly because of the interference of preoccupations external to the task; second, the near total absence of the feeling of logical necessity in the responses. Concerning the first point, the digressions noted provoked breaks in the response argumentation but these never transformed in appearance the significance of the experimental content (which does not exclude the possibility that the latter may have a particular meaning for each subject) and were simply added to the responses more directly linked to the task. The content of these digressions included aggression, weather, food, animal themes, etc.

Concerning the second point, we were struck by the number of justifications given that expressed merely personal certitude: "I know it's like that, I guessed, it must be like this." More sophisticated arguments do not attempt to explain what happened. Few subjects express their response in terms that justify the experimental result and only after much insistence do they emit arguments that suggest adequate logical reasoning possibilities. The spontaneous responses are mainly affirmative: "It's more, it's less, it's the same," "It's more because I can see it's more." The subject "knows." An exchange of points of view is not necessary.

Overt Behavioral Reactions During the Experiment. Certain particularly interesting procedures that indicate the subject's tendency to seek less or minimally conflicting situations were noted during the experimentation. The most frequent procedure was to answer questions only in the presence of two identical objects. Thus, when the clay ball is transformed into a sausage, the subject claims not to be able to answer unless the same transformation is applied to the other clay ball. This is immediately carried out by the subject. This is not a verification procedure as noted with operatory level children. Our subjects feel more secure after this second transformation and they express this by saying, "You can't know before they're the same."

A second procedure consisted in displacing the center of interest onto the less relevant elements of the experiment. The subjects, before answering, thus build symmetrical patterns with the objects or use certain evaluatory gestures with reference to their own body as a standard of measure or even orient the object in some specific way.

Finally, a less frequent procedure consists in the subject creating a situation of inequality (he removes part of the quantity of an object) only to reproduce the equality by adding the removed part. This more complex behavior enables the subject to formulate an opinion as to the invariance or not of the quantities implied.

Effect of Suggestion and Reading of Experimental Results (in the Case of Anticipations). Three reaction types were noted that were frequent and characteristic of this group of subjects.

1. Massive opposition to any suggestion implying the point of view of a different child: "He's not right, he tells tales, he doesn't know." In this case we had demanded that the subjects judge the opinions of other children but this had no particular problem-solving effect. Each subject asserts the righteousness of his own opinion.

2. The reading of an experimental result (weighing or immersion of a transformed object) always confirms the subject's prediction: "That's what I said, I was right," and this was indeed sometimes the case.

3. The subject deforms the reading of the result or questions the starting point. This is the most frequent type of response. The subject sees the scales as unequal or the water levels as different, and asserts that previously, when they were equalized, there was a difference.

REACTIONS TO INTERROGATION

The most striking fact is the difficulty we encounter in using such an éxperimental procedure with these children. As much as our mentally retarded subjects seem to respond to a certain extent to the relational demands of our interrogations, so do the psychotic subjects seem to feel this procedure as inflicted upon them. Several of the latter's reactions betrayed the fact that the interrogation and the task materials (and often both) coupled with the concommitant dialogue and justifications were experienced as a real aggression. This may in part explain why these subjects never progressed during the sessions. But the problem remains open since we have yet to show how these subjects acquire certain notions even though they remain unstable and also that the fluctuating types of response are precisely not the result of such interrogations.

REACTIONS TO THE CONTROL SITUATIONS

Three control tasks were presented to 13 subjects of the group (two being already at the highest level of acquisition of conservation notions). Our aim was twofold: to account for the subject's possibilities of using some help on the one hand, and on the other, his ability to reach some degree of stability in his acquisitions. Our intervention turned out to be particularly difficult in view of the resistance the majority of the subjects offered to the facilitation attempts. As their reasoning possibilities precluded their making a firm choice within the different types of argument, it was impossible for them to select in order to assert conservation once and for all. Our attempts were somewhat more fruitful with control 1; they showed us that in fact the reasoning possibilities of some of our subjects were better than what had been revealed in spontaneous behavior.

Control 1. Eight subjects out of 13 definitely assert that nothing must be added or taken away from the quantities presented as these different actions would upset the equilibrium: "There will be too much," "If you take away, there won't be enough." These refusals are expressed overtly despite the fact that certain judgments continue to be of the fluctuating type. But the interpretation of this refusal remains delicate. Is it a form of behavioral or intellectual opposition? Since several of their arguments justify at times the conservation of the quantity in question, we are tempted to believe that in the face of these corrections demanded, the comprehension of conservation remains predominant. But quite obviously the control task has not brought about the desired state of equilibrium since the return to a normal interrogation procedure does not bring about the disappearance of the fluctuating type of responses.

Four out of five remaining subjects either add or subtract from the quantities involved; after that, they nonetheless assert that the result obtained "is not right, because there is too much or too little." Only one 9-year-old subject remains at the conservation level after such a procedure.

Generally speaking, the subjects who accept additions or subtractions evidence a certain difficulty in controlling these actions. They tend to add or subtract too much. The regulation of such behavior appears to be very difficult. The experimenter has to intervene constantly to bring the subject back onto the task.

Controls 2 and 3. These controls proved to be nearly impossible to carry out as all the subjects had enormous trouble producing and assessing a slowed down transformation. We thus noted discontinuous and excessive transformation movements, flights into phantasmatic activity, reinforcement of the discontinuous aspect of assessments. Everything happened as if it were impossible for the subject to take into account both the continuous aspect of the succession of the different stages of the transformation which supposes a feedback process and to adapt a type of continuous assessment. The subjects are not able to regulate their actions on the task material as they are unable to build stable notions.

Classification and Arrangement Notions

Group of Mentally Retarded

Spontaneous Activity

With the classification task the subject must organize a totality of objects in terms of certain resemblance criteria. In the first part of the experiment, the subject is called upon at the verbal level only (after visual exploration) while in the second phase he is called upon verbally and on the level of active manipulation.

Exploration and Verbalization of Classes of Objects. Of our 15 subjects, eight manage to describe exhaustively the characteristics of the objects. This corresponds to the higher levels of conservation reasoning. The other seven give only a few characteristics, the size of the objects being for them the hardest criterion to identify. In these subjects we noted a certain difficulty in spontaneously exploring in a complete manner the board on which the different objects were glued. They rapidly declare they have "seen everything."

Concerning the construction of object classes:

(a) Five subjects use a considerable number of envelopes (eight to ten on the average) and are incapable of putting all the objects into less. These subjects do not discover a single classification criterion. In each envelope they place one, rarely two, objects justifying their choice by color, shape, or even size.

(b) Four subjects start by using six envelopes using for the objects two criteria "color and size" or "shape and size." Only one subject later forms fewer "heaps" using three envelopes according to the "color" criterion. (In this group, three subjects are at the level of conservation of liquids, and the fourth at the level of conservation of matter).

(c) Six other subjects form a single classification in three envelopes, four in terms of color and two in terms of shape. Despite certain suggestions by the experimenter, the subjects never change their classification criterion. While correctly identifying another criterion, they persist in carrying out the original classification. No subject is able to announce the classes he intends to create.

Construction of Classes by Object Manipulation. Table 17.2 best illustrates our results.

The results described here represent the subjects' maximal productions. For instance, one of the subjects listed under (b) began by assembling figural collections but upon request to do better grouped his objects according to size and color. Similarly, in group (c), the subject who reaches

Table 17.2. *Construction by Manipulation*

ANTICIPATORY BEHAVIOR	NO HEAP	FIGURAL COLLECTION	PARTIAL GROUPS	6 HEAPS	1 CRIT.	2 CRIT.	3 CRIT.
(a) More than 6 heaps	2	1	2				
(b) 6 heaps				2	2		
(c) 1 criterion					1	5	

Code: The figures indicate number of subjects giving such a response. crit. = criterion.

a one criterion classification first produced six subgroups in his classification. In general, we may note the following: the subjects' sorting activity was exhaustive; a certain number of spontaneous corrections were possible; there were few digressions during these activities. For nine subjects, manipulatory behavior lead to more success than verbal behavior.

Anticipation and Contruction of a Series of Numbers. With the number arrangement task, a certain spontaneous construction was possible only with three of the above (c) group subjects; the others manifestly not understanding what a number represented. Certain subjects were able to identify a number, i.e., read it, but could not recall even two others or identify them when presented on separate boards. In each case two digit numbers are read separately.

With our three subjects who were able to recall two digit numbers, the spontaneous contructions remained very limited. The most important difficulty is in the notion of limitation of series, these subjects tending to reproduce mentally and in manipulation the same number several times. And when they are asked to make a different number without repetition of the previous figures, the subjects respond by changing the spatial arrangement of the numbers (vertical positions instead of horizontal for instance). It must, however, be noted that once they have produced certain numbers, they are nonetheless able to place them in a correct ascending order (for example, 11, 12, 13, 21, etc.).

REACTIONS TO THE CONTROL SITUATIONS

Concerning the classification task, it is apparently only group (b) that at least partly benefits from the help that is offered. Group (a) does not admit the diminishing of the number of "heaps" since, according to them, the objects bear little resemblance to each other. Only one subject admits that one could group objects such as a square and a triangle because "they all have edges." Two subjects of the (b) group reach a better comprehension of the classes involved (as evidenced two weeks later) by building three object classes based on color out of the original six subclasses.

The cognitive level of our mentally retarded subjects did not enable them to make any significant progress in the number arrangement task using our control tasks. Thus, not one of our three best subjects was able to avoid number repetition despite our suggestions.

Group of Infantile Psychoses

SPONTANEOUS ACTIVITY

This group is once again characterized by an output which is extremely difficult to classify into a definite hierarchy.

Exploration and Verbalization of Object Classes. Out of the 15 subjects, 13 were not able to describe exhaustively the different characteristics of the objects. Frequent repetitions, halts, and hence a lack of continuity in visual exploration were noted. Eleven subjects correctly announce a first classification criterion with the correct number of envelopes for separating the objects, seven subjects announce two criteria, and only two subjects predict the three criteria. Four subjects never go beyond a simple description of the objects. On the other hand, when asked to distribute the objects into the envelopes, most subjects were able to label them correctly but only two subjects did so systematically indicating the objects belonging to each class (these two subjects presented no difficulty in the conservation tasks). All other subjects evidenced enormous difficulty in exploring systematically. We noted frequent breaks in activity obliging the experimenter to intervene, deviations from an announced criterion (from color to shape for instance), comments on the possible significance of the objects (house, man, . . .). While this behavior suggests some kind of total disorganization, it is interesting to note that the naming of total classes remains possible for the subject which suggests a certain remaining ability of abstraction.

We wished to verify this ability and to dispel the idea that the object classes are built merely on one object to which the label "all" has been applied. Consequently, 13 subjects underwent a task of logical inclusion (the task material was comprised of six daisies and two tulips). Ten subjects performed correctly, making correct assessments of the total class and justifying their answers. While this is not surprising in view of the age of the subjects, it is interesting in view of the difficulties encountered in the classification task.

Construction of Classes by Object Manipulation. The aforementioned difficulties also arose in object manipulation. We could even hypothesize that they would be all the more predominant owing to the spatial element introduced by the disposition of the objects and by the subjects' successive actions upon them. The classificatory activities are thus sidetracked by certain associations or preservations (a red object may sidetrack a classification based on shape onto one based on color). The subject evidenced great difficulty in making his choices (decision making). Sorting activities were not systematized. There were no postcorrections or verification of what had been elaborated. The subjects often abandoned their activity after several manipulations and certain sudden reactions of the type "putting in a heap" were noted.

In consequence, the experimenter was continually called upon to intervene. Difficulties of the same order were encountered in the number arrangement task. Ten subjects were tested on this as the remaining five did not sufficiently understand the nature of the problem. Of these ten, seven correctly anticipated series up to three numbers while the other three refused to announce anything at all. During the effective construction of the series, only two subjects behaved systematically enough to discover the law. The others evidenced difficulties of the type already mentioned. These subjects attained a general level of juxtaposition of elements without any postcorrections.

REACTIONS TO THE CONTROL TASKS

Owing the lack of constructive activity evidenced by most of these subjects, the experimenter's interventions were numerous and directive. Thus the control tasks merely confirmed the behaviors noted on the other tasks. The psychotic subject manages certain constructions only when he is directed to do so and his own transformatory activities are controlled. Left to himself, the psychotic subject evidences enormous difficulties in executing cognitively correct intuitions.

DISCUSSION

The analysis of our results may seem lacking in that it does not refer to what we know about the course of normal cognitive development. This is in fact deliberate, and for two main reasons:

1. In the Piagetian framework, the "epistemic" subject studied presents no typology or individual discordance since he is the result of an abstract construction (he represents for instance a child of 7 to 9 years of age or an adolescent from 12 to 16). This hypothetical coherence at the structural level is not always evidenced in the normal concrete subject and even less so in the concrete deviant subject who undergoes a series of tasks. We must underline the generality of Piaget's theoretical and experimental preoccupations: to study the dynamic processes of equilibrium in thinking, to discover general thought structures, and to demonstrate the structural isomorphism between knower and what is known.

Piaget's experimental method suggests that normality is sufficiently homogeneous in its many aspects so that individual differences compensate themselves and may consequently be ignored. This is certainly not the case for subject groups in pathology presenting a more or less well defined syndrome and whose modes of organization, whether cognitive or affective, we know little about. While this experimental method is of interest in that it may enable a better comprehension of modes of organization of thinking in pathologic subjects, it does not, because of its mainly epistemological preoccupations, present sufficiently precise references for an analysis of cognitive activity in the individual subject.

2. The constant reference to the normal child, while difficult to

avoid entirely, may be dangerous in that one may be led to formulating negative judgments on the productions of pathologic subjects, and this is all the more the case when the reference subject is "epistemic." As we are attempting to analyze the organization modes of these children's thinking, we therefore decided to remain on the mainly descriptive level in order to gain knowledge of experimental facts. We have formulated certain interpretative hypotheses merely to indicate new directions for research. The following important facts may be gathered from our comparative study.

Hierarchy of Behaviors

Such a hierarchy seemed possible with the mentally retarded subjects. Inhelder's study has already shown that the retarded subject goes through the normal pathways in the contruction of his thought operations even if these are slowed down or remain at the half-way stage. The psychotic children on the other hand have a widespread difficulty in attaining stable operatory constructions even at developmentally lower levels. Concerning the latter's behavior types, considering our incomplete knowledge of all the procedures used by normal children, we can say that it seems unlikely that these are part of the normal development of thinking in children.

Organization of Procedures Leading to Solutions of Problems

Despite the limited nature of his intellectual productions, the retarded subject nonetheless exhibits adequate reactions to the demands made by the experimental problem and the form of interrogation. He thus attains a certain level of operatory construction using forms of groping and generalization that prepare a form of stable equilibrium even if the latter is characteristic of a lower developmental level. The activity of these subjects is regulated in terms of successive discoveries and a fixed goal. Even if the deductive process seems limited, there is nevertheless a certain logical necessity evident in their actions. The contrary is noted for the psychotic subjects where the regulation of activity is particularly discordant and does not lead to stable acquisitions either in the logical or in the physical domain. Our analysis of the fluctuation behaviors and of their cognitive content does not evidence an absence of constructions (most of the arguments were of a higher level than those given by the retarded subjects) but a fundamental difficulty in attaining a definite logical structural level. The reasoning processes are linked to spatial and temporal considerations and are formed by simultaneous construction. Each action seems to contain its own causality which prevents the coordinations of the actions necessary for the logical structuring of thought. One problem remains unsolved: what is the meaning of certain adequate logical constructions in the anticipation tasks? We have to investigate whether the psychotic subject is dependent upon particular interactions during experimentation which prevent him from displaying his true cognitive acquisitions.

CONCLUSION

The control tasks which were designed to facilitate the discovery of the solutions to our problems enabled us to grasp the construction processes of each of our experimental groups. We were thus able to show that the retarded subjects were to a certain degree able to go beyond their spontaneous productions as would normal subjects nearing levels of stable but higher acquisitions. Certain regressive behaviors were noted, however, in the situations where the cognitive elements were too few and our intervention then took on a drill aspect.

The control tasks enabled us to underline the adequate form of the reactions of the retarded within the limits of their assimilation capacities. In the case of the psychotic children, our interventions merely stressed in most situations the discordant elements that had appeared in spontaneous behavior. Despite certain opposition reactions that betrayed a higher level of comprehension, it was impossible to center the subject on his contradictions in order for him to overcome them. His actions, coupled with digressions and refusals, suggest that only in this way does he dominate his conflicts and thus maintain their causal significance which in turn prevents definite logical structuring. This reminds us of what Bettelheim (1969) says of psychotic children in a different context, namely that the latter act not to better their condition but to exclude further dangers.

FIVE

Cross-Cultural Research

18

Need and Significance
of Cross-Cultural Studies in
Genetic Psychology

JEAN PIAGET

Genetic psychology is the study of the ontogenesis of cognition. The study of child development may provide an explanation, or at least additional information as to the cognitive mechanisms in the adult. In other words, genetic psychology uses developmental psychology to solve general psychologic problems.

It becomes more and more obvious that, from such a point of view, developmental psychology is an essential tool of psychologic investigation. But it has been less often realized that its role could be almost as important in sociology. Auguste Comte maintained with good reason that the formative action of one generation upon the next is one of the most important phenomena of human societies, and Durkheim inferred from this that ethical feelings, judicial norms, and logic itself must have a collective origin. But there is only one experimental method to verify such hypotheses: the study of the progressive socialization of the individual, that is to say, the analysis of his development as a function of general or particular social influences.

Any comparative research, bearing on different cultures and social environments, leads one initially to consider the problem of the delineation of factors which are specific to the spontaneous and internal development of the individual, and of social and cultural factors which are specific to the society under study. But this delineation, which must be

259

done initially, can produce unexpected results. In the field of psychoanalysis, for example, the first Freudian doctrines provided a model of endogenous individual development in which the various stages (in particular that of the so called "Oedipal" reactions) were seen as essentially due to the successive manifestations of a single "instinct," that is to say, of internal tendencies independent of society. On the other hand we know that a large group of contemporary psychoanalysts, called "cultural relativists" (e.g., E. Fromm, K. Horney, Kardiner, Glover, joined by some anthropologists, such as R. Benedict and M. Mead) maintains the hypothesis of a close interdependence between the various Freudian complexes, and notably the Oedipal tendencies, and the social environment.

DEVELOPMENTAL FACTORS

In the field of cognition, the main advantage of cross-cultural studies is to allow a dissociation of the sociocultural and individual factors in development. But it is essential to distinguish which factors are to be considered.

1. Biologic Factors

First of all there are biologic factors linked to the *epigenetic system* (interactions between the genotype and the physical environment during growth), which appear especially in the maturation of the nervous system. These factors, which owe nothing to society, play an as yet little-known role. But their importance probably remains crucial in the development of cognitive functions, and it is thus important to consider their possible influence. In particular, the development of this "epigenetic system" implies from a biologic point of view, the occurrence of *sequential stages*, the existence of *creodes*, and the intervention of a mechanism of *homeorhesis*. These stages are of a sequential nature, each one being necessary to the next in a constant order. The creodes are necessary channels or paths in the development of each particular area of the organism. Homeorhesis is a dynamic equilibration by which a deviation from the creodes is more or less compensated for by a return to the normal path.

We have considered it possible to recognize these characteristics in the development of the operations and the logicomathematical structures of intelligence. If this is so, it would naturally mean a certain constancy or uniformity in development, whatever the social environments in which individuals live. On the other hand, inversions in the succession of stages, or major modifications of their characteristics, from one milieu to another, would mean that these basic biologic factors do not intervene in the cognitive development of individuals. This is the first fundamental problem, the solution of which requires extensive cross-cultural studies.

2. Equilibration Factors

In numerous Western countries, where the study of our stages has been undertaken, the investigation of the development of intellectual operations shows that the psychobiological factors are, by far, not the only ones. Indeed, if there were a continuous action of the internal maturation of the organism and of the nervous system alone, the stages would not only be sequential but would also be bound to relatively constant chronologic ages, as are, e.g., the coordination of vision and prehension (around 4 to 5 months) and the appearance of puberty. One finds in children of the same town, depending on the individuals, and on the social, family, or school environments, advances or delays that are often considerable. These do not contradict the order of succession, which remains constant, but show that other factors are added to the epigenetic mechanisms.

A second group of factors must therefore be introduced: these are equilibration factors, seen as an autoregulation closer to homeostasis than to homeorhesis. In principle these still depend on activities specific to behavior in general, in its psychobiologic as well as sociocultural aspects. We must reserve judgment on the possible links of these factors with social life.

Individual development is indeed a function of multiple activities exercising, experiencing, or acting upon the environment. Among these actions, there arise particular, followed by more and more general coordinations. This *general coordination of actions* presupposes multiple systems of autoregulation or equilibration, which depend upon the environmental circumstances as well as on epigenetic potentialities. The operations of intelligence can be considered as the highest form of these regulations; this shows the importance of the factor of equilibration as well as its relative independence of biologic givens.

But if the equilibration factors can be hypothesized to be very general and relatively independant of the social environment, this hypothesis requires cross-cultural verification. Equilibration processes can be observed in particular in the formation of the concepts of conservation, the stages of which show, in our society, not only a sequential order, but also systems of *compensations*. The intrinsic characteristics of the latter are typical of regulations according to successive levels. But are these particular stages found everywhere? If so, one would not yet have a confirmation of the hypothesis, but at least a more or less favorable indication. If not, it would be, on the contrary, the sign of particular cultural and educational influences.

3. Social Factors of Interpersonal Coordination

In the psychobiologic field we have made a basic distinction between the epigenetic potentialities and equilibration factors. With regard to the sociocultural factors, it is necessary to introduce a distinction, just as essential, between the general social or interpersonal interactions or coordinations, which are common to all cultures, and cultural and educational transmissions, which change from one culture to another, or from one specific social environment to another.

Whether one studies a child in Geneva, Paris, New York, or Moscow, or in the mountains of Iran, the center of Africa or a Pacific island, one finds social exchanges among children or between children and adults. These operate by themselves, independently of educational transmissions. In any environment, individuals ask questions, exchange information, work together, argue, object, etc. This constant interpersonal exchange occurs during the whole of development, according to a socialization process which involves the social life of children among themselves, as well as their relations with elders.

Durkheim referred to general social mechanisms, and maintained that "under civilizations is Civilization." In the same way, it is indispensable, in order to discuss the relations between cognitive functions and social factors, to start with opposing the *general coordinations of collective actions* and particular cultural transmissions which have crystallized in a different way in each society. In case one were to find, in all the societies studied, our stages and results, it still would not prove that these convergent developments are of a strictly individual nature. Just as it is obvious that, everywhere, a child has social contacts from a very early age, it would also show that certain common socialization processes exist, which interact with the equilibration processes discussed in the previous section.

These interactions are so highly probable, and likely to be so close, that one may readily put forward the hypothesis (which should be confirmed or refuted by future cross-cultural studies) that, at least in the field of cognitive functions, the general coordination of actions affects interpersonal actions as well as individual ones. The progressive equilibration of this general coordination of actions seems to be the basis of the formation of logical or logicomathematical operations. In other words, one should find the same laws of coordination and regulation in individual actions or in social interactions involving, e.g., exchanges, cooperation, and competition. These laws would result in the same final structures of operations or of cooperations, as "co-operations." One could thus consider logic as a final form of equilibration, as being simultaneously individual and social; individual since it is general and common to all individuals, and social since it is general and common to all societies.

4. Factors of Educational and Cultural Transmission

On the other hand, besides this functional and partly synchronistic (constant or universal) nucleus, one must naturally consider the mainly diachronic (divergent or culturally relative) factor constituted by traditions and the educational transmissions which vary from one culture to another. When one speaks of "social factors," one in fact is usually referring to these differential cultural pressures. Insofar as cognitive processes can vary from one culture to another, it is obvious that one ought to consider this group of factors which is distinct from the former. To start with, one could look at the various languages which are likely to have a more or less strong influence, if not on the operations themselves, at least on the detail of the conceptualizations (e.g., content of classifications, relations).

CROSS-CULTURAL STUDIES IN THE FIELD OF COGNITIVE PROCESSES

Once we have agreed on this classification into four groups of factors, according to the types of relations between the individual and the social environment, we must try to define the usefulness of cross-cultural studies for our understanding of cognitive processes. The main problem in this respect is that of the nature of intellectual operations, and particularly of logicomathematical structures. Several hypotheses are possible which correspond, among other things, to the four factors distinguished previously, eventually with some additional subdivisions.

Biologic Factors and Factors of Coordination of Actions

One could interpret these structures, if not as innate, at least as the exclusive result of biologic factors of an epigenetic nature (e.g., maturation). K. Lorenz, one of the founders of contemporary ethology, tends toward this interpretation: he believes in the *a priori* nature of knowledge, and interprets it as instinctual.

From the point of view of cross-cultural data already collected, or still to be obtained, one should distinguish between two questions: (a) Shall we always find the same stages of development, considering of course the possibility of corrections and improvements to the theory? (b) Shall we always find them at the same average ages? To answer these two questions, it is useful and almost necessary to have available a point of reference, in comparing the development of the response to operational tests (e.g., conservations, classification and inclusion, seriation, numerical correspondence) with the development of the response to tests of intellectual performance, such as those generally used to determine an IQ.

Cross-cultural studies are only beginning, and it would be very unwise to draw conclusions, given the available information, and the great difficulties, linguistic and others, which there are in multiplying these studies. An additional difficulty is the long training necessary to master the testing methods, which become more difficult to use as they get closer to operational functions. But the results of the first studies, assuming they can be generalized, indicate at least a possible line of interpretation.

In Iran, for example, Mohseni (1966) examined schooled children of Teheran and young rural illiterates on conservation tests on the one hand, and on performance tests on the other (e.g., Porteus Maze, graphical tests). The three main results obtained with the children (aged 5 to 10 years) are as follows: (a) On the whole, the same stages are found in both city and country, in Iran, as in Geneva (succession of the conservations of matter, weight, volume). (b) One notes a systematic delay of two to three years for the operational tests between country and city children, but about the same ages in Teheran as in Europe. (c) The delay is greater, sometimes four but usually five years, for the performance tests, between country and city children, to the extent that the country children would appear mentally defective without the operational tests. For the performance tests, schooled children of Teheran are one to two years behind European and American children.

Assuming that such results are found elsewhere, one would be led to make the following hypotheses:

(a) A more general verification of the constancy in the order of the stages would tend to show their sequential characteristic. Until now, this constant order seems to have been confirmed in Aden by Hyde (1959), in Nigeria by Price-Williams (1961), in Hong Kong by Goodnow (1962), and in the Martinique by Boisclair (personal communication). But it is obvious that we need to have much more data.

Now, if the sequential order were to be verified cross-culturally, one could see an analogy with the epigenetic development (according to Waddington), and consequently a certain probability of the intervention of biologic factors (factor 1). But up to what point? In order to involve biologic factors of maturation with certainty, one ought to be in a position to establish the existence not only of a sequential order of stages, but also of certain average ages of appearance. Mohseni's results, however, show a systematic delay of the country children compared to those of the city, which means, of course, that factors other than maturation intervene.

On the other hand, in the area of figurative thinking, one could possibly find everywhere the same age for the appearance of the *semiotic function* (e.g., symbolic play, mental images, and the development of language), which develops in our culture between one and two years of age. Apparently the main factor which makes this semiotic function possible is the interiorization of imitation: at the sensorimotor level, it already constitutes a sort of representation in action, a motor copy of a model, in such a way that its prolongations, first in delayed imitation, then in interiorized imitation, allow the formation of representation in images. But the existence of delayed reactions, and of interiorization, naturally implies certain neurologic processes, such as the freezing, at a certain level of connections, of the actualization of action schemes. A cross-cultural study of the sensorimotor forms of imitation and of the ages of appearance of the semiotic function from delayed imitation, could show some chronologic regularities, not only in the sequential order of stages, but also in the more or less fixed ages of formation. In this case we would get closer to the factors of maturation, which are related to the epigenetic system (e.g., intervention of the language centers).

(b) The second clear result of Mohseni's study is the fairly general delay of country children, compared with those of Teheran, on the operational tests (conservations) as well as on the performance tests. This delay proves the intervention of actors distinct from those of simple biologic maturation. But here one hesitates to decide among the three other groups of factors named above: (2) factors of equilibration of actions, (3) factors of general interpersonal interaction, and (4) factors of cultural and educational transmission. Indeed each one of these could intervene. Concerning factor 2, Mohseni noticed the astounding lack of activity of the young country children who do not go to school and who have no toys, except stones or sticks, and who show a constant passivity and apathy. Thus one finds at the same time a poor development of the coordinations of individual actions (factor 2), of interpersonal actions (factor 3), and of educational transmissions (factor 4), which are reduced since these children are illiterate. This implies a convergence of the three groups of factors. But how are they to be differentiated?

(c) In this respect, the third result obtained by Mohseni is interesting. In spite of the dismal situation of the country children, their responses to the operational tasks are superior to their results on the performance tests; whereas one should consider these children as moderately or even severely mentally defective on the basis of the intellectual performance tests alone, they have but two to three years of delay on the conservations tasks, compared with Teheran school children. Here again, it is obvious that we should not risk a generalization before collecting data from many more cultures. But, in order to show the interest of the problem, and the multiplicity of the various situations still to be studied, let us point out that Boisclair, with Laurendeau and Pinard, has examined school children in Martinique who are not at all illiterate, since they are attending primary schools with a French curriculum, but who show nevertheless a delay of about four years on the main operational tasks. In this case, the delay seems to be attributable to the general characteristics of social interactions (factor 3, in connection with 2), more than to a lack of educational transmissions (factor 4).

In the case of Iran, the better results on the conservation tasks (indicative of operational mechanisms), compared to the performance tests, seems to indicate a difference in nature between the fairly general coordinations necessary to the functioning of operational structures, and the more special acquisitions relative to performance on particular problems. In the case of a confirmation of such results, this could help to distinguish between factors 2 and 3 taken together (general coordinations of actions, whether individual or interpersonal) and factor 4 (educational transmission). In other words, operational tasks would yield better results because they are bound to the coordinations necessary to intelligence itself, which are the products of progressive equilibration and not of innate biologic conditions. Performances would be influenced by special cultural factors, which, in this case, are particularly deficient.

Such are, on the whole, the possibilities of interpretation of cross-cultural studies, such as Mohseni's, provided that the number of these studies be increased. But these are only the broad outlines, and it is important now to examine in detail the role played by the sociocultural factors (factors 3 and 4).

Cultural Factors of Educational Transmission

If the operational structures could not be explained by the laws of the general coordination of actions, according to our hypothesis, one would have to think of more specific factors. Two of the main ones would be: (a) educational activities of adults, and (b) language itself, as a crystallization of syntax and semantics which, in their general forms, involve a logic.

(a) The hypothesis of a formative action of education by adults certainly contains a part of the answer. Indeed, even from the perspective of the general coordination of actions (either as overt behavior or interiorized as operations), the adult, being more advanced than the child, can help him and speed up his development, during educational processes in the family or in the school. But the question is whether this factor plays an exclusive part: this was Durkheim's idea, for whom logic emanates (as do ethics and law) from the total structure of society, and is imposed on the individual, through social and especially educational constraints. This is partly Bruner's (1964) idea too, who maintains that one can teach anything, at any age, if one goes about it adequately; but Bruner thought of educational processes less in terms of schooling and more in terms of the American models of learning. With regard to Durkheim's perspective, and not that of Bruner's, which is dependent on laboratory experiments* more than on cross-cultural studies, facts like those observed in Martinique by the Canadian psychologists seem to indicate that an ordinary schooling, with a French curriculum that facilitates comparison, is not sufficient to ensure a normal development of operational structures, since there are, in this case, three or four years of delay in comparison with Western

---

* These have been done in Geneva by Inhelder and Bovet (Inhelder *et al.*, 1966; Pascual-Leone and Bovet, 1966); they are far from verifying Bruner's hypotheses.

cultural environments. But here again one should not conclude hastily: one still should differentiate the influences of the family from those of the school. We can simply assert that the cross-cultural method is, on this point as on others, likely to provide the desired solutions.

(b) The important problem of the interactions between language and operational development has been clarified by the studies of Inhelder and Sinclair on the linguistic development of the child, and on the role of language in the learning of operatory structures.

Without going into the details of the methods and results, which have been described elsewhere (Sinclair, 1967a), we shall limit ourselves to emphasizing the perspectives opened by Sinclair's studies from a cross-cultural point of view. Let us recall, for example, the experiment with two groups of children: one group of older children definitely mastered conservation structures (giving explicit justifications) and one group of younger children were unequivocally nonconserving. The subjects of these two groups are asked to describe some objects (e.g., a short and thick pencil, another one long and thin; several little marbles, a smaller number of bigger marbles). The language used in the two groups differs as to the comparatives used: whereas the nonconserving subjects make use largely of what the linguist Bull has called *scalaries* (e.g., "big," "small," "a lot," or "a little"), the subjects at the operational level use *vectors* ("more" or "less," etc.). Furthermore, the structure of the expressions differs: the conservers use binary modes (e.g., "this one is longer and thinner"), whereas the nonconservers use quaternary modes (e.g., "this one is thick and the other one is thin; this one is long and the other one is short"). Thus there is a very close correlation between operativity and language, but in which direction? Learning experiments, with which we are not directly concerned here, show that, in conditioning the preoperational subjects to use the expressions of their elders, one obtains only a slight improvement in operational thinking (1 case out of 10). However, there remains to be established whether it is an action of language as such or an influence of the practice in analysis induced by learning, and if a certain progress would not have taken place without this learning through the development of schemes as a function of various activities. Thus it seems that operativity leads to the structuration of language (of course through a choice among preexisting linguistic models), rather than the reverse.

One immediately sees the great interest there would be in multiplying experiments of this type with various languages. Sinclair found the same results in French and English, but one should turn to very different languages. In Turkish, for example, there is only one vector, which corresponds to our word "still"; to say "more," one says "still much" and to say "less," "still little."

Evidently one will find many other combinations in other languages. In this case it would be of great interest to examine the delay in the development of operational structures as a function of the language used by subjects, and one ought to repeat Sinclair's experiments with children of different levels. The development of the similar structures of thought, in spite of linguistic variations, would argue in favor of the factors of progressive and autonomous equilibration. On the contrary, if we should find modification of operations according to the linguistic environments, we ought to examine closely the meaning of these interactions according to Sinclair's experimental model.

CONCLUSION

Psychology elaborated in our environment, which is characterized by a certain culture and a certain language, remains essentially conjectural as long as the necessary cross-cultural material has not been gathered as a control. We would like to see cross-cultural studies of cognitive functions, which do not concern the child only, but development as a whole, including the final adult stages. When Lévy-Bruhl raised the problem of the "pre-logic" of "primitive mentality," he undoubtedly overemphasized the opposition, in the same way as his posthumous recantation exaggerates perhaps in the other way the universality of structures. It seems to us that a series of questions remains unanswered by the excellent work of Lévi-Strauss: for example what is the operational level of adults in a tribal organization, as far as the technical intelligence (completely neglected by Lévy-Bruhl), verbal intelligence, the solution of elementary logicomathematical problems, are concerned? The developmental data relative to the lower age levels will attain full significance only when we know the situation of the adults themselves. In particular it is quite possible (and it is the impression given by the known ethnographic literature), that in numerous cultures, adult thinking does not proceed beyond the level of *concrete operations,* and does not reach that of propositional operations, eleborated between 12 and 15 years in our culture. It would thus be of great importance to know whether the preceding stages develop more slowly in children of such cultures, or if the equilibrium level which will not be exceeded is reached around 7–8 years, as with our children, or only with a small delay.

19

Piaget's Theory of Cognitive Development and Individual Differences

MAGALI BOVET

Dr. Uzgiris has summed up clearly the hierarchical aspect of the organization of the processes of intellectual development as argued by Piaget. She has also underlined the importance of continuous interaction between the organism and the environment, mentioning the complementary role played by the fundamental processes of assimilation and accommodation in this interaction. She has rightly maintained that Piaget is mainly concerned with the development of the intellectual of a normal subject "in an ideal generalized case." The generalization is evidently made from studies carried out under the normal conditions obtaining in modern Western civilization. She has recognized that Piaget regards the role of experience and of sociocultural factors as indispensable in addition to those of maturation. Moreover, Piaget also introduces a general factor of equilibration, which is at work within each of the specific factors and which also regulates their respective influence. It is this equilibratory factor which explains the fact that development necessarily moves toward more extended and stable stages of reasoning. But in fact, though Piaget's theory provides a general theoretical framework for the study of individual differences, these fields of psychology have not given rise to any explicit application of his theory.

A great deal of research on the learning of elementary logical structures has been undertaken for many years in various countries. The aim of these experiments may vary. A strictly pedagogic point of view would aim at the desired result as such and would involve the manipulation of various methods of didactic learning procedure in order to discover the most efficient one for a particular acquisition. But such methods will reveal little about the action-acquisition process. An example of a totally different approach is provided by the research of the Center for Epistemology directed by Piaget in 1957. Here the problem is to study the learning of logical structures with the emphasis on the relations between the laws of learning, in the strict empirical sense of the word, and those responsible in a more general way for intellectual development. Piaget concluded that the latter dominated the former.

At present, Genevan research on learning takes an intermediate position by studying in detail the psychologic processes which underlie the acquisition of logical operations and by concentrating on the transition from one stage to the next in each individual subject (see Inhelder *et al.*, 1967).

In these experiments we are mainly concerned with the following problems:

1. We have undertaken a series of experiments to study specifically the rate of the transition from one level to the next as it takes place in the course of several learning sessions. We are thus trying to clarify the regulating mechanisms inherent in development.

2. A second series of experiments deals with developmental coherence, i.e., the homogeneity of the behavior patterns in relation to a particular, logical, structural level. There is constant interaction between cognitive structures in the process of development. Here our aim is to arrive at a psychologic analysis of such interrelationships (a logical analysis only provides a model). The problem concerns the psychologic synchronism between various concepts. To study this we have initiated a series of experiments in which a child is presented with a variety of problems belonging to different fields of cognition.

3. Finally, through yet another series of experiments, we are attempting to analyze the branching relationships between concepts and their possible derivation one from the other.

In spite of the different nature of each of these three kinds of learning experiments, all procedures have certain basic principles in common. They are all based on what we already know about spontaneous development and about the difficulties or specific obstacles presented by different concepts. These obstacles are deliberately introduced into a learning procedure. The experimenter's task is to lead the child to a progressive awareness of what the problem involves. There is no question of either masking the obstacles or of forcing the child to adhere to specific methods of action—which would only result in an improved "performance" and not better understanding. To sum up, the various procedures aim at encouraging the child to relate and coordinate his own actions for himself.

The effects of these learning sessions are judged through pretests and posttests comprising at least two problems of the same logical level, and their durability is checked through an identical test which takes place after an interval of several weeks. The manner in which answers are justified is considered an important criterion. We think that the reactions taking place during the learning sessions are as important (if not more important) as the actual answers given to the different tests, which indicate whether progress has taken place. This is obvious since we are more interested in better understanding the actual developmental mechanisms than in speeding up development itself. The results of this research has been the subject of a detailed study.

Thus, these learning experiments provide insight not only into general developmental processes but also into the way these processes are observable in the individual child.

Apart from our learning studies, several other lines of research concern, to a certain degree, individual differences. Longitudinal studies have been carried out on different age groups and have concentrated on the progressive structuring of concrete operations.

Moreover, a certain standardization of Piagetian tests has been effected. Different age groups have been systematically questioned, and several groups of subjects have been presented with an extensive series of problems. This has enabled us to draw developmental curves for certain concepts and also to verify the correlations between different concepts.

Another series of experiments using Piagetian tests has been carried out in different fields of psychology. As early as 1943, efforts were made to relate Piaget's theory of the development of intelligence to problems of mental retardation (see Inhelder, 1963). Later on, the research was extended to infant psychosis, mental deficiency, and senile dementia (see Ajuriaguerra *et al.*, 1964, and Sinclair de Zwart, 1967a).

Finally, various cross-cultural Piagetian studies are being carried out in different countries. They concern the comparison between urban and rural dwellers and that between those who have been to school and those who have not in Algeria, Ghana, and in Sicily (planned). We shall give details of some of our own studies in connection with this research.

The different directions in which we are orienting our research provide proof, we feel, of our determination to analyze the individual process of cognitive development and to pave the way for a study of the different factors which intervene in intellectual development.

THE EFFECT OF CULTURAL FACTORS

We shall briefly describe and discuss certain results which we obtained through research in Algeria.

Children from four age groups (6–7, 7–8, 8–10, and 9–11 years) were asked questions concerning the conservation of physical quantities and of length.

Physical Quantities

We began by asking the first two age groups the most usual questions concerning the conservation of liquids and of matter. We obtained nonconservation results in the youngest group, but the 7–8-year-old children gave correct answers. The latter children seemed to have stopped basing their answers on the configurations resulting from the transformations. As we could not discover the reasoning processes behind their correct answers by asking for verbal explanations, we introduced complementary items. The subjects were asked to pour two quantities (as equal as possible) of liquid into two glasses of different diameters, and also to anticipate the height of the level when a quantity of liquid was transferred from one container to another of different dimensions.

The youngest group gave wrong solutions, as do our Genevan subjects without conservation. To our amazement, however, we found that most of the 7–8-year-old children with conservation also gave wrong solutions. They judged the quantity by the "fullness" of the containers regardless of their dimensions, or they guessed the answer without really understanding the relationship between the diameter, the container, and the liquid levels. The results of the anticipation of the levels were inconsistent and did not improve after the subjects were shown what actually happened. Such behavior patterns do not correspond to those of Genevan subjects, who give correct answers in the usual conservation tests. The latter arrive at correct solutions by coordinating the different dimensions.

These results led us to question older children. In an 8–10-year-old group, in contrast with the preceding one, the answers to conservation problems were sometimes right and sometimes wrong. The subjects hesitated a great deal and seemed to realize spontaneously the importance of the dimensions without being able to coordinate them in a stable way. It was only at 9–11 years that most subjects gave consistently correct answers. The 8–10 group tried to solve the complementary problem of constituting equal quantities by equalizing the levels or else admitted that the levels must be a little different. Their solutions to the problem of anticipating the level of a liquid which was poured from one container to another were often not immediately correct, but improved after they had watched what actually happened. In the oldest age group, the majority of the solutions were immediately correct or became so at the end of the experiment.

After these complementary items, we returned to our conservation tests and asked at least one of the questions the subject had already answered at the beginning of our experiment. The following comparative curves were obtained by comparing the initial replies with the final results:

1. The 6–7 age group's behavior did not change.

2. The 7–8 year group gave answers which were less correct in the final test than in the initial one. Their final answers showed that they were beginning to base their judgments on figurative appearances, i.e., the levels of the liquid and the different shapes of the glasses.

3. The 8–11-year-old children gave more consistently correct answers in the final test.

4. The oldest subjects not only gave correct answers in the final test but were able to justify them verbally.

It might be supposed that if the first correct answers at the age of 7–8 years and the final ones at 9–11 bear witness to the same reasoning structure, the only difference between the age groups lies in the child's ability to express himself, i.e., the ease with which he can justify his arguments. Several factors, however, lead us to believe that there is also a difference in the nature and levels of cognitive development:

1. In the answers given in the initial conservation tests, we were struck by a "relapse" of the 8–10 group after the correct answers of the 7–8 group, which then gradually reappeared between 9 and 11 years.

2. The 7–8 group, when faced with the complementary problems, behaved differently from the 9–10 group. Their answers showed that there were indeed different cognitive processes at work.

3. Finally, the complementary problems constituted a form of "operatory learning," or at least enabled the subjects to become familiar with the type of questioning. What we found particularly interesting was that these problems had an apparently contradictory effect on the behavior of the 7–8 group and on the two older groups. The children in the first group tended to give wrong answers in the final nonconservation tests, whereas the children in the two older groups made gradual progress.

We feel justified in concluding from these three main points that there exists a form of conservation at 7–8 years which is not completely operatory. It does not imply the existence of a structure enabling the child to perform additive and multiplicative operations involved in the understanding of reversibility. By contrast, the 9–11 group does appear to have reached this stage. The "regression" of the conservation answers seems to us in reality to constitute progress as regards the operatory development of the 7–8 group. These subjects, who initially did not seem to take into account perceptual indices such as level of the liquids and dimensions of the glasses, which are indispensable for operatory understanding of the conservation problem, seem, in the final test, to pay attention to these factors. This leads at first to nonconservation answers which are consistently based on one of the perceptual indices.

Conservation of Length

We carried out experiments in this field in very much the same way as those on physical quantities. We asked questions regarding conservation of length starting from a situation in which two rods of equal length $(A = B)$ were cut up; the fragments of A were placed in a straight line while those of B formed a zigzag. The children were also given complementary tasks: They were asked, for instance, to build a straight road of the same length as a model which was in the form of zigzag. The conservation questions were asked a second time after the children had completed the complementary tasks (which could be considered a sort of exercise).

These results may be summarized as follows:

1. In the first two age groups there were a majority of children without conservation who presented solutions to the complementary items which were characteristic of the same level of reasoning, i.e., their judgment of length was based on "which line went farthest" and they paid no attention to detours.

2. From 8–10 years, behavior patterns of the children confronted by the two types of problem showed the beginnings of coordination between the "shape" of the paths and their terminal point, but these subjects were still hesitating in their answers.

3. In the oldest age group, better coordination led to better solutions, but these children still did not give consistently correct answers.

When we repeated the conservation test, all the groups except the youngest improved their answers.

To sum up, the following may be observed:

1. In the initial tests, we observed a regular course of development in the reactions of the different age groups to the conservation problem. In this case, the different substages were exactly the same as those obtaining in Geneva.

2. Answers to the complementary questions were of a level corresponding to that of the solutions to the conservation problems.

3. Generally, the "operatory exercise" constituted by the complementary tasks enabled the child to make steady progress.

In short, we observed that in these problems on conservation of length, the children's development corresponded to that observed in Geneva.

A comparison of the Algerian children's reactions to these two problems (conservation of matter and of length) with those of Genevan children reveals two important facts. As regards the conservation of matter, Algerian children exhibited a type of conservation (the correct answers of the 7–8 group) which has never been encountered in Geneva. This deviant stage was followed by an intermediate stage and then a final stage of conservation which were both similar to what is typically found in Geneva.

By contrast, no such deviations in the course of development were observed in the reactions to problems of conservation of length. As we have mentioned, the difference in this field was one of developmental rate. All substages were reached at a slightly later age than in Geneva, but the course of development was exactly the same.

How can we account for the difference between the results in the field of conservation of matter and those in the conservation of length? It is evident that, in day-to-day life, children's activities as regards their handling of matters are quite different from their activities as regards measurement and comparison of length. Could we find an explanation of our results in cultural differences? Methods of handling food and distributing goods vary from country to country. All over the world, children handle matter from a very early age. Food is a most essential part of their lives, and its distribution at meals is an important event. Children are also present on occasions when adults buy and sell and discuss price and quality. In different societies, bargaining is based on different value judgments. It seems possible that the earliest concepts of quantity are influenced by the way a society regulates the distribution of goods and by the values it places on different items. Moreover, inside the structure of the family, food may be distributed in many different ways—authoritarian, egalitarian, subject to discussion, etc. If the situation is such that the mother distributes, in an authoritarian way, food which is not plentiful, and if moreover, containers of various shapes and sizes (bowls, plates, etc.) are used, it is possible that the child pays far more attention to the initial authoritarian act of distribution than to the perceptual indices, i.e., the appearance of the food in the container. Since there are no containers of exactly the same size and shape, perceptual comparison between amounts is impossible. This could explain the fact that, at a certain age, indifference regarding the appearance of the quantity, i.e., the "shape" of the liquid in the glass, results in correct conservation answers, based on the initial act of distribution which was accepted without question as fair.

This way of solving the problem is already slightly more advanced than that used by younger subjects. As we have said, the peculiar type of conservation of the 7–8-year-old children in Algeria follows a stage of frank nonconservation which is similar to that found in Geneva. As in Geneva, the younger subjects neglect the action of fair distribution and judge the amount on the basis of its appearance in the container, i.e., they judge according to whatever dimension is the most striking. The 7–8-year-old children, on the other hand, are already capable of detaching themselves from the immediate aspects and of basing their judgment on the initial distribution, that is, they are capable of a certain mental flashback. However, this flashback leads them to the correct answer only because they ignore the appearance of the liquid after it has been poured into a different container and not because they integrate the modifications in appearance into a coherent system of conservation. During the next substage, there is an apparent regression due to the fact that now the child becomes conscious of the apparent contradiction between the modification of shape and the initial act of fair distribution. This taking into account of the dimensional aspects of the final state is a necessary step toward genuine conservation in which initial and final states are linked together by an understanding of the "transformation" as such.

On the other hand, the reactions of Algerian children to problems of length followed the same developmental pattern as in Geneva. It is only the rate of development which is different, and not its course. In this case, we think that the slower rate may be explained by the fact that little importance is attached to comparisons of length and height and to measurement in general. Clearly, school children in Western educational systems are made aware of differences in height at a very early age and are taught to compare length. In kindergarten, they stack blocks, nest bowls one into the other, and in general, are taught to pay close attention to the perceptual characteristics of objects. In primary school, the teaching of reading and writing involves careful comparison between shapes of different letters, the disposition of words on a page, and so forth. In short, children in less sophisticated environments lack the kind of stimulation which results in more developed perceptual strategies, at least in this particular respect.

We have done no more than suggest some quite general factors which may be invoked to explain the slower rate of development. However, it is important to mention how our observations fit in with those made by Greenfield and Bruner (Bruner *et al.*, 1966) in their cultural study of the same problems. These authors appeared surprised to discover that the unschooled Wolof children, when faced with conservation problems, concentrated on what these authors called the "action aspect." Secondly, they emphasized that one of the results of schooling is that children become better able to analyze the figural aspects of a given situation. Both observations fit in exactly with our own; the "action aspect" is what we have called "the initial act of fair distribution" and the inadequate analysis of figural aspects is present as the cause of the deviant type of conservation of our 7–8-year-old subjects.

CONCLUSION

The cross-cultural studies show that two distinct processes may exist. On the one hand, we observe what we have called differences in the course of development, as for instance the deviant type of conservation of matter. On the other hand, we observe differences in the rate of development, as for instance the slower development of the concept of conservation of length without any change in the developmental pattern itself. Such a slowing-up of development can no doubt be explained by the less stimulating quality of the environment, particularly in the case of the absence of all schooling.

The learning experiments, the standardization of tests, and the longitudinal studies show the regularity of the rate of normal cognitive development. Our learning procedures have a certain accelerating effect, but only within definite limits.

IMPLICATIONS FOR THE UNDERSTANDING OF MENTAL RETARDATION

Can the results of these many-sided studies and experiments throw some light on the processes involved in mental retardation? The answer would seem to be in the affirmative. In fact, in mental retardation, two aspects at least have to be distinguished: the rate of and the course of development. Both a slowing-up and an acceleration of the developmental rate have been observed in cross-cultural and learning studies. Slowing-up may be caused by lack of stimulation, and acceleration can be achieved, within certain limits, by teaching methods which closely follow the normal course of development. Changes in the course of development have also been observed, and they have a positive as well as a negative aspect. As we have mentioned, the deviant type of conservation is a substage that has to be overcome; on the other hand, this behavior pattern shows a certain mobility of cognitive structure which can no doubt be used to further progress. In fact, the complementary items of our conservation tests had just this effect of accelerating development and of leading it back to the normal course.

We have to emphasize that we have hardly ever studied the re actions of subjects older than 12 years of age; therefore, the question of a possible acceleration or modification of cognitive processes in adults remains open. It is possible that the early intuitive processes become crystallized in adults and that they result in irreversible modes of thought after a certain age. In fact, a few interviews with Algerian adults who had never been to school point this way. As regards conservation of weight, which is particularly subject to an intuitive approach, these adults showed non-operational behavior patterns. In problems of temporal relationships, the reactions were even more peculiar: these adults seemed to have concepts of duration and time profoundly different from ours. As Piaget (1966) states: ". . . crosscultural research which is most important does not only concern child development but development in general including the final adult stages [p. 13]." It seems reasonable to suppose that, the more firmly the adult modes of thought are established and the longer the lack of environmental stimulation has lasted, the more difficult it is to correct deviations or to close the gap.

Until now we have only discussed research carried out on normal subjects. We certainly agree with Uzgiris when she says, referring to mental retardation, "limiting the experiential opportunities of already limited individuals would be the least desirable course."

Certain results of a long-term learning procedure using operatory exercises with a group of 10 mentally retarded children in Geneva are worth mentioning in this context. This group of subjects was far from homogeneous, their ages ranging from 7 to 11 years and the degree of mental retardation from slight impairment to a massive handicap (corresponding, roughly, to an IQ of 45 to 50). The most striking results of two training sessions per week per child during an entire academic year were the following.

Those children who in the initial tests performed in at least one specific field (e.g., logic, spatial relationships, etc.) at a higher level than in other fields attained, at the end of the year, a homogeneous level corresponding to their best performance in the initial tests. One subject (10 years old) performed initially at a completely homogeneous level (his was the lowest IQ). This massive impairment apparently prohibited any progress; at the end of the year his reactions were exactly the same as at the beginning. Two other children had specific instrumental deficiencies (language and motor impairments), and both progressed to an almost normal level. Only one subject performed in a nonhomogeneous manner at the end of the year. However, he did not succeed better in one field than in the others, but he changed his level inside one field from session to session. Some instability of the reasoning processes seemed to cause frequent regressions to lower levels and an incapacity to consolidate momentary insights.

It would seem that well-designed exercises, based on what is already known of normal development, can have a beneficial effect in certain cases of mental retardation. No doubt there are limits to the usefulness of such exercises, and, in any case, they would have to be used as early as possible. The example of our cross-cultural research would indicate that even deviations in the course of development are amenable to correction up to a certain point and that optimal conditions of learning can bring about a higher level of development than might have been thought possible. Piaget's theory of cognitive development certainly provides a conceptual framework for teaching methods which would result not in parrotlike rote learning but in genuine cognitive progress.

References

AHRENS, R. (1954). Beitrage zur Entwicklung des Physiognomon und Mimik erkennes. Z. Exp. Angew. Psychol. 2, 412–454, 599–633.

AJURIAGUERRA, J. DE, DIATKINE, A., and KALMANSON, D. (1959). Les troubles du développement du langage au cours des états psychotiques precoces. Rev. Psychiat. Enfant 2(1), 9–65.

AJURIAGUERRA, J. DE, JAEGGI, F., GUIGNARD, F., KOCHER, F., MAQUARD, M., PAUNIER, A., QUINODOZ, D., and SIOTIS, E. (1963). Organisation psychologique et troubles de développement du langage. (Etude d'un groupe d'enfants dysphasiques). In Problèmes de Psycholinguistique. Paris: PUF, pp. 109–140.

AJURIAGUERRA, J. DE, REY–BELLET–MULLER, M., and TISSOT, R. (1964). A propos de quelques problèmes posés par le déficit opératorie des vieillards atteints de démence dégénérative en début d'évolution. Cortex 1, 103–132, 232–256.

AJURIAGUERRA, J. DE, INHELDER, B., JAEGGI, A., ROTH, S., and STIRLIN, M. (1969). Troubles de l'organisation de désorganisation intellectuelle chez les enfants psychotiques. Psychiat. Enfant 12(2).

AUBIN, H., MESTAS, C., and CLAVEIROLE, G. (1956). Les schizophrenies infantiles. Rev. Neuropsychiat. Infant. 4(11–12).

BARTLETT, F. (1932). Remembering. London: Cambridge Univ. Press. London.

BENDER, L. (1953). Childhood schizophrenia. Psychiat. Quart. 27, 663–681.

BENVENISTE, E. (1958). De la subjectivité dans le langage. J. Psychol., 257–265.

BEVER, T. G. (1970). The cognitive basis for linguistic structures. In Cognition and Development of Language, (Hayes, J. R., Ed.). New York: Wiley.

BOVET, M. (1968). Etudes interculturelles du développement intellectuel et processus d'apprentissage. Rev. Suisse Psychol. Pure Appl. 27(3–4), 189–200.

BOWER, T. G. R. (1966). The visual world of infants. Sci. Amer. 215, 80–92.

BRONCKART, J. P., and SINCLAIR, H. (1973). Tense, time and aspect. Cognition 2(1), 107–130.

References

BRUNER, J. S. (1964). The course of cognitive growth. *Amer. Psychol.* **19**, 1–15.

BRUNER, J. S., OLVER, R. R., and GREENFIELD, P. M. (1966). *Studies in Cognitive Growth.* New York: Wiley.

CHOMSKY, N. (1957). *Syntactic Structures.* The Hague: Mouton.

CHOMSKY, N. (1964). *Current Issues in Linguistic Theory.* The Hague: Mouton.

CHOMSKY, N. (1965). *Aspects of the Theory of Syntax.* Cambridge, Mass.: MIT Press.

CLAPARÈDE, E. (1898). La perception stéréognostique. *L'intermédiaire des biologistes* **I**, 432–437. Also in *Perceptual and Motor Skills* **24**, 35–41. (1967).

COLE, M. and MALTZMAN, X. (1969). *Handbook of Contemporary Soviet Psychology.* New York: Basic Books.

DASEN, P. (1970). Cognitive development in aborigines of Central Australia. Unpublished doctoral dissertation. Canberra, Australian National University.

ERVIN, S. M. (1964). Imitation and structural change in children's language. In *New Directions in the Study of Language* (Lenneberg, E. H., Ed.). Cambridge, Mass.: MIT Press.

FANTZ, R. L. (1961). The origin of form perception. *Sci. Amer.* **204**, 66–76.

FANTZ, R. L. (1963). Pattern vision in newborn infants. *Science* **140**, 296–301.

FERREIRO, E. (1971). *Les Relations Temporelles dans le Langage de l'Enfant.* Geneve: Droz.

FURTH, H. G. (1966). *Thinking Without Language.* New York: Free Press.

FURTH, H. G. (1970). On language and knowing in Piaget's developmental theory. *Human Develop.* **13**, 241–257.

GARONNE, G., GUIGNARD, F., RODRIGUEZ, R., LENOIR, J., KOBR, F., and DEGAILLER, L. (1969). La débilité mentale chez l'enfant. *Psychiat. Enfant* **12**(1).

GASCON, J. (1969). Modèle cybernétique d'une sériation de poids chez les infants. *Modeles Cybernétiques de la Pensee* **2**. Université de Montreal.

GIBSON, E. J. (1969). *Principles of Perceptual Learning and Development.* New York: Appleton.

GIBSON, J. J. (1968). *The Senses Considered as Perceptual Systems.* London: G. Allen.

GILLIES, S. (1965). Some abilities of psychotic children and subnormal controls. *J. Ment. Def. Res.* **9**.

GOLDFARB, W. (1961). *Childhood Schizophrenia.* Cambridge, Mass.: Harvard Univ. Press.

GOLDFARB, W., BRAUNSTEIN, P., and LORGE, I. (1956). A study of speech patterns in a group of schizophrenic children. *Amer. J. Orthopsychiat.* **26**.

GOLDFARB, W., BRAUNSTEIN, P., and SCHOLL, H. (1959). An approach to the investigation of childhood schizophrenia. The speech of schizophrenic children and their mothers. *Amer. J. Orthopsychiat.* (3).

GOODNOW, J. J. (1962). A test for milieu effects with some of Piaget's tasks. Paper read at Eastern Psychological Association, Atlantic City.

GOUIN-DÉCARIE, T. (1966a). *Intelligence and Affectivity in Early Childhood.* New York: International Univ. Press.

GOUIN-DÉCARIE, T. (1966b). Intelligence sensori-motrice et psychologie du premier âge. In *Psychologie et Épistémologie Génétiques: Thèmes Piagétiens.* Paris: Dumod, pp. 299–306.

HALLE, M. (1962). Phonology in a generative grammar. *Word* 18, 54–73.

HATWELL, Y. (1960). *Privation Sensorielle et Intelligence.* Paris: PUF.

HATWELL, Y. (1966). A propos des notions d'assimilation et d'accomodation dans les processus cognitifs. In *Psychologie et Épistémologie Génétiques, Thèmes Piagétiens.* Paris: Dumod, pp. 127–136.

HEUYER, G., SCHENTOUB, V., JAMPOLSKY, F., RAUSCH, N., and RIVET, M. (1956). Examen psychologique de la schizophrenie juvénile. *Rev. Neuropsychiat. Infant.* 4 (11–12).

HYDE, D. M. (1959). An investigation of Piaget's theories of the development of the concept of number. Doctoral thesis, University of London.

INGRAM, T. T. S. (1962). Clinical significance of the infantile feeding reflexes. *Develop. Med. Child Neurol.* 4, 159–169.

INHELDER, B. (1963). *Le diagnostic du Raisonnement chez les Débiles Mentaux,* 2nd ed. Neuchâtel: Delachaux et Niestlé.

INHELDER, B. (1965). Contribution des études génétiques à l'examen des fonctions intellectuelles des enfants présentant des troubles du langage. In *Jahrbuch für Jugendpsychiatrie und ihre Grenzbebiete* (Stutte, Ed.). Bern and Stuttgart, IV, (11–22).

INHELDER, B. (1968). *The Diagnosis of Reasoning in the Mentally Retarded.* New York: John Day.

INHELDER, B., LÉZINE, I., SINCLAIR, H., and STAMBAK, M. (1972). Les débuts de la fonction symbolique. *Arch. Psych.* 163 (Vol. XLI), 188–243.

INHELDER, B. and PIAGET, J. (1958). *The Growth of Logical Thinking from Childhood to Adolescence: An Essay on the Construction of Formal Operational Structures.* New York: Basic Books.

INHELDER, B. and SINCLAIR, H. (1969). Learning cognitive structures. In *Trends and Issues in Developmental Psychology* (Mussen, P., Langer, J. and Covington, M. Eds.). New York: Holt Rinehart and Winston.

INHELDER, B. and SIOTIS, E. (1963). *Observations sur les Aspects Opératifs et Figuratifs chez les Enfants Dysphasiques.* In: *Problèmes de Psycholinguistique.* Paris: PUF.

INHELDER, B., BOVET, M., SINCLAIR, H., and SMOCK, C. (1966). Comments on Bruner's course of cognitive development. *Amer. Psychol.* 21, 160–164.

References

INHELDER, B., SINCLAIR, H., and BOVET, M. (1967). Développement et apprentissage. *Rev. Suisse Psychol.* **26**, 1–23.

KANNER, L. (1943). Autistic disturbances of affective contact. *Nerv. Child.* **32**, 217–250. Also (1968) *Acta Paedopsychiat.*

KANNER, L. and EISENBERG, L. (1955). Notes on the follow up studies of autistic children. In *Psychopathology of Childhood* (Hoch, P. and Zubin, J., Eds.). New York: Grune & Stratton.

KATZ, J. J. (1966). *The Philosophy of Language.* New York: Harper and Row.

KLIMA, E. S. and BELLUGI, U. (1966). Syntatic regularities in the speech of children. In *Psycholinguistic Papers* (Lyons, J. and Wales, R. J., Eds.). Edinburgh: Edinburgh Univ. Press, pp. 183–208.

KURYLOWITZ, J. (1956). Apophonie en Indo-Européen. *Polska Akad. Nauk Prace Jezyk. Nog.*

LANG, J. L. (1969). Psychoses infantiles à expressions déficitaires et "arriéation-psychose." *Confrontation Psychiat.* (3).

LECUYER, R. (1967). Diagnostic différentiel entre arriération mentale et psychose chez l'enfant. *Rev. Neuropsychiat. Infant.* **15**(1–2).

LESTANG-GAULTIER, E. and DUCHE, D. J. (1967). Contribution à l'etude du diagnostic et de l'évolution des psychoses infantiles (enfants de moins de 7 ans). *Rev. Neuropsychiat. Infant.* **15**(1–2).

LÉVI-VALENSI, A. E. (1970). Adaptation et valeur. Les perspectives psychanalytiques. *Econ. Soc., Cahiers I.S.E.A.* **IV**, 12.

LOCKYER, L. and RUTTER, M. (1970). A five-to-fifteen year follow-up study of infantile psychosis: IV. Patterns of cognitive ability. *Brit. J. Soc. Clin. Psychol.* **9**.

LOMOV, B. F. (1966). Manual interaction in the process of tactile perception. In *Psychological Research in the USSR, Vol. 1.* Moscow: Progress Publishers, pp. 267–309.

LUQUET, G. H. (1927). *Le Dessin Enfantin.* Paris and Neuchâtel: Delachaux et Niéstlé, (2nd ed., 1967).

LURIA, A. R. (1961). *The Role of Speech in the Regulation of Normal and Abnormal Behaviour.* London: Pergamon Press.

MANDELBRODT, J. and MOUNOUD, P. (1971). On the relevance of Piaget's theory to the visual arts. In *Leonardo*, Vol. 4.

McNEILL, D. (1970). *The Acquisition of Language.* New York: Harper and Row.

MEHLER, J. (1969). La psycholinguistique. *Langages.* **2**(16), 3–15.

MEHLER, J. and BEVER, T. G. (1968). The study of competence in cognitive psychology. *Int. J. Psychol.* **3**(4), 273–280.

MILLER, G., GALANTER, E., and PRIBRAM, K. (1960). *Plans and Structure of Behavior.* New York: Holt Rinehart and Winston.

Misès, R. and Perron-Borelli, M. (1972). Essai d'approche psychopathologique de la déficience intellectuelle. Lés déficits dysharmoniques. *Psychiat. Enfant*, **14**(2).

Mohseni, N. (1966). La comparaison des réactions aux épreuves d'intelligence en Iran et en Europe. Thesis. Univ. of Paris.

Monod, J. (1970). *Le Hasard et la Nécessité*. Paris: Seuil.

Moor, L. (1968). Critères psychologiques des psychoses chez les oligophrènes. *Rev. Neuropsychiat. Infant.* **16**(3).

Mounoud, P. (1968). Construction et utilisation d'instruments chez l'enfant de 4 à 8 ans: intériorisation des schèmes d'action et types de régulations. *Rev. Suisse Psychol.* **27**(1).

Mounoud, P. (1970). *Structuration de l'Instrument chez l'Enfant*. Neuchatel and Paris: Delachaux et Niestlé.

Norman, E. (1948). The play of a psychotic child. *Brit. J. Med Psychol.*, **21**.

O'Connor, N. (1961). *Recent Soviet Psychology*. New York: Liveright.

Oléron, P. (1957). *Recherches sur le Développement Mental des Sourds-muets*. Paris: CNRS.

Pascual–Leone, J. and Bovet, M. (1966). Apprentissage de la quantification de l'inclusion et la théorie opératoire, 1. *Acta Psychol.* **25**.

Perrimond, J. (1965). L'examen intellectuel dans les "schizophrénies" de l'enfant. Unpublished doctoral thesis. Univ. of Marseille.

Piaget, J. (1923). *Le Langage et la Pensée chez l'Enfant*. Neuchatel and Paris: Delachaux et Niestlé.

Piaget, J. (1936). *La Naissance de l'Intelligence chez l'Enfant*. Neuchâtel and Paris: Delachaux et Niestlé.

Piaget, J. (1937). *La Construction du Réel chez l'Enfant*. Neuchâtel and Paris: Delachaux et Niestlé.

Piaget, J. (1945). *La Formation du Symbole chez l'Enfant*. Neuchâtel and Paris: Delachaux et Niestlé.

Piaget, J. (1954a). La langage et la pensée du point de vue génétique. In *Thinking and Speaking, a Symposium*. (J. Revesz, Ed.). Amsterdam: North-Holland.

Piaget, J. (1961a). *Les Mécanismes Perceptifs*. Paris: PUF.

Piaget, J. (1961b). *Play, Dreams and Imitation in Childhood*. London: Heinemann.

Piaget, J. (1962). *Comments on Vygotsky's Critical Remarks*. Cambridge, Mass.: MIT Press.

Piaget, J. (1963). Langage et opérations intellectuelles. In *Problèmes de Psycholinguistique*. Paris: PUF.

Piaget, J. (1965). Language et pensée. Tome XV. *La revue du Praticien* **17**, 2253–2254.

PIAGET, J. (1967a). *Biologie et Connaissance*. Paris: Gallimard.

PIAGET, J. (1967b). *Six Psychological Studies*. New York: Random House.

PIAGET, J. (1970). *L'Epistémologie Genetique*. Paris: PUF.

PIAGET, J. (1970b). *Structuralism*. New York: Basic Books.

PIAGET, J. (1971a). *Biology and Knowledge. An Essay on the Relations between Organic Regulations and Cognitive Processes*. Chicago, Ill.: Univ. of Chicago Press.

PIAGET, J. (1972). *The Principles of Genetic epistemology*. London: Routledge and Kegan Paul; New York: Basic Books.

PIAGET, J. (1975). L'équilibration des structures cognitives. Problème central du développement. *Etudes d'Epistémologie Génétique*, Vol. 33. Paris: PUF.

PIAGET, J. and GARCIA, R. (1971). Les explications causales. (*Etudes d'Epistémologie Génétique*, 26.). Paris: PUF.

PIAGET, J. and INHELDER, B. (1948). *La Représentation de l'Espace chez l'Enfant*. Paris: PUF.

PIAGET, J. and INHELDER, B. (1951). *La génèse de l'Idée du Hasard chez l'Enfant*. Paris: Presses Univ. de France. (English translation forthcoming, New York: Norton).

PIAGET, J. and INHELDER B. (1956). *The Child's Conception of Space*. London: Routledge and Kegan Paul.

PIAGET, J. and INHELDER, B. (1959). *La Génèse des Structures Logiques Élémentaires. Classifications et Sériations*. Neuchâtel: Delachaux et Niestlé.

PIAGET, J. and INHELDER, B. (1962). Le développement des images mentales chez l'enfant. *J. Psychol. Norm. Pathol.* **1–2**, 75–180. Also, *Traité de Psychologie Expérimentale*, Vol. 7. Paris, PUF, 1963.

PIAGET, J. and INHELDER, B. (1966a). *L'Image Mentale chez l'Enfant. (Etude sur le Développement des Représentations Imagées)*. Paris: PUF.

PIAGET, J. and INHELDER, B. (1966b). *La Psychologie de l'Enfant*. Paris: PUF, QSJ.

PIAGET, J., INHELDER, B. (1969). *The Psychology of the Child*. Routledge and Kegan Paul and Basic Books.

PIAGET, J. and SZEMINSKA, A. (1941). *La Génèse du Nombre chez l'Enfant*. Neuchâtel: Delachaux et Niestlé.

PIAGET, J. and SZEMINSKA, A. (1952). *The Child's Conception of Number*. London: Routledge and Kegan Paul.

PIAGET, J., INHELDER, B., and SZEMINSKA, A. (1960). *The Child's Conception of Geometry*. New York: Basic Books.

PICK, H. L. (1964). Perception in Soviet psychology. *Psychol. Bull.* **62**(1), 21–35.

POSTAL, P. M. (1968). *Aspects of Phonological Theory.* New York: Harper and Row.

PRECHTL, H. F. R. (1958). The directed head turning response and allied movements of the human body. *Behaviour* 13, 212–242.

PRICE-WILLIAMS, R. R. A. (1961). A study concerning concepts of conservation of quantities among primitive children. *Acta Psychol.* 18, 293–305.

SCHMID-KITSIKIS, E. (1969). *L'Examen des Opérations de l'Intelligence: Psychopathologie de l'Enfant.* Neuchâtel: Delachaux et Niestlé.

SINCLAIR, A., SINCLAIR, H., O. DE MARCELLUS. (1971), Young children's comprehension and production of passive sentences. *Arch. Psych.* 161 (Vol. XLI), 1–22.

SINCLAIR, H., AJURIAGUERRA, J. DE, BOEHME, M., and TISSOT, R. (1966). Quelques aspects de la désintégration des notion de temps à travers des épreuves morpho-syntaxiques chez des vieillards atteints de démence dégénérative. *Bull. Psychol.* (Paris).

SINCLAIR DE ZWART, H. (1967a). *Acquisition du Langage et Développement de la Pensee.* Paris: Dunod.

SINCLAIR DE ZWART, H. (1967b). Conduites verbales et déficits opératoires. *Acta Neurol. Psychiat. Belg.* 67(11), 852–861.

SINCLAIR, H., FERREIRO, E. (1970). Etude génétique de la compréhension, production et répétition des phrases au mode passif. *Arch. Psych.* 160 (Vol. XL), 1–42.

SLOBIN, D. I. (1973). Cognitive prerequisites for the development of grammar. In *Studies in Child Development* (Ferguson, C. A. and Slobin, D., Eds.). New York: Holt, Rinehart and Winston.

SOKOLOV, J. N. (1966). Orienting reflex as information regulator. In *Psychological Research in the USSR, Vol. 1.* Moscow: Progress Publishers, pp. 344–366.

SPITZ, R. (1952). *La Première Année de la Vie de l'Enfant.* Paris: PUF.

SPITZ, R. A. (1968). *De la Naissance à la Parole.* Paris: PUF.

STAMBAK, M., HERITEAU, L., AUZIAS, M., BERGES, J., and AJURIAGUERRA, J. DE, (1964). Les dyspraxies chez l'enfant. *Psychiat. Enfant.* 7(2), 381–496.

THORPE, W. H. (1969). A retrospect. In *Beyond Reductionism*, (Koestler, A., and Smythies, J. R., Eds.). London: Hutchinson.

TISSOT, R., LHERMITTE, F., and DUCARNE, B. (1964). Etat intellectuel des aphasiques. *Encéphale* 4, 285–320.

VAN DEN BOGAERTS-ROMBOUTS, N. (1966). Projection spatiale d'une série temporelle. In *L'Epistemologie du Temps* (Grize, J. B., Ed.) (*Etudes d'Epistémologie Genetiques*, XX). Paris: PUF, pp. 137–148.

VEKKER, L. M. (1961). Some theoretical problems of the image in touch. In *Recent Soviet Psychology* (O'Connor, N., Ed.). New York: Liveright.

VIITAMAKI, R. O. (1964). Psychosis in childhood. A psychological follow-up study. *Acta Psychiat. Scand.* 40, 173.

References

Vinh-Bang, N. (1965). *De l'Intuition Géométrique. (Etudes d'Epistémologie Génétique*, **XIX**). Paris: PUF, pp. 39–58.

Vinh-Bang, N. Une échelle de développement du raisonnement. In preparation.

Wassing, H. E. (1965). Cognitive functioning in early infantile autism. An examination of four cases by means of the W.I.S.C. *Acta Paedopsychiat.* 32(4).

Watkins, C. (1969). *Indo-European Origins of the Celtic Verb*. Dublin: Dublin Institute for Advanced Studies.

Watt, W. C. (1970). On two hypotheses concerning psycholinguistics. In *Cognition and the Development of Language* (Hayes, J. R., Ed.). New York: Wiley.

Author Index

O

Odier, C., 71
Oléron, P., 194

P

Plato, 56
Papert, A., 68
Pascal, B., 55
Pavlov, I., 19, 106, 179
Perron-Borelli, M., 235
Piaget, J., 1–4, 37–42, 72–74, 102, 121–122, 145, 149, 151–156, 164, 167,
        173–175, 177, 179–180, 184, 189–193, 197, 201–203, 205–210, 217,
        236, 253, 279.
Picasso, P., 185
Pierce, W., 158
Pinard, A., 265
Postal, P. M., 214
Prechtl, H. F. R., 174
Pribram, K., 67
Price-Williams, R. R. A., 264

Q

Quine, W. V., 28

R

Rensch, B., 52
Rosenfeld, L., 72
Rutter, M., 235

S

Saussure, F. de, 34, 198, 211
Schmalhausen, R., 52
Schmid-Kitsikis, E., 7, 225, 235
Sinclair, H., 6, 69, 97, 104, 130, 160, 224, 231, 267–268, 271
Skinner, B. F., 27
Slobin, D. I., 215

Subject Index

C

Categories, of knowledge, 38, 151
Catharsis, 68–69
Chance, concept of, 73, 79, 85
Classification task, 240, 249
Cognition: animal, 47; control of, 48–49, 60–61; intelligent, 47
Compensations, logical, 96–97, 131–132, 145, 261
Competence, linguistic, 150–151, 204
Composition, of transformations, 90
Concepts, Piagetian theoretical, 37, 39, 167, 208–210, 253, 269
Conflicts, cognitive, 132
Conservations: operative, 54, 89–91, 96, 99, 123, 230–231, 239, 273;
        organic, 53
Construction, notion of, 13, 57, 213
Contiguous composition scheme, 42–43
Co-operations, 262
Coordination: of actions, 15, 156–157, 207–208, 261; of schemes, 49;
        of social or collective actions, 262
Correspondence: one-to-one, 93, 110, 112, 123, 239; direct, 93; logical, 93;
        reciprocal, 93
Covariations, functional, 96–97
Creodes, 22, 260
Cybernetics, 165

D

Decentration, 21, 154, 191
Development: 44; biologic, 27; changes in, 277; cognitive, 42, 51, 129;
        deviations in, 275; of epistemology, 122; genealogic, 55; of identity,
        93; organic, 55; of psychology, 27, 122; of the structural model, 132
Differentiation: process, 175; between assimilation and accommodation, 49;
        between signifier and signified, 192
Discordance, between operative and figurative aspects of thought, 226–227
Disintegration, of thought processes, 227
Dissociation: process, 175; between form and content, 177–178
Drawing, 179

E

Egocentrism, 21
Empirical return, 97

Reasoning: in mentally retarded, 221–222; in prepsychotic children, 225
Reciprocity, 93
Reconstruction: cognitive, 61; conceptual, 68; memory, 118.
Reflexes, 172–173
Regression, 132, 255, 273
Regulation: cognitive, 48–50, 53, 58, 165; interindividual, 55;
    systems of, 167
Relations: horizontal, 42; oblique, 42; vertical, 42
Relationships, functional, 92
Representation: 179; collective, 62; system of, 41, 169; unconscious, 38–39,
    68
Repression, unconscious, 67
Response, 25–26
Reversibility, operative, 54, 97
Rule of couples, 40

S

Schema, 14, 33, 102, 119
Scheme: 14, 33, 43, 102, 104, 106, 112, 118–119, 156–157, 174, 177;
    conceptualization of, 40; hereditary, 173; preoperational, 107–108;
    sensorimotor, 35, 114
Semiotic function, 34, 158, 178, 190, 210, 264
Signals, 34
Signifiers: 34, 178; development of, 160, 192
Signs, 34, 192, 232
Smiling reaction, 176
Societies, human, 55
Stages: cross-cultural verification of, 264–265; in deaf–mute children, 194;
    of development, 22, 71, 261; in embryogenesis, 22, 260;
    maturational, 22, 204; in mentally retarded, 222; in senile
    dements, 224; transition between, 123, 227, 270
Strategies: constructive, 182–183; imitative, 182
Structuralism, transformational, 28, 216
Structures: cognitive, 52, 64, 120; formal, 35; general, 15, 121; logico-
    mathematical, 16, 28–29, 37, 51; acquisition of syntactic, 196
Subject: epistemic, 55, 253; per se, 56; transcendental, 56
Symbols, 34, 192, 217, 232
System: autoregulatory, 54; closing of 47–48; living, 57; open, 47

T

Theory of development: 15, 164; biological, 122; cognitive, 209–210;
    learning, 122

Deborah K. Keller

(NOTES)